Korean Studies of the Henry M. Jackson School of International Studies

EDITED BY CLARK W. SORENSEN,
University of Washington

FIGHTING FOR THE ENEMY

Koreans in Japan's War, 1937–1945

BRANDON PALMER

UNIVERSITY OF WASHINGTON PRESS | *Seattle and London*

KOREA FOUNDATION 한국국제교류재단 The Korea Foundation has provided financial assistance for the undertaking of this publication project.

This publication was also supported in part by the Korea Studies Program of the University of Washington in cooperation with the Henry M. Jackson School of International Studies.

The University of Washington Press also gratefully acknowledges the support of the Association for Asian Studies, Inc. (AAS), which provided assistance through its First Book Subvention Program.

University of Washington Press
PO Box 50096, Seattle, WA 98145, USA
www.washington.edu/uwpress

Library of Congress Cataloging-in-Publication Data
Palmer, Brandon, 1970–
Fighting for the enemy : Koreans in Japan's war, 1937-1945 / Brandon Palmer.
    pages cm. — (Korean studies of the Henry M. Jackson School of International Studies)
Includes bibliographical references and index.
ISBN 978-0-295-99257-0 (hardcover : alk. paper) — ISBN 978-0-295-99258-7 (pbk. : alk. paper)
1. Korea—History—Japanese occupation, 1910-1945 2. World War, 1939–1945—Korea. 3. World War, 1939–1945—Participation, Korean. 4. World War, 1939–1945—Conscript labor—Korea.
I. Title.
DS916.54.P363 2013   940.540089'957—dc23   2013011466

All photographs courtesy of the Truth Commission on Forced Mobilization under Japanese Imperialism.

CONTENTS

ACKNOWLEDGMENTS

I have finally come to the end of this journey. I know that my friends and family feel it is about time. My debt to my friends, family, colleagues, and mentors who have contributed to *Fighting for the Enemy* is enormous. This project would not have come to fruition without the generosity of Dr. Kim Do-hyŏng (of the Independence Hall of Korea), who sent me research materials and provided me room and board during my visits to Korea. I also thank my wife, Sunny, for all her patience and assistance.

When I was a graduate student at the University of Hawaii, the History Department, the Center for Korean Studies, and the Center for Japanese Studies provided support that was invaluable to the formation of this research topic and to the progression of my academic career. Namely, I extend my appreciation to Yŏng-ho Choe and Peter Hoffenberg for the extra time they took to provide quality feedback; to Margot Henriksen and George Akita for the advice and humor that sustained me during some difficult times; and to John Haig and Kakuko Shoji, who gave freely of their time to double-check translations (saving me from myself). Of course, any errors in writing, translation, or interpretation are my own. Funding for the publication of this project was made possible through the Association for Asian Studies First Book Subvention Program and the Korea Foundation's Publication Support Program.

I wish to thank my colleagues in the history department at Coastal Carolina University, especially Amanda Brian, Aneilya Barnes, and Carolyn Dillian, for their support (and for the free meals). I hope that our lottery numbers come up soon. Also, I wish to extend my gratitude to the faculty and staff at the University of Washington Press for their careful proofreading and insight that have been critical to the refinement of this project. Thanks to Lorri Hagman, Clark Sorensen, Mary Ribesky, and the outside readers for their advice throughout the editing process.

ABBREVIATIONS

CDR company-directed recruitment

GDR government-directed recruitment

GGK government-general of Korea

ICCCSC *Ilcheha chŏnsi ch'ejegi chŏngch'aek saryo ch'ongsŏ* (Historical document collection of the policies of the wartime regime under Japanese imperialism)

LMP Labor Mobilization Plan

NGML National General Mobilization Law

POW prisoner of war

SAJAN *Selected Archives of the Japanese Army-Navy, 1868–1945*

STCSGDS *Senji taiseika Chōsen Sōtokufu gaikaku dantai shiryōshū*

(Collection materials of extragovernmental organizations of the Korean government-general under the war system)

TGSS *Teikoku gikai setsumei shiryō*

FIGHTING FOR THE ENEMY

INTRODUCTION

On June 22, 1939, a Japanese brigade captured Wanshan, a small village in Shanxi in northern China. By nightfall, however, Chinese nationalist forces regrouped and launched a series of counterattacks that drove the Japanese from their positions. One of the Japanese casualties in this battle, private Yi In-sŏk, an ethnic Korean, was fatally wounded by a hand grenade. In the last moments of his life, Yi allegedly grabbed the hand of a fellow soldier and cried out, "Tennō heika banzai!" (Long live the emperor!).[1] Private Yi was the first Korean soldier to die in the Asia-Pacific War (1937–1945). Few people realize that Koreans served in the Imperial Japanese Army and Navy during the last global conflict.

The story of Yi's death begins with Japan's annexation of Korea in 1910. As the ruler of Korea, it was the Japanese government's prerogative to mobilize its colonial subjects for war—a practice common among Western colonial powers. According to Japanese and Korean sources, from 1937 to 1945, Japanese colonial authorities mustered at least 360,000 Koreans to serve in the Japanese military as soldiers or civilian employees, another 750,000 Koreans to work in mines and wartime industries in Japan, and a million more industrial laborers within Korea. By the end of World War II, between four and seven million Korean men, women, and students had been mobilized throughout Japan's wartime empire.[2] Given the colossal number of people who served Japan, the Koreans' participation in Japan's war effort, which has received extensive treatment in Korean and Japanese languages, remains a major lacuna in English historiography.

Fighting for the Enemy fills this void by accentuating Japan's mobilization of Korean human resources for war from 1937 to 1945. By analyzing the multifarious ways that Koreans served imperial Japan, scholars of modern Korea and Japan can develop a fuller understanding of one of the most tumultuous periods in Korean history. Japan's exploitation of

Koreans during the war period, while undeniable, should not be the sole focal point of analysis. Instead, the totality of experiences related to imperial Japan's mobilization of Koreans, such as volunteer soldiers, conscript soldiers, industrial laborers, and civilian employees of the military, need to be included to portray Korea's wartime history in a more complex light.

Japan's populace and bureaucracy considered the Korean population educationally and ideologically unprepared to contribute to Japan's war efforts, and, as a result, Japanese bureaucrats were hesitant to include Koreans as an integral part of Japan's war effort. Underlying the Japanese hesitancy was decades of negative publicity within Japan proper that highlighted the Koreans' social and cultural backwardness. In this context, it was no simple task to incorporate hundreds of thousands of Korean soldiers and laborers in the mobilization process. An important part of this story is that Japan cautiously implemented wartime policies to marshal Koreans in a way that minimized ethnic resistance and prevented a sense of entitlement among the Korean population. Japan's control over Korea, while heavy-handed, was not absolute. In fact, the Japanese state began recruitment by eliciting Korean cooperation and compliance; this gave Koreans a choice to participate. Thus, Koreans were active agents (not passive victims) throughout the mobilization processes. Of course, if Koreans opted against cooperation, the colonial regime exerted pressure on the unwilling.

An examination of the Japanese colonial regime's policymaking process reveals that wartime manpower laws for Koreans were watered-down versions of policies used to mobilize Japanese citizens. The average Korean subject was educationally and culturally unprepared to contribute to the war effort on a level comparable to that of the average Japanese; and the mobilization had to account for this. The alteration of laws provides a window through which much knowledge can be gained. These differences indicate that Koreans were not completely trusted and that Korea held an ancillary position in Japan's wartime empire.

The mobilization of Korea was not an automatic feat at the outbreak of war in 1937, nor was it a knee-jerk reaction to the declining war fortunes of Japan in the 1940s. The decision to involve Korean manpower, especially as soldiers, was plagued with anxiety and much hand-wringing by Japanese authorities. The dilemma for Japanese authorities was that they needed Korean soldiers and laborers to enhance Japan's fighting capacity, but colonial bureaucrats had reservations about the readiness and usefulness of Koreans for wartime service because they considered Koreans ideologically and educationally unsound. A fundamental political concern harbored by many Japanese citizens was that Korean military service would remove a major obstacle to the granting of citizenship and political equality to Koreans.[3] By forbidding military service, the conservative Japanese could keep clear the boundaries between imperial citizen and colonial subject; Japanese authorities realized that including Koreans in the war effort as soldiers would empower the Korean population, which then might demand political autonomy or equality, as happened in India during World War I. Thus, Japanese bureaucracies in Tokyo and Seoul carefully fashioned and implemented mobilization laws that would not provoke Korean support for Korean nationalists or communists.

Analysis of the implementation process reveals that Japan sought to secure Korean loyalty and cooperation through indoctrination (propaganda and education), tangible benefits (social and material), and coercion (if the other two failed). Indoctrination and propaganda, as part of the assimilation policies, were primarily designed to promote Korean support for Japan's war, or to at least weaken Korean resistance. The Government-General of Korea (GGK) and the war industries sought to win Korean cooperation through inducements that included stable wages, military glory, and improved social status. When enticements failed, the colonial regime coerced Koreans by manipulating the socioeconomic nexus of power to ensure the cooperation of individuals and families. The Japanese colonial regime had tremendous ability to coerce Koreans to comply, as well as to strike fear into Korean society, but its power should not be mistaken for absolute power.

The Japanese regime acted carefully throughout most of the war period to not antagonize the Korean population excessively; colonial authorities and businessmen thought that the regime could best marshal Korea's human resources by offering economic and social opportunities. The Korean response to mobilization ranged from active cooperation to determined resistance. Many took advantage of the multifarious jobs and social positions created by the war economy; they opted to work as laborers in factories, to serve as policemen, and so forth. Conversely, uncounted numbers were coerced into serving the Japanese state, and still others completely evaded wartime demands. But the vast majority of Koreans quietly acquiesced to mobilization policies as a fiat accompli in order to avoid coercion and unwanted attention from the bureaucracy. The point here is that Koreans were not solely victims of the colonial state; instead, they were, as a whole, agents in the state-society relationship. Japan's efforts to win the support of the Korean populace, along with the GGK's inability to police noncompliance, show that the colonial regime was not an all-powerful monolithic bureaucratic organ; it had vulnerabilities that the Korean people exploited to their own benefit.[4]

Japan's mobilization of Koreans is placed in a more global context in order to show that Japan's colonial policies were consistent with Western colonial practices. One of the great ironies that imperial powers, including Japan, faced when mobilizing subaltern peoples was that the "superior" races entrusted the welfare of their empires to the colonized races. The British and French used their colonial troops from Africa and Asia to expand, police, and sustain their empires. European powers had few qualms about utilizing colonial subjects as an expendable resource; the Japanese, on the other hand, were much more reluctant to delegate the responsibility of soldiering.

Comparison of Japan's mobilization of Korea with European colonial practices shows that the Korean experience was not unique in global history. In fact, Japan's policies and actions were not as far-reaching as many Western colonial policies. Specifically, the French utilized hundreds of thousands of Africans and Indochinese as soldiers or laborers, and the British recruited even greater numbers of colonial subjects from India, Africa, Malaya, and wherever else the Union Jack flew. These analogies highlight the similarities and differences between the methods used by the Western and Japanese empires to mobilize their colonies for war. Acknowledging the exploitation of other colonies in no way diminishes the suffering that is such a large part of Korea's historical remembrance; nor does it justify Japan's actions, but it is instead an indictment of all colonial powers' wanton abuse of their colonial subjects.

HISTORICAL VIEWS ON COLONIAL KOREA

The discussion of wartime Korea is best understood as part of the wider historical narratives on modern Korea. South Korea's collective national memory of the colonial period, including scholarship, has since the 1970s been dominated by the nationalist historical paradigm (elsewhere called the "internal development theory," K: *naejaejŏk palchŏn non*), which describes Korea's colonial experience in value-laden terms. This paradigm draws heavily on a revisionist history from the perspective of the common people (K: *minjung*) that highlights the exploitation of the average peasant.[5]

These studies portray the colonial regime as a totalitarian and fascist political machine that wrung out the lifeblood and economic vitality of the Korean people, who were powerless victims. In support of these claims, individual suffering is extrapolated into national suffering, and individual acts of resistance are represented as national resistance. Korean historiography continues the binary representations of imperial repression and colonial resistance, colonial exploitation and national development. Some authors label the colonial era a period of "enslavement."[6] No room is left for a middle ground.[7] The nationalist historical paradigm has strong vested interests within Korean society and is the nationalized version of history taught in public schools, displayed in museums, and shown on television.

One branch of the nationalist historical paradigm that relates to scholarship on the wartime use of Koreans as laborers, soldiers, and prostitutes is forced mobilization studies (K: *kangje yŏnhaeng*; J: *kyōsei renkō*). *Kangje yŏnhaeng* (literally, "forced taking [by the police]") is an emotive word used by scholars to describe Korean and Chinese laborers taken to Japan during the war. The first scholar to undertake a serious examination of Korean wartime labor was Pak Kyŏng-sik, a Korean resident in Japan. His *A Record of the Forced Displacement of Koreans* (J: *Chōsenjin kyōsei renkō no kiroku*), published in 1965, is a seminal work on wartime Korea. Pak, evoking the themes of the nationalist historical paradigm, stated that Koreans suffered "inhumane slavelike labor conditions" and were victims of "colonial semifeudal fascist oppression."[8] Forced mobilization studies include coverage of the forcible recruitment of foreign laborers for work in Japan.

Subsequent Asian and English works on wartime Korea have adopted the above themes and have focused on Japan's exploitation, coercion, and victimization of Koreans. Forced mobilization studies accentuate the inhumane treatment of the comfort women and of Korean workers by focusing on unequal pay, harsh working conditions, poor housing, discriminatory treatment at the hands of Japanese, and so forth.[9] In other words, the wartime colonial relationship is shown in a wholly negative light. These works frequently urge the Japanese government to correct past wrongs. For example, Pak Kyŏng-sik, Miyata Setsuko, Hayashi Eidai, and Utsumi Aiko use their academic studies as a polemic to prod the Japanese government to apologize and to pay restitution to Koreans who suffered as a result of their involvement in Japan's war.[10]

The forced mobilization paradigm remains prominent in Korean- and Japanese-language scholarship on colonial Korea. Books and journals continue to disseminate the nationalist historical paradigm by highlighting compulsory labor (K: *kangje nodong*), the comfort women, and other issues related to the exploitation of Koreans.[11] The South Korean government provides financial support to museums, public monuments, and research centers, such as the Truth Commission on Forced Mobilization under Japanese Imperialism (K: Ilche Kangjŏmha Kangje Tongwŏn P'ihae Chinsang Kyumyŏng Wiwŏnhoe) and Independence Hall of Korea (K: Tongnip Kinyŏmgwan), to propagate this paradigm to the Korean public. The perception created by forced mobilization studies is that all Korean men, women, and children, with the exception of a handful of collaborators, suffered during the war.

The Japanese military's exploitation of Korean industrial workers and comfort women dominates Korean- and Japanese-language historiography of Korea during World War II. Kim Min-yŏng's *Research on Japan's Korean Manpower Exploitation* (K: *Ilche ŭi Chosŏnin nodongnyŏk sut'al yŏn'gu*, 1995) and Chŏng Hye-gyŏng's *Korean Forced Displacement, Forced Labor* (K: *Chosŏnin kangje yŏnhaeng, kangje nodong*, 2006) are representative studies of this paradigm; each places the exploitation and suffering of Korean workers at the center of attention but provides limited analysis of the structural conditions in which mobilization took place. This is also true of collections of oral histories. Personal accounts, unedited, provide terrific insight into how policies were implemented and how people responded to state demands, although the bureaucratic level of analysis is ignored. However, most editors of these personal narratives are selective as to which accounts are included; only the most damning accounts are published. English-language works that substantively address wartime Korea often adopt the themes of forced mobilization by highlighting the suffering of Korean miners and comfort women, but pay little attention to Korean soldiers or to structural isses.[12] Few works within this field address the international and historical context of colonial subjects mobilized for war.

Coverage of Korean soldiers has slowly grown over the past two decades. The most prolific authors in the Japanese language are Higuchi Yūichi and Utsumi Aiko; while in Korea, Kim To-hyŏng has numerous studies about Korea's military participation in the war. Higuchi's *Koreans Who Were Forced to Be Imperial Army Soldiers* (J: *Kōgun heishi ni sareta Chōsenjin*, 1991) and *Korean People and Conscription during the War* (J: *Senjika Chōsen no minshū to chōhei*, 2001) are meticulously researched studies that focus on Japan's program of military mobilization in Korea, making them the most important secondary works in this field. Utsumi's study, *The Korean "Imperial Army" Soldiers' War* (J: *Chōsenjin "kōgun" heishitachi no sensō*, 1991) provides a nice survey of Korean soldiers; she has also published extensively on the postwar conditions of Korean soldiers and laborers. And Kim's numerous articles and pamphlets published through the Independence Hall of Korea and the Truth Commission on Forced Mobilization stress the plight of Koreans in New Guinea, Burma, and the Philippines.

Critics of forced mobilization studies note that South Korean scholarly efforts blur the lines between critical and popular understandings of Korea's modern history.[13] One outcome of this approach is that Korean scholarship protects and promotes the nationalist Korean political and social identity.[14] The marriage of scholarship and wider society has increased this scholarship's rigidity to such an extent that all other historical explanations are ignored.[15] In other words, counternarratives or contradictory evidence are generally dismissed.

In recent decades, the nationalist historical paradigm has been challenged by Korean and Western scholars who advocate the colonial modernization theory, which contends that Japan's colonization of Korea, including the wartime mobilization, was critical to the modernization of the peninsula. This revisionist approach moves beyond a rigid nationalist view and explores the ways that Koreans encountered modernity within Japanese colonialism. Studies in this field examine educational advancement, technical training, industrial development, modern infrastructure, and legal systems as Japanese contributions that helped Korea's postwar growth. Since the early 1990s there has been a growing movement to examine colonial modernity as yet another alternate view of the colonial era. Colonial modernity moves beyond the rigid interpretations of nationalism and colonialism found in the historiography of modern Korea by analyzing the formation of Korean identity under colonialism. These studies claim that the use of emotive terms obscures our understanding of the colonial era, as well as the options available to the Korean people. More significantly, this paradigm challenges the binary explanations (exploitation versus resistance) of nationalist history by adopting a more pluralistic approach to historical studies.

Studies of modernity evaluate the intricate relationship between the Korean people and the colonial regime, between colonialism and modernity, and between personal and national motives. Yun Haedong is one of the best scholars in this field. His works *Another Reckoning of Modern Times* (K: *Kŭndae rŭl tasi ingnŭnda*, 2006) and *A Rediscovery of History before and since Liberation* (K: *Haebang chŏnhusa ŭi chaeinsik*, 2006) are examples of recent Korean scholars' willingness to recognize positive outcomes of the colonial era. English-language works such as Carter J. Eckert's *Offspring of Empire* (1991), Soon-won Park's *Colonial Industrialization and Labor in Korea* (1999), and Theodore Jun Yoo's *The Politics of Gender in Colonial Korea* (2008) offer a revisionist understanding the colonial era. While addressing larger issues of capitalism, industrialization, and gender, respectively, these works provide insight into the role Koreans played in shaping their own lives under Japan's rule; they show that Koreans participated in the creation of a modern society. These scholars maintain that, while morally objectionable, the colonial era was not necessarily detrimental to Korea.

In terms of wartime mobilization, a majority of English-language works recount the experiences of the comfort women, placing emphasis on their victimization. One welcomed exception to these studies is C. Sarah Soh's *The Comfort Women* (2008). Her study provides an anthropological interpretation of the comfort women's victimization that resulted from Japanese and Korean patriarchy. Soh terms their experience as "gendered structural violence."[16] Beyond *The Comfort Women*, there are no English-language monograph-length studies focused solely on Korean industrial labor or soldiers; most of the published research on wartime Korean soldiers and laborers have been book chapters or journal articles. For example, Utsumi

Aiko has published articles in *Asian Labor in the Wartime Japanese Empire* (2005) and *Perilous Memories* (2001), but, unfortunately, none of her books have been translated into English.

The most significant works on Koreans in the Japanese military have been by Takashi Fujitani, who has published articles in *Senri Ethnological Studies* (2000) and *Representations* (2007), as well as a monograph, *Race for Empire* (2011). His works compare the biopolitical policies and discourses of the Japanese toward Koreans in the Japanese Army and the United States toward Japanese Americans in the United States Army.[17] Fujitani provides excellent coverage of the volunteer soldier and conscription systems, as well as insightful chapters on war-era movies and literature. However, Fujitani's works rely almost exclusively on English- and Japanese-language sources. The result is that his works do not incorporate Korean opinions and responses to Japan's policies. *Fighting with the Enemy*, on the other hand, utilizes a variety of Korean sources and explores in much greater detail the Korean wartime experience.

Revisionist and postcolonial studies portray Koreans as active agents in the creation of Korean history, not as victims of unmitigated exploitation. The colonial regime was not capable of imposing its unabridged policies upon the Korean people. *Fighting for the Enemy* differs from Higuchi's, Utsumi's, and other major works in two important ways: It moves beyond an emphasis on the suffering of Koreans, and it places Korea's mobilization in a global context. Furthermore, it contributes to the field of colonial modernity by arguing that the economic and social conditions accompanying wartime industrialization created opportunities for Koreans who cooperated with and worked within the colonial system. Countless Koreans at the local and national level *chose* to become policemen, educators, soldiers, bureaucrats, laborers, heads of local neighborhood units, and businessmen.

THE COLONIAL REGIME'S POWER

Many Korean and Western scholars implicitly or directly portray the GGK as a monolithic, hegemonic, and demonic structure. This misrepresentation needs to be replaced by a more nuanced treatment that judiciously questions the limits of the colonial regime's powers. In 2005 a Korean scholar stated to the author that the colonial bureaucracy had absolute power over every aspect of every Koreans' life, and that any resistance was "due to Korean ingenuity." While this opinion does not hold universal support among Korean scholarship, widespread misconceptions such as this are common in this field. Any claim that the GGK held absolute power should be questioned. Michel Foucault aptly noted, "Power is not something that is acquired, seized, or shared, something that one holds on to or allows to slip away; power is exercised from innumerable points."[18] And no government, including the Japanese colonial regime in Korea, can control every point of power. For example, despite an all-out assimilation policy to force Koreans to speak Japanese, less than one-quarter of Koreans were able to do so. Quite simply, the GGK, like other colonial regimes, had weaknesses. The colonial state was not monolithic, nor was it omnipotent. It lacked the foresight to predict its future needs, and instead reacted to circumstances as they arose.[19] The GGK realized its vulnerabilities and adapted the way it dealt with the Korean population throughout the period under examination. These weaknesses left room for Koreans to act, with limitations, of their own volition.

Colonial regimes, while powerful entities, were neither monolithic nor omnipotent organisms. They controlled many aspects of life within their colonies, but that power had limitations and vulnerabilities. The actions of all colonial bureaucracies were shaped by a nervousness that colonial subjects would rise up against the imperial power, as happened in India in 1857. Imperial powers learned quickly that colonized peoples could not be forced to abandon their indigenous political consciousness, history, or loyalties. Colonial regimes understood that colonies were better ruled through laws and cooperation from native elites than by a reliance on brute force. Of course, military action was necessary from time to time. For example, in the 1890s the British in India reacted to frequent peasant uprisings by passing tenancy acts—which were haphazard and ineffective. The British did not have the manpower to properly patrol the provinces to prevent uprisings; they reacted to events as they arose.[20] Colonial regimes focused on policing outward behavior and demanding obedience, but were powerless to control personal thoughts and behavior behind closed doors.

Consider the extreme example of African slaves in the American South. They were chattel, and therefore politically and legally powerless. Yet they retained a degree of agency and, by extension, power within the relationship. Even in enslavement they "developed effective protest techniques in the form of indirect retaliation."[21] Slaves would feign illness, make themselves lame, run off for a short while, destroy their master's property, abuse the animals, and malinger. Slaves could be beaten, locked up, and sold, but some masters feared that severe punishment would provoke greater resistance. The same may be said of the Japanese bureaucrat's apprehension about Korean workers and soldiers who lived in conditions that were far from enslavement. Japan attempted to force conformity on the everyday behavior of Koreans through a colonial bureaucracy that utilized local officials, hundreds of semigovernmental organizations, and 23,000 police, one-third of which were Korean. Despite these powerful political and social tools, resistance remained an option for Koreans—and resistance, of any sort, exposed cracks in the colonial regime's hegemony.

Resistance, in a colonial setting, is any action that runs counter to the ideals or goals of the state. It can be undertaken by individuals or groups; it can be enacted in public or in private.[22] This definition fits colonial Korean resistance quite well, because most Korean resistance consisted of small, individual acts that, taken by themselves, are insignificant. A mosaic of economically motivated individual and occasional group resistance was exhibited through feigning ignorance, conveniently disappearing, and so forth. Resistance is not inevitable or accidental; it is a choice. More importantly, the colonial regime was unable to prevent or effectively respond to everyday forms of resistance, thereby showing that the GGK lacked complete power over the Korean people.

Everyday forms of resistance are undertaken by the socially and politically weak. Such people employ "foot dragging, dissimulation, desertion, false compliance, pilfering, feigning ignorance, slander, arson, sabotage, and so on." Additionally, those lacking power can pretend to be ill or incompetent, or can damage equipment to slow work.[23] The weaker classes of people use everyday forms of resistance because these require little or no coordination or masterminding and are impossible to police. While these activities cannot change the status quo, they are often the only options available to the dispossessed. These forms of protest are obvious and significant only when done in large numbers, as happened in Korea.

This subject is a sensitive subject, and it is not my intention to support either the Korean or the Japanese viewpoint. Some may consider the findings detailed herein to be objectionable or insensitive. The suffering and exploitation of the Korean people cannot be denied or ignored, nor should it be minimized. Rather, the best way to approach this subject is to examine the historical documents, the legal foundations of Japan's mobilization of Koreans, and the impact that those policies had on individual Koreans. This approach unveils the intersections between the colonial regime and the Korean people during the last years of Japan's rule in Korea, and shows that the process used to marshal Koreans for war was more complex than was previously supposed.

1 | KOREA'S MOBILIZATION IN CONTEXT

Japan's wartime mobilization of Korea during the Asia-Pacific War (1937–1945) was an unprecedented event in Korean history that affected every aspect of its society and economy: Hundreds of thousands of Koreans were uprooted and sent overseas to work and fight in foreign countries, Japanese and Korean industries proliferated throughout the peninsula, and state control extended more completely to the local levels. Korea underwent social and economic change that greatly effected subsequent history. Remarkably, despite the extent of this mobilization, the Korean nation was, by Japanese standards, not prepared for the demands placed upon it by the Japanese war machine. In order to better understand the unpreparedness of Korea, and its position within the Japanese wartime empire, it is necessary to review the history of colonial Korea.

THE COLONIAL GOVERNMENT: ITS CHARACTER AND POWER

Japan made Korea a protectorate in 1905 and a colony in 1910, establishing the Government-General of Korea (GGK) as the sole policymaking organ in Korea with legislative, judicial, and executive powers. The GGK was a powerful, highly institutionalized bureaucratic regime headed by a governor-general who was appointed by the central government in Tokyo. The GGK generally acted independently of the cabinet and diet, but on matters of importance worked in conjunction with them to determine colonial policies, especially after the outbreak of war with the United States.

The nature of Japan's colonization of Korea, like all colonial ventures, was designed to politically, economically, and strategically bolster the colonizer, often at the expense of the colony. Japan's demands on Korea grew increasingly burdensome over the thirty-five years Korea was a colony. Initially, Japanese colonization was a preventive measure to forbid Korea's colonization by another imperial power; later, Korea became a supplier of raw materials to the Japanese metropole as well as a market for Japanese products. In the 1910s, Japan acquired Korean land for Japanese farmers; in the 1920s, it exploited Korea for rice; in the 1930s, it requisitioned labor for Japanese-owned industries; and in the 1940s, it asked Koreans to sacrifice their lives for the Japanese empire. Yet the GGK invested insufficient resources in the prewar era to prepare Korean society for industrial and martial contributions to a total war.

The GGK, like most structures of domination, was not static. The colonial administration was not a unified, single-minded organism; instead it was plagued by innumerable contradictions and internal debates.[1] It adapted to new circumstances in response to Japan's evolving economic and political needs. Japan utilized wartime policies and organizations to meet its own needs, but the use of Korean human resources was mitigated by a fear of igniting Korean nationalism, pushing Koreans into the arms communist agitators, or sparking another demonstration similar to the March First Independence Movement in 1919.

Japan's rule in Korea was predicated upon a strong military presence. In fact, all governor-generals were career generals or admirals. The Imperial Japanese Army stationed an army unit in Korea (Chōsen-gun, referred to hereafter as the Korean Army) to safeguard Japanese rule. The blatant use of force early in the colonial period, as well as the Koreans' long-standing animosity toward Japan, culminated in Korean resistance to colonial rule. The two largest movements for Korean independence were the "righteous armies" (K: *ŭibyŏng*) and the March First Movement. From 1907 to 1912, small bands of righteous armies took up arms to fight against Japan's colonization of Korea. Upwards of 17,600 Korean soldiers and civilians were killed during the suppression of these armed groups. After the formal colonization of Korea, effective policing rooted out most nationalist resistance, with notable exceptions.

The second movement, the March First Independence Movement of 1919, was a peaceful peninsula-wide demonstration with nearly a million participants. Demonstrators hoped, in vain, to win international recognition for Korean self-determination, in accordance with Woodrow Wilson's Fourteen Points. The Japanese military and police brutally suppressed this demonstration, killing at least 553 demonstrators and arresting another 12,000.[2] These two incidents, and numerous smaller ones, reflect Koreans' widespread discontent with Japanese colonial rule. More importantly, Japan's leaders recognized that Japan could not rely solely on naked coercion to govern Korea; instead, the colonial regime needed Korean agents to gain the compliance of other Koreans.

In Korea, the GGK controlled nearly all avenues to economic, social, and political power. Prasenjit Duara's concept of the "cultural nexus of power" offers insight into state-society relations in colonial Korea. Analyzing the state's use and control of cultural symbols and norms (religious, kinship, and social networks) to control society in Republican China, Duara argues that social status and community influence were equally important for individuals who sought leadership positions.[3] And in Korea the Japanese dominated all avenues to power. The GGK permitted Koreans of all socioeconomic classes to take part in the cultural nexus, but at the will and whim of Japanese bureaucrats who gained cooperation through the manipulation of Korean culture; Korean values were twisted, and the purse strings threatened in some cases. As a result, the colonial regime gained the cooperation of subaltern agents through financial and social inducements.

When inducements failed to effect the desired response, the GGK resorted to coercion to control and mobilize the Korean masses. "Coercion" must not be confused with the use of brute force or destruction.[4] "Coercion" is the process of getting another to act in a certain way without resorting to actual force. It is one step shy of brute force, although it can be difficult to differentiate between the two.[5] And so it was with Japan's coercion of wartime Korea. The Japanese found the appropriate social and economic pressure points and manipulated them to gain compliance to mobilization policies.

Following the March First Movement, Japan initiated a decade of cultural rule (J: *bunka seiji*) that allowed Korean nationalists an open forum, but in a strictly regulated environment. The moderacy of the cultural rule was tempered by an expanded police force and surveillance of suspected Korean patriots. In the 1930s, Japan's militarist adventurism in northern China resulted in the rise of martial rule and the suppression of Korean nationalist elements.[6] Furthermore, expressions of Korean nationalism were banned, and Korean-language newspapers and journals were closed. Individuals targeted by the state were subjected to random police visits, groundless arrest, long periods of imprisonment, and even torture without legal recourse. Renowned Korean scholar Yi Ki-baik wrote in a tone reflective of the national historical paradigm,

> The leading figures in the Korean Language Society were arrested in October 1942, on charges of fomenting a nationalist movement, and as a result of the severe torture to which they were subjected by the Japanese police, Yi Yun-jae and some others among the Korean linguists died in prison. Novelists, poets and other creative writers were forced to produce their works in Japanese, and in the end it was even required that Japanese be exclusively used in the schools and in Korean homes. Not only the study of the Korean language but also of Korean history was regarded as dangerous.[7]

One reason for the suppression of the Korean ethnicity was that the Japanese government advocated the spiritual unity between the Koreans and Japanese to legitimize its rule and to reduce dissent. The Japanese were concerned that another rebellion (similar to the March First Movement) would erupt if disaffection among Koreans was too great. The GGK was forced by political and military considerations to strike a balance between incentives, flowery propaganda, and outright oppression. Consequently, bureaucrats preferred to enforce policies through moral suasion and indoctrination instead of nightmarish oppression, massacres, and banishment to Sŏdaemun Prison.[8] Moral suasion entailed the use of corporatism, the organization of government-sponsored groups that acted as intermediaries between the state and the people.[9] In other words, the colonial regime established a plethora of semiofficial organizations, such as the Chōsen League (J: Kokumin Sōryoku Chōsen Renmei), to propagate state-sponsored policies and apply coercion to ensure state supremacy.

Additionally, Japan had a strong legal tradition that inclined the GGK to avoid overt oppression by establishing an intricate law code through which it exercised and legitimized its power. The Japanese legalist tradition and mentality impelled the Japanese to create, revise, and enforce laws to internally and externally legitimize the mobilization of Korea, if for no other reason than appearance. The military conscription of Koreans was delayed over two years because the GGK needed to straighten out bureaucratic red tape. However, by the end of the war, Japan was so desperate that it did not bother to alter laws to justify its coercion and underhanded recruiting methods in Korea.

Laws in Korea were enforced by a police force of 22,715 (in 1943), of whom one-third were Korean.[10] The police performed a broad spectrum of tasks in order to maintain Japan's hegemony in Korea. Officers collected data, spread propaganda, enforced laws and court decisions, improved public health, and visited the homes of average Koreans.[11] Furthermore, police compelled physical and spiritual obedience by subduing Korean nationalists and enforcing mobilization policies. The Peace Preservation Law empowered the police to make preventive arrests and to suppress anything they deemed heretical or a threat to the Japanese national polity.[12]

The colonial apparatus had uncontested control over the colony's nexus of power, namely the economic, social, political, judicial, and educational systems. The GGK used its resources to buy, bully, and belittle individuals to comply with state policies. The colonial bureaucracy and its affiliated organizations used a carrot-stick approach, offering enticements such as a stable salary. If inducements failed, the state then resorted to iron-fist measures. The name-change policy is a prime example. During the state's push to make Koreans take Japanese names, Koreans were first given the option to change their names—an act presented as a gift from the emperor—then those who were reluctant to comply faced increasing pressure from bureaucrats. For example, students were harassed at school as a way to pressure families to take Japanese names. Some government-run schools even refused to allow Korean students to attend school unless they had Japanese names.

The colonial regime exercised extensive power over the lives of individual Koreans but was far from omnipotent. The GGK's greatest weakness was that it was unpopular among the Korean people. On the surface, Koreans complied with colonial policies, but, in their hearts, most resented the heavy-handed governance of the GGK. Herein is a paradox of Japan's mobilization of Koreans during the Asian-Pacific War: Japanese bureaucrats needed to marshal Koreans to defend Japan's wartime empire, but knew that Koreans harbored antipathy toward Japan. Historical animosity between the Koreans and the Japanese was at the foundation of the Koreans' unwillingness to give their full support to Japan during the war. The average Korean harbored distrust of and disdain for the Japanese, whom they considered shifty, condescending, and untrustworthy. This animosity can be traced back to the Japanese invasion of Korea in 1592, as well as to Japan's meddling in Korean politics after Korea and Japan established modern diplomatic relations in 1876. Furthermore, Koreans blamed Japan for the assassination of Queen Min in 1895 and for the dethronement of King Kojong in 1907. Korean nationalists felt humiliated and infuriated by Japan's colonization of Korea in 1910 and the subsequent imposition of heavy-handed colonial policies.[13] Essentially, many Koreans viewed Japan as a historical enemy.

Conversely, the Japanese in Korea exhibited an ethnocentric (if not xenophobic) attitude toward Koreans and were uneasy with relying on "peninsulars" (J: hantōjin) for national defense. Discrimination and ethnic prejudice are at the foundation of all forms of colonialism, and Japan's colonization of Korea was little different. While Korea's proximity to Japan, coupled with the cultural ties between the two peoples, mitigated some of the more extreme colonial racial discourses and practices that are found among Europeans in African and Asia, ethnocentrism was an inherent part of Japan's colonial rule.

Nevertheless, given the historical ties between the two countries, Japan promoted racial unity as part of its colonial discourse, but into the 1930s highlighted Koreans' cultural shortcomings (such as crudeness, clannishness, and talkativeness), which Japanese officials claimed was caused by centuries of social stagnation.[14] Up to the late thirties, the Japanese asserted that Koreans had defects in their character, intellect, and abilities that justified the colonization of Korea and exempted Koreans from military service. These negative portrayals complemented the first wave of Koreaphilia that swept Japan in the 1930s, in which the Japanese populace was drawn to elements of exotic Koreana.[15] While some Koreana was positive, much of it reinforced negative stereotypes of Koreans. The negative discourse contributed to discrimination against and distrust of Koreans in the workplace. Japanese managers stereotyped Koreans as lazy and poor workers. One colonial-era journal claimed that Koreans "habitually transgress the law, run away, have a brutal character, are kleptomaniacs, gamblers, or are agitators."[16] Another author regarded the Koreans as "having an anti-Japanese consciousness."[17]

In Japan, the Japanese bureaucracy viewed the Koreans as a special social problem, which it called the "Korean problem" (J: *Chōsen mondai*). At the heart of the Korean problem were the distinctive features of Korean culture, language, and social habits that the Japanese considered threatening to public peace and security.[18] Japanese businessmen and officials used these negative perceptions to justify paying Koreans less than Japanese for the same work and depriving them of equal political rights. The cabinet denied citizenship to Koreans until late in the war. This discrimination also contributed to uneasiness among Japanese officials and the general public about mobilizing Koreans, especially as soldiers, during the Asian-Pacific War.

Japanization had been a long-standing goal of the GGK, but little effort had been invested in enacting it as a full-fledged policy. But in the late 1930s Japanese authorities implemented in earnest assimilation policies to correct the Koreans' supposed shortcomings, and the war brought an even greater urgency for a more forceful assimilation. Japanese colonizers reasoned that if Koreans were made loyal subjects, Korea's twenty-five million people would offer less opposition and, more importantly, would more willingly labor, sweat, fight, and die for the empire.[19] Unfortunately for Japan's war efforts, the GGK's prewar social policies contributed to the lack of preparedness among Koreans to fill industrial positions requiring technical training or to become war-ready soldiers.

Assimilation efforts were based on assertions of universal brotherhood (J: *isshi dōjin*) between Koreans and Japanese. Propagandists, playing on pan-Asianism, claimed that a common racial and cultural heritage (J: *dōbun dōshu*) between the two people made possible Korean nationalization into the larger Japanese society.[20] Japan's pan-Asianism attempted to build a unified Asian identity by hearkening to the cultural similarities of Asian peoples, the racial kinship of all Asians, and the common historical experiences of the East, as well as a shared Asian destiny.[21]

In July 1938, one year after the outbreak of the Second Sino-Japanese War, a new era of indoctrination was inaugurated with the founding of the National Spiritual Mobilization Movement (J: Kokumin Seishin Sōdōin Undō) in Korea.[22] This movement was implemented as part of the assimila-

tion (J: *naisen ittai*; K: *naesŏn ilche*) and imperialization (J: *kōminka*) policies. In practice, these policies required Koreans to speak Japanese, visit
Shintō shrines, recite imperial rescripts, and take Japanese names. In other
words, Koreans were asked to abandon 3,000 years of Korean customs and
adopt Japanese culture. One colonial authority euphemistically called the
process a second creation of Korean culture.[23] The Japanese government
established an emperor-based state ideology for the Japanese citizenry and
attempted to impose it onto the Korean population. This effort floundered
because Koreans, with their Confucian-based culture, found it difficult to
relate to the many aspects of Japanese culture—namely the centrality of
the military and the deification of the emperor. Japan's goal to incorporate
Korea as part of Japan proper, much as it had with Okinawa, was originally planned to take several generations. However, hostilities with China
and America stymied this process. The assimilation process was acceler-
ated to an unrealistic degree, and, while the goal of assimilation was still
envisioned at the highest levels of government, at the individual level of
state-society relations, its implementation was not wholly sincere, nor was
it practicable in such a short period. Wartime assimilation was largely a
rhetorical goal rather than a practical possibility.[24] In other words, the Japanese who interacted with Koreans did not earnestly pursue the complete
incorporation or equality of Koreans as part of the Japanese national polity (J: *kokutai*). Nevertheless, the GGK, under wartime pressures, pushed
upon the Korean people the duties of Japanese citizenry without offering
significant concessions in return.

The functional arm of the imperialization movement, established in
1933, was the Chōsen League. The colonial regime utilized branches of
the league in each province, county, city, and village, as well as in some
workplaces, as a system of municipal governance.[25] The lowest level of the
Chōsen League were patriotic units (J: *aikokuhan*) that consisted of ten to
twenty households. By 1942 there were an estimated 350,000 to 420,000
patriotic units throughout Korea.[26] The patriotic units functioned much
like the neighborhood associations (J: *tonarigumi*) in Japan. Patriotic unit
heads, who were both Korean and Japanese, were responsible for executing
government surveillance and policies within households during the war.
They located and recruited laborers, encouraged applications for military
service, informed the police of potential resistors, and helped to suppress

Korean cultural practices. Unit heads, as representatives of the government, had authority over people's lives. In particular, they controlled food rations, which were basic yet powerful levers of state control. Thus, families had to comply with state demands if they wanted to eat.[27]

The colonial education system was also central to the GGK's assimilation and spiritual mobilization policies. Education authorities created a school curriculum to spiritually unify the Koreans with the Japanese, which meant aligning the Korean people's daily practice with Japanese culture; the key mechanism of this process was Japanese-language education in public schools. Bureaucrats hoped that the propagation of the Japanese language would weaken Korean cultural identity. Schools were the ideal places for the Japanese regime to indoctrinate Korean youths with the Japanese language and culture, but as of 1937 only one-third of school-aged Koreans were enrolled in school.[28]

On the world stage, Japan's colonial policies, including assimilation, were not unique. French educational facilities in Africa taught African children to speak French at school to enlighten them about Western civilization as well as make them obedient subjects. The French demanded the cultural rebirth of their colonial subjects as a way to citizenship.[29] The United States attempted to force Native Americans to accept American culture throughout the 1930s, and used more coercion to assimilate the Native Americans than Japan used in Korea. For example, Native American children were taken from their parents, put in boarding schools, and punished for speaking their language. The same practices took place in Australia with the Aborigines. Interestingly, the French offered citizenship to some of its African and Vietnamese subjects, although very few were eligible. Citizenship was a benefit that Japan denied Koreans until 1945, the last year of the war. Such colonial examples help us better understand the global historical processes in which Japan participated; they do not deny or lessen the suffering and exploitation of the Korean people.

During the Asian-Pacific War, the GGK used the Korean elite to tighten and deepen its control over Korean society. Beginning in the 1930s, the GGK increasingly required the upper classes at local and national levels to cooperate with government assimilation policies. By 1940 most of Korea's educators, technocrats, businessmen, socialites, monks, and other elites were drawn into the orbit of state power and, eventually, openly supported

Japanese policies.[30] The GGK required them to serve as the spokesmen for
and enforcers of state policies. Korean cooperation was essential to Japan's
efforts because it helped legitimize Japan's unpopular policies by being the
hand and fist of the regime. The actions of the elites during the war were at
variance with their actions in the 1920s, when many elites participated in
the cultural nationalist movement. Cultural nationalists worked within the
stringent boundaries set by the GGK, but their activities were designed for
the betterment of Korean society.

Koreans who cooperated with the colonial bureaucracy helped mobilize
the masses in various ways that included publishing articles in newspapers
and journals, traveling on lecture circuits, offering donations, and head-
ing semigovernmental groups. Korean notables such as literary figure Yi
Kwang-su, scholar Ch'oe Nam-sŏn, businessman Kim Sŏng-su, social
activist Pak Ch'un-gŭm, army colonel Kim Sŏg-wŏn, and American educated reformer Yun Ch'i-ho lent their names and energies to Japan's war
effort. Members of the Korean royal family also participated in propaganda
efforts. Princes Yi U and Yi Kŏn, both graduates of a Japanese cadet school,
were officers in the Japanese military, although their posts were largely
ornamental.[31] By cooperating, elites weakened their credentials as national
leaders among the Korean populace. The colonial regime probably understood and exploited this paradox. This ploy decapitated potential Korean
resistance because most of the Korea's leadership was caught up in Japan's
nexus of power. As a result, Korea did not have a recognized national leader
on the peninsula on a par with India's Gandhi, and this contributed to
Korea's postwar chaos.

More useful to Japan than national elites were the tens of thousands of
Koreans at the local level who were activists for Japan's war effort. The activities of pro-Japanese Koreans (K: *ch'inilp'a*) fostered a social environment in
which Koreans were expected to submit to government demands. Japanese
officials would have had great difficulty ruling Korea without the assistance
of the thousands of ethnic Koreans who served as educators, policemen,
and patriotic unit heads. Koreans took bureaucratic positions in colonial
government in increasing numbers during the war to replace conscripted
Japanese.[32] Korean authorities who actively cooperated with Japan played a
critical role in the mobilization of Korea because they helped recruit fellow
Koreans for war, often betraying the trust of neighbors and friends.

Koreans who cooperated often did so for a multitude of reasons. Suffice it to say that some elites were coerced; others acted with Korea's long-term interest (namely independence) at heart; and some cooperated to gain social status and economic benefits. Underlying the actions of many were self-preservation and the enrichment of their families. Businessmen such as Kim Sŏng-su knew that financial opportunities depended on close alignment with the colonial state. Scholars and poets had agendas that were more difficult to decipher. Ch'oe Chŏng-hŭi used some of her writings to attack male dominance in Korean society.[33]

Ardent supporters of assimilation policies, such as Hyŏng Yŏng-sŏp and Yi Hang-nyŏng, sought equality for Koreans. Yi, in expectation of equality, assailed the Japanese for continuing to discriminate against Koreans.[34] Some sincere nationalist Koreans felt that Japan's tutelage was critical to the progression of Korean modernity; in such cases, they blamed the lower classes for the overall lack of progress in Korean rights.[35] Given the plethora of motives Koreans had for cooperating with the colonial regime, it is impossible to delineate who was truly pro-Japanese because nearly all Koreans, on a daily basis, acted in ways that supported Japan. Hundreds of thousands cheered Japanese troops during parades and at train stations, used the Japanese language on a daily basis, or purchased Japanese goods. Such activities do not necessarily qualify individuals as being pro-Japanese. The larger point is that Koreans, from the businessman to the bureaucrat down to the tenant farmer, merely sought to survive and better their lives, and the only way to do so meant submitting to Japanese policies.[36]

Those who resisted faced economic, social, or legal repercussions from the colonial regime. Korean nationalists were imprisoned or subjected to surveillance or loss of economic privileges. The difficulty of remaining true to Korean independence, or even indifferent to Japan's assimilation policies, was summarized by Yun Ch'i-ho, who wrote in his diary on July 24, 1938, "We must make up our mind to be the Japanese subjects or else to immigrate to Europe or America or heaven. It is very dangerous to straddle the fence."[37]

KOREAN READINESS FOR WAR

The worldwide depression of the 1930s had bankrupted thousands of farmers, many of whom were illiterate, who then moved to urban centers in Korea and Japan to search for jobs as manual laborers. Korea's largest cities possessed a surplus of untrained, uneducated day laborers. To alleviate Korean unemployment and reduce migration to Japan, the GGK launched the Official Employment Promotion Policy (J: Kan Assen Shokugyō Seisaku) in April 1934. Employment introduction offices (J: *shokugyō shōkaijo*), the engine of this policy, provided occupational assistance to the unemployed and to recently graduated students in Korea. This policy diverted surplus labor from Korea's rural southern provinces to the industrializing north.[38] During the Asia-Pacific War these offices helped secure Korean labor (mostly unskilled) for businesses in Korea and Japan, as well as comfort women for military brothels.

Like other colonial powers, Japan had not invested in the human resources of her colonies. In the prewar period, the GGK did not have the resources to build large numbers of schools, fund social programs, or significantly improve the overall health of the Korean populace.[39] These deficiencies in colonial social and educational policies led to qualitative deficiencies within Korean human resources that hindered Koreans' wartime contribution. Specifically, there was no compulsory education for Korean children, and the quality of education offered in Korean schools was far inferior to Japanese schools. Korean schools were designed to secure Japan's hegemony over Korean society, not to empower and train it. Furthermore, until 1938 the Korean education system focused on civic and moral training (J: *kōmin kyōiku*) and did not teach students technical skills or offer the martial and national training (J: *kokumin kyōiku*) that was provided to Japanese students.[40]

Statistics emphasize how Japan's prewar education policies unwittingly limited the wartime usefulness of the Korean people. A low school attendance rate (65.5 students per 1,000 children, compared to 109.5 for Formosans and 184.7 for Japanese), resulted in inadequate Japanese language skills among Korean youth.[41] Low levels of Japanese language comprehension reduced the effectiveness of Koreans who worked as laborers in Japan. The colonial government remained doubtful of Koreans' loyalty and capabilities, and, as a result, was hesitant to provide Koreans with weapons, real or intellectual, that could be used by the independence movement. As a result, workers had lower educational qualifications and fewer options for higher education, which meant that Korean workers were best suited for manual labor and nontechnical positions, but not to be technicians, machinists, or engineers. This dearth of skilled laborers hurt wartime production as unskilled Koreans replaced skilled Japanese workers who were sent to war.

The industrialization of Korea and the growth of an industrial workforce began in earnest following the Manchurian Incident in 1931. Korea became a continental logistics base (J: *heitan kichi*) for Japan's military's exploits in China. By 1936 the number of Korean wage laborers reached 594,793 workers, and by 1940 had grown to 702,868. Three years later this number more than tripled to 2,122,374.[42] The growth was especially notable in mining and construction. In a decade, the number of laborers in factories and mines nearly quadrupled, while construction workers increased nearly ninefold. Table 1.1 shows the distribution of labor in Korea in the last two years of the war, as well as the rapid industrialization of Korea. These numbers do not reflect the hundreds of thousands of Korean laborers mobilized in Japan.

TABLE 1.1   Korean Labor from 1943 to 1945

Type of Industry	Number of Workers
Construction	437,752
Manufacturing	591,494
Transportation	179,544
Forestry	205,911
Marine Products	211,520
Metal Mining	273,863
Coal Mining	72,561
Agriculture-Related	130,377
Mariners	19,352
Total	**2,122,374**

Source: Pak Kyŏng-sik, *Nihon teikoku shugi*, vol. 2, 162.

Koreans were not conscripted into the army prior to 1937 for several reasons. First, Koreans had a cultural aversion to martial activities that had originated in the Korean Confucian elite class's exemption from military obligations.[43] Japan, on the other hand, had a warrior elite class (*samurai*). Thus, Korean and Japanese culture had disparate views on the social value of soldiers. Late in the colonial era, Japan attempted to impose its *samurai* tradition upon Korea through an education system.

A second reason Koreans were forbidden from enlisting in the army was that too few young men spoke Japanese. Colonial and military officials were deeply concerned that Koreans' Japanese language proficiency levels were deficient. Table 1.2 shows that late in the colonial period, less than one-quarter of all Koreans could communicate effectively in Japanese.[44] Proficiency rates were higher among young men than in the general populace because the youth were more likely than their elders to have attended school. Nevertheless, these language deficiencies troubled the Japanese army because men who could not speak Japanese would be unable to take orders and therefore useless on the battlefield. One education official opined that Korean soldiers without Japanese language skills might just as well be deaf and mute.[45] The low Japanese comprehension levels reveal the deficiencies of prewar education in Korea. To promote the Japanese language and transform Korean youth into better Japanese subjects, the Japanese revised their educational laws in 1938 and eliminated the Korean language in schools.

TABLE 1.2   Japanese Language Ability among Koreans, 1920–1943

Year	Total Speakers
1920	367,365 (2.12%)
1925	947,146 (5.11)
1930	1,627,136 (8.27)
1936	2,103,962 (9.84)
1940	3,573,338 (15.57)
1943	5,722,448 (22.15)

Source: *Chōsen Sōtokufu Teikoku Gikai setsumei shiryō*, Diet 86, 1944; in ICCCSC 22, 231. The number in parentheses is the percent of the Korean population.

A third problem hindering Korean military service was a plethora of legal barriers. The Military Service Law stipulated that a man must have graduated from a six-year elementary school in order to serve in the military. The school curriculum and the classification of the schools in Korea disqualified Koreans from soldiering.[46] Korean education focused on morals and loyalty to the Japanese emperor, but lacked the martial training offered to Japanese students. Furthermore, attendance rates for all Korean youth during the war never reached more than 55 percent, and never surpassed 75 percent for young men.[47] The overall impoverished circumstances in rural Korea, in which families could not afford the school fees, contributed to the low attendance rates.[48] Still, those who attended school were ill-prepared to serve in the military. This underscores the larger issue at hand: Japan's prewar policies shortchanged the Japanese empire in the long run because Japan could place only limited effective demands on Korea. During World War II, Korea possessed too few skilled laborers for industrial labor, and too few men were prepared to join the army or navy.

INTERNATIONAL CONTEXT OF MILITARY MOBILIZATION

The historiography of the nationalist historical paradigm omits references to Western imperialist and colonial practices. This sort of tunnel vision erroneously leads the reader to believe that imperial Japan was uniquely barbaric and that the suffering of the Korean nation is unparalleled in modern history. Recent revisionist studies on colonial modernity have helped to correct this blind spot by looking to Taiwan and other colonial situations as part of an examination of Korea.[49] The following discussion on the global practice of wartime mobilization of colonial peoples shows that Japan's enlistment of Koreans through a volunteer soldier system (1938–1943) and a conscription system (1944–1945) has been common in imperial systems.

Japan, like European imperial powers, was apprehensive about randomly enlisting a large number of subjects into the military because of the politicizing effect it could have on them. Imperial overlords understood that subalterns would not forget the skills they learned in boot camps and factories, no matter how helpless and incompetent the colonial discourse portrayed them to be.[50]

The conundrum that colonial powers confronted when enthralled in a war of survival was that the metropole worried that it might lose the war without the assistance of the colony, yet mobilizing the colony altered the dynamics of the ruler-subject relationship by empowering subalterns with technical and military skills that could be used in a struggle for independence. More importantly, these wars awakened within subjugated peoples the mentality that the metropole was not invincible. This meant that the master-and-servant relationship could not last. For example, during World War I, Indians bargained for political concessions from Britain, forcing the

British to announce that they would roll back imperial control over India to encourage cooperation among the Indian population. Likewise, the Japanese cabinet promised Koreans representation in the diet starting in 1946 as a nonofficial concession. Japan surrendered before this actualized.

Western European nations had a longstanding practice of marshaling for war their colonial subalterns from Africa, South Asia, and Southeast Asia. By the twentieth century, the military mustering of subject peoples was practiced by the British, French, Germans, Dutch, and other European colonial powers. The irony of colonial soldiering was that Western powers mustered their subjects to expand and to defend the imperial empire— which, by extension, prolonged and deepened the oppression of the subaltern peoples, including those in the colonial armies.[51] Colonial soldiers were not fighting to preserve Western civilization, nor were they preserving democracy—instead, they were merely expendable pawns of imperialism.

The international practices of colonial mobilization provide a revealing and often ignored backdrop to Japan's utilization of Korean manpower. By global colonial standards, Japan's usage of colonial manpower for military service was comparatively late. The Japanese government was aware of Europe's precedence when it mobilized Koreans as laborers and soldiers. The impact of Europe's practices upon Japan's decision-making process is not clearly outlined in government documents or publications; Japanese officials rarely justified the mobilization of their colonies based on existing colonial precedence. Nevertheless, Japanese authorities could not ignore the ubiquitous presence of Indian troops throughout the British Empire and the usage of African troops in World War I. In fact, the Japanese were in a minority among colonial powers because Japan's peacetime army was made up exclusively of Japanese citizens.[52]

European powers maintained colonial armies to enhance the colonizers' military and political power within the colony and at the international level. These armies policed the colony to prevent or suppress internal uprisings, maintained internal security by reducing banditry, and guarded borderlands from encroachment by rival imperial powers. Native armies had the added benefit of being cheaper than European troops and were treated as more expendable than Caucasian troops. As a result, colonial powers frequently used colonial soldiers to expand their empire and to fight in savage wars of peace.[53] For example, France had to rely on colonial armies to handle overseas possessions because soldiers in the metropolitan army could not be sent overseas without the approval of the army and the French legislature.[54] History is filled with accounts of empires that utilized the manpower of conquered peoples for military purposes. Imperial Rome, the Mongol Empire, and the Ottoman Empire, to name a few, required subjugated populations to supply soldiers. For our present purposes, a brief examination of colonial armies in the Age of Imperialism (1850–1914) is useful for understanding the global climate in which Japan acted.

Most early colonial mobilization of native troops was undertaken by joint-stock trading companies. For example, the British East India Company employed Indian sepoy as early as the 1740s. By 1800 the company employed over 100,000 sepoy, and by the 1840s had close to 200,000 sepoy in the Indian presidency armies. Most soldiers originated from the Bengal and Madras regions.[55] In fact, the British conquest of India was largely accomplished by Indian regiments. These troops, however, mutinied against British rule during the Indian Mutiny (1857–1858), leading to the direct rule of India under the British Crown.[56]

Britain was shaken by the mutiny but established firmer control over India through fundamental changes to their colonial practices. The British restructured the sepoy units to create the Indian Army, which consisted of fewer artillery units. Also, the ethnic composition drastically changed. Instead of Bengali troops, the military recruited Sikh and Ghurka ethnic minorities, with smaller numbers from Yamuna and Madras. By 1900 over half of the Indian Army originated from the greater Punjab area of northern India. The British considered the Sikh and Gurkha to be India's martial races, and these soon became the "sword arm of the Raj." Some Gurkha originated from Nepal, which was not formally a British possession.[57]

The Dutch East India Company (Vereenigde Oostindische Compagnie, VOC) was another European trade company that recruited soldiers from its colonial possessions. The Dutch VOC employed Southeast Asian soldiers within the Spice Islands as early as the 1670s, showing preference to the Christian ethnicities from Timor and Moluccas over the Muslim majority. Native troops were segregated by ethnicity and locally commanded by natives, but the high command in the larger units consisted of European officers.[58] By one estimation, two-thirds of the Dutch East India colonial army was Asian.[59]

By the mid-1800s government-run colonial regimes replaced trading companies. The colonial governments confronted several paradoxical problems when recruiting and training indigenous armies: first, how to entice subjects to participate in military service at the expense of the sovereignty of the native states; second, how to secure sufficient manpower for military projects, especially during times of war; and, third, how to maintain control over colonial subjects who, through their employment in the military, were empowered by skills they learned. On the first count, colonial armies relied on economic factors to entice colonial soldiers to willingly serve in the military. Regular pay and bonuses were often sufficient to attract recruits. In underdeveloped regions with surplus populations, the lure of economic gain generally outweighed a desire for ethnic or national independence. Men from all over India attempted to deceive recruiters by changing their names to conform to Gurkha traditions so they could serve in the military.[60] Other factors that facilitated recruitment included three meals a day, the social prestige of wearing a uniform, and adventure.[61] In some cases, men hoped to learn marketable skills that, along with their veteran status, would contribute to their postwar economic advancement.[62]

European colonial regimes did not always attract sufficient numbers of volunteers with socioeconomic incentives. Under the duress of war, too few colonial subjects volunteered for military service. Simple factors hindered widespread recruitment, namely that indigenous men feared traveling overseas, considered the pay to be too low, or did not want to risk their lives in a white man's war. European militaries responded to the shortfalls by turning to conscription and coercion. The French established a conscription system in West Africa in 1912, and later in Algeria and Tunisia, to compensate for the military imbalance with Germany.[63] During wars, colonial regimes mustered for service all young healthy men who met the minimum requirements.[64] Recruitment systems occasionally degenerated into raiding villages and shanghaiing young men into the military if legal recruitment yielded too few recruits.

Colonial armies, in order to maintain control over colonial troops, segregated nonwhite troops into their own units and kept these units under the command of European officers. The British and French utilized this command structure to ensure that no colonial soldier, African or Indian, had command over a European. And in the military courts, nonwhites could not punish Caucasians. Furthermore, indigenous soldiers had to yield to whites if they were of the same rank.[65] Native troops, when compared with their European counterparts, were promoted more slowly, encountered a lower glass ceiling, and were offered lower salaries. That said, the French promoted a higher proportion of Africans to be officers within their units than did the British in Africa. White soldiers were paid better and given better quality rations than were nonwhite soldiers of equal rank.[66] The rigid racial lines established by the Western imperial powers were based on racial stereotypes and cultural factors. In some instances, colonial subjects were noted to lack the proper education, sufficient intelligence, or the correct character to have command over Caucasians.[67]

Colonial authorities worried that Africans, when removed from their villages, would be uncontrollable, and that African soldiers and laborers, when they returned to their homeland, might clamor to seek improved conditions within the colony—or even political equality. Also, European imperialists feared that African soldiers might rebel and use their military skills to fight for independence. In essence, imperial powers feared that martial training might spark an ethnic pride among natives that would challenge white supremacy.[68] A colonial army was a double-edged sword: it served to expand and stabilize the empire, but those troops, like the sepoy of India, might mutiny or challenge European supremacy.

Europeans passed laws and spread propaganda to overcome opposition to military service and to limit unwanted influences such as pan-Africanism. The French promoted assimilation, while the English allowed cultural diversity within military units. The French required indigenous troops to learn and speak French, while British commanding officers often used the native tongue of the men they commanded. In Africa and India, European colonial regimes allied with one tribe or group and used them to police the wider population. France's African armies used the Berber of North Africa, who were considered a warrior race, to control other ethnicities.[69] And the British relied on the Sikh and Gurkha from Northeastern India following the sepoy mutiny. A telling example of this divide-and-rule tactic is found in Burma. In 1925 the India Army discharged all Burmese from the military because the British believed that Burmese nationalists posed a threat to British rule. Thereafter, the India Army in Burma recruited only Chin, Karen, and Kachin minorities.[70] The benefit of this policy was that it pitted colonial subjects against one another.

European powers successfully employed their colonial armies to expand

and stabilize their territorial possessions. The British used Indian troops as a fire brigade to deal with crises in China, Africa, and Southeast Asia, as well as for the occupation of most of its Asian possessions. Indian soldiers took part in all three Afghan wars (1839–1842, 1878–1880, and 1919), the conquest and occupation of Burma, and Britain's victory in the Opium War (1839–1842) with China. African troops were equally important to Britain. Over half of the British army that defeated the Zulu in South Africa in 1879 were from the Natal Native Contingent from British South Africa. In British East Africa, the British organized the King's African Rifles in 1902 as a constabulary force manned by African soldiers (*askari*). And the West African Gold Coast Regiment defended frontiers, assisted the civil government, and provided military assistance to other territories.[71]

Similarly, the French mobilized colonial subjects in the French Colonial Forces and the Army of Africa, a division of the French Metropolitan Army.[72] The French mobilized irregular units (*goums*) and light infantry (*tiraillers*) from Morocco, Tunisia, Algeria, Senegal, and the Ivory Coast. The light infantry and riflemen from Algeria and Senegal who served France as early as the 1840s and 1830s, respectively, participated in the conquest of Madagascar in 1895. Algerian infantrymen fought alongside the French as early as the Franco-Prussian War in 1870 and as late as the Battle of Dien Bien Phu (Vietnam) in 1954. The French also used irregular units from Morocco and French Sudan.

WORLD WAR I AND THE INTERWAR ERA

World War I was the first worldwide mobilization of European colonies, transforming a local continental war into a global conflict. All European colonial powers involved in the war, including the Belgians, Germans, and Portuguese, used colonial manpower as soldiers, laborers, and other auxiliary roles to assist in the defense of the imperial homeland or of African colonies. Britain's Caucasian settler communities from her colonies contributed significantly to the war effort. Canada, New Zealand, South Africa, and Australia sent close to a million men overseas to fight in the war, and 140,884 of these lost their lives.[73] More importantly, European powers drew just as heavily from their African and Asian colonies. Great Britain and France mobilized nearly one million black Africans as soldiers and another million as porters and construction workers for military campaigns in Africa, on the western front, and in the Middle East. For example, the British mobilized nearly 30,000 East Africans in the King's African Rifles, and 25,000 soldiers in British West Africa.

The recruitment methods used by the British and the French differed. The French, concerned with growing German power, began a prewar build up of its African colonial armies as early as 1909 and implemented a conscription system in 1912. This allowed the French to move soldiers from Africa to the western front at the outbreak of war. By the end of 1914 over 160,000 men in the Senegal Rifles were serving in the French military. To quell and prevent revolts, as happened in Tunisian and Vietnamese, the French imposed martial law and censored news media in its colonies.[74]

The British made up for their shortage of manpower through existing social networks that included village chiefs, administrators, and businessmen. Colonial authorities assigned traditional rulers and chiefs with quotas for soldiers and laborers that were filled by accepting volunteers and, when necessary, acquiring soldiers by force. Traditional rulers cooperated with the British to preserve their status as well as for financial gain. The British paid bonuses to chiefs in West Africa for each soldier and laborer.[75] When chiefs failed to meet their quotas, however, the British rounded up men for military and portage service.

France used colonial subjects, regardless of their color, to work and fight on all fronts manned by the French Army. Asians and Africans were stationed at the Dardanelles, on the Bulgarian front, and on the Western Front. France mobilized between 500,000 and 818,000 colonial subjects as soldiers, another 223,000 North Africans as industrial laborers, and untold thousands of others as porters and nonindustrial laborers. The French raised approximately 34,000 Moroccans, and 173,000 Arabs and Berbers in Algeria as soldiers during World War I. By war's end, the French had imported 215,000 colonial troops for service in France.[76] The French also mobilized tens of thousands of African laborers in Greece, Mesopotamia, and throughout Africa. However, the French government segregated African industrial workers from the French population in order to maintain a proper racial hierarchy.

The British were not as liberal as the French in their use of African colonial subjects; they mobilized African troops only within Africa. The British were uncomfortable with the presence of Indian soldiers on the British Isles, and it was unthinkable to them to bring black colonial soldiers into the heart of the empire. The one exception to this was the British loosening the color bar for the Royal Flying Corps and Royal Air Force during World Wars I and II, to allow men of non-European descent to become pilots. But once the wars ended, the peacetime restrictions were reinstated.

Europe's Asian colonies were also called upon to supply military manpower. The Indian Army supplied Britain with 1,440,437 soldiers. Over one-third of India's combat troops came from Punjab.[77] The Indian Army was deployed to the Western Front and against the Ottoman Empire in Mesopotamia and Gallipoli. However, Britain's reliance on a handful of ethnicities for recruitment limited the pool of available for servicemen. Thus, as the war continued, recruitment in India slackened, leading the British to consider implementing a conscription system in Punjab. The idea was rejected out of fear that a draft might lead to political unrest.[78]

The British employed hundreds of thousands of Africans in noncombatant roles. During the East African Campaign in World War I, 327,000 men in the Egyptian Labor Corps worked for Britain. And by 1918 roughly 200,000 men in Britain's East Africa Protectorate (modern Kenya) served as laborers; it is estimated that one in five died.[79] Although China was not a European colony, Britain recruited around 100,000 Chinese for the war at Wei-hai-Wei, a small British concession territory on the Shandong Peninsula. These workers dug trenches, laid railways, and carried provisions. The French also transported 140,000 Vietnamese to France as laborers and porters.

An estimated one million Africans served as laborers, porters, or construction workers during military campaigns on the Western Front and in the Middle East, and these units suffered 200,000 casualties. Other estimates claim that 50,000 African soldiers and porters died, with tens of thousands of others wounded.[80] French colonial soldiers on the Western Front suffered 25,000 casualties, a casualty rate around 14.5 percent, which was comparable to the rate for French soldiers.[81] Indian and Nepalese troops suffered 62,056 deaths.

After World War I the colonial powers demobilized their colonial soldiers and laborers, although the French used Senegalese troops to occupy the German Rhineland. Most colonial corps reverted back to their traditional roles, but with a fueled anticolonial nationalism. Colonial rulers remained vigilant to protect their domination over their empires. After the war, the French regime passed a peacetime conscription act in 1919 to recruit 50,000 men a year. In Africa, the King's African Rifles continued its prewar roles by policing intertribal warfare and preventing banditry, as well as hunting cattle thieves and rogue lions.[82] These troops protected Kenya and other British possessions from an invasion following the Italian occupation of Ethiopia.

The British implemented a volunteer system in Malaya that offers a useful touchstone for contextualizing Japan's actions in Korea. The Royal Malay Regiment, a volunteer unit, was created in 1933 to replace Indian troops that were costly to the Straits Settlements. The regiment accepted only ethnic Malays, despite a large Chinese and Indian population in Malaya. Over 1,000 men applied for the corps in 1933, and twenty-five recruits were enlisted into the Experimental Company that became the Malay Regiment. In 1935 the regiment expanded to 380 men, and by 1942 grew to 1,400 volunteer soldiers. Throughout the training process, British colonial methods exhibited a cultural sensitivity that was lacking in the Japanese in Korea. The British adapted the uniforms and some conditions of military service to reflect Malay culture, which was possible because the rank and file were all Malay. Commands were in English, but most other communication was in Malay. Nevertheless, the officer corps of the Malay Regiment were all white.[83] Japan, by comparison, required all communication be in Japanese, and Koreans did not form their own units.

Europe's wartime use of colonial manpower differed from Japan's in several ways. Unlike the segregated Euro-American battalions, the Japanese army integrated Koreans into the regular units and even promoted them to ranks where they were in direct command over Japanese soldiers. Of course, the integration of Korean soldiers was done to maintain surveillance and control over Koreans. In fact, one purpose of Korean military service was to force the assimilation of the inductee. The Japanese were unable to use divide-and-rule tactics in Korea because Korean society was ethnically and linguistically homogeneous. Instead, Japan recruited a cross section of Korean society.

COLONIAL TROOPS IN WORLD WAR II

The United States was among the imperial powers to establish a colonial army. The United States military used Filipinos as irregulars and scouts during the Philippine-American War (1899–1902). These forces were reorganized in 1935 when General Douglas MacArthur was appointed to build the Philippine Army so that the Philippine Commonwealth could defend itself when it became independent in 1946. The commonwealth government proclaimed that all twenty-year-old men had to register for military training. MacArthur hoped to train 40,000 reservists a year who could be called up to defend the islands. On July 27, 1941, President Franklin Roosevelt nationalized the Philippine Army and made MacArthur commanding general of US forces in the Philippines, essentially combining the United States and Philippine militaries, but in segregated units. On November 24, 1941, MacArthur ordered 140,000 Philippine reservists to report for active duty.[84] During the Japanese invasion, approximately 120,000 Filipino soldiers and reservists fought for the American military. Most troops on the Bataan Death March were Filipino. And on the American mainland, more than 7,000 Filipinos enlisted after the outbreak of war and were placed in the two segregated Filipino Infantry Regiments.[85]

During World War II, European colonial powers once again mobilized their colonies. Prior to the surrender of France in June 1940, the French mustered nearly 500,000 colonial troops in French North and West Africa, and another 116,000 from Indochina.[86] However, the war ended for many of these with the fall of France in 1940. The war continued for others because Free France continued to recruit colonial troops to fight with the Allies, recruiting 385,000 soldiers from North Africa, including Moroccan, Algerian, and Tunisian irregular troops and infantry. French West Africa contributed another 150,000 troops to the Allied war effort.

The British used the greatest numbers of colonial subjects for war. Nearly 200,000 soldiers and laborers were recruited from West Africa for campaigns in East and North Africa. The King's African Rifles from East Africa contributed nearly 325,000 troops and laborers, and another 65,000 joined the Royal West African Frontier Force and served in East Africa and Burma. And South Africa, as part of the commonwealth, provided 200,000 troops, one-third of whom were unarmed black soldiers, for the reconquest of Ethiopia. In the case of South Africa, government officials were keen to prevent the politicization and empowerment of black subjects by arming only Caucasians. Britain's African contingent was dwarfed by 1.8 million Indian soldiers. South Asian troops served in North Africa, Singapore, and

Burma, as well as in the invasion of Italy. Interestingly, Britain's concerns over the loyalty of its colonial subjects were made manifest when the Japanese succeeded in enlisting 20,000 of the 45,000 captured Indian troops for the Indian National Army under Chandra Bose.[87]

The British and French used millions of nonskilled African laborers to increase food production, and hundreds of thousands of skilled workers in industries to sustain wartime production. The British mobilized about 100,000 Africans in central Nigeria to work on plantations and in tin mines, often in appalling conditions. Furthermore, 184,000 Indians served overseas as technical, skilled, and medical personnel. The industrial usefulness of colonies to their imperial overlords during both world wars was limited by the lack of industrialization within the colonies. India's light industries produced tailored items, shoes, and parachutes, but few, if any, tanks, ships, or artillery. The lack of industrialization was logical during peacetime, because it prevented the long-term economic empowerment of the colony, but these actions contributed to the underdevelopment of the colony's economy and society. During war the colonies provided little industrial assistance. For example, India's economy, much like Korea's, was ill-suited to supply the metropole with modern weaponry such as tanks, airplanes, and warships.

Nazi Germany was another European combatant to use labor from conquered territories. Germany experienced labor shortages early in the war and, as a result, implemented short-sighted labor mobilization policies. The Germans, like Japan, remedied labor shortages internally by first recruiting unemployed labor, then shifted workers from nonstrategic industries to strategic factories, and finally drew on youth, women, and the elderly. After internal resources were exhausted, Germany mobilized large numbers of foreign laborers, including prisoners of war. As early as 1939 the Nazi regime used Polish workers and prisoners of war to harvest crops and work in factories. Without the use of foreign labor, the agricultural and industrial production of Germany would have faced severe labor shortages by 1942. The German war economy, therefore, had no choice but to depend on millions of forced laborers.[88] Later, the Third Reich imported Russians, French, Danes, and other nationalities. The Nazis also forced 800,000 Hungarians to build military fortifications. By 1944 foreigners from twenty-six countries constituted upwards of one-fifth (8.1 million total) of the German workforce. However, the Nazi economy suffered for want of skilled labor.

Nazi and Japanese mobilization of the manpower in conquered territories differed in several ways. Japan's demands on Korean labor were less extreme and arbitrary than were Nazi Germany's in Eastern Europe. And, unlike the Nazis, Japan had no sanctioned slave labor camps for Koreans, but the conditions of Southeast Asian laborers in Japan's military was very close to slavelike. Paul H. Kratoska's *Asian Labor in the Wartime Japanese Empire* (2005) provides an excellent account of Japan's treatment of peoples in occupied China, Indonesia, Philippines, and other areas. This volume of edited articles provides an informative although general account of Japan's exploitation of Asian populations during the Asia-Pacific War.[89] Japan's treatment of peoples in newly conquered territories was much worse and less legally founded than the mobilization of its long-established colonies of Korea and Taiwan.

The use of colonial soldiers continued after World War II. British colonial troops (specifically the Punjabi Cavalry) were sent into Indonesia after the war to fight the insurgency on behalf of the Dutch, and the King's African Rifles were used to suppress communist insurrection in Malay colonies in 1960. The French used Moroccans in Vietnam and Algeria to suppress independence movements.

JAPAN AND COLONIAL TAIWAN

Japan gained control of Taiwan from Qing China at the end of the First Sino-Japanese War (1894–1895). Japan's rule of Taiwan provided the Japanese government with administrative experience; however, differences between Taiwan and Korea obviated the direct translation of lessons learned in Taiwan to Korea.[90] Japan's rule in Taiwan was complicated by the cultural connections between mainland China and Taiwan. The significant ethnic and historical connections between mainland China and Taiwan were not found in Korea.[91] Korea, on the other hand, had a centuries-long history of independence and had a strong ethnic identity, whereas Taiwan had been part of China's political orbit. As a result, the Taiwanese lacked a cohesive national identity. Despite this, the Japanese regime in Taiwan faced significant resistance during its first decade of rule. During pacification campaigns from 1898 to 1902 the Japanese killed 11,950 Taiwanese resistance fighters and sentenced another 3,000 to death.[92] Intermittent indigenous resistance continued until 1930.

In Taiwan, the Japanese implemented assimilation policies similar to those in Korea. The anchor of assimilation in Taiwan was the education system. Compulsory education began in Taiwan on April 1, 1943, and by the end of the war over 70 percent of school-age children were attending school, with 81 percent of school-aged boys and 61 percent of girls enrolled in elementary school.[93] Official statistics, although unreliable, claim that by 1945 over 80 percent of Taiwanese were conversant in Japanese.[94] Later in the colonial era, the Japanese introduced the imperialization movement in Taiwan and Korea. This movement stressed the political duties as well as the obligations of the subaltern. The Japanese hoped to educate and assimilate Taiwanese and Koreans before introducing military service.

The methods and goals of assimilation in Taiwan and Korea were similar but had differences to account for the cultural and historical distinctions between the two colonies. For example, the name change policy, which the Koreans despised, was limited in Taiwan to a select number of willing families, with as few as 7 percent of families adopting Japanese names. The Taiwanese name change policy, unlike the Korean system, applied to households, not individuals, so the whole family had to meet the qualifications to take a Japanese name. As a result, name changes took place mostly among the upper classes.[95] In Korea there was considerable pressure on family heads to take Japanese names, resulting in nearly 81 percent of individuals adopting Japanese names.

Taiwan, as a stepping stone to the conquest of the south, housed military supplies and military-related industries. Shortly after the outbreak of the Sino-Japanese War, Taiwan's government-general recruited Taiwanese as nurses, porters, and interpreters. Japan also recruited thousands of volunteers for military-run farms in China. The mobilization of Taiwanese as soldiers began with the formal announcement of the volunteer system in June 1941 and the induction of soldiers in April 1942. This came four years after a similar system in Korea. During the first year of the volunteer system, 425,921 Taiwanese, out of a male population of three million, applied for 1,000 available slots. The second round of applications reached 601,147 applications for 1,000 positions. In 1944, 759,276 applied, and 2,497 were enlisted.[96] A naval volunteer system was announced in Taiwan at same time as in Korea (August 1943), and the Imperial Japanese Navy received 316,097 applications.[97] Despite Taiwan's smaller population, the volunteer system garnered more applications than the comparable system in Korea. There is debate over the degree to which these applications indicate a spirit of volunteerism because of the pressure on young men to apply that came from local government authorities, educational officials, and semigovernmental organizations.

The military mobilization of Taiwan expanded as the war worsened for Japan. By the end of the war, over 200,000 Taiwanese had worked overseas as civilian laborers for the Japanese military. The Japanese implemented conscription in Taiwan in January 1945. Japan enlisted 207,183 men, 80,433 of which were deployed overseas; the rest remained in Taiwan to prepare for an Allied invasion. These statistics include only the survivors, and are therefore a low-end estimate. Unfortunately, the full scope is not known. During the war, an estimated 3.4 million students were mobilized as laborers.[98] The Taiwanese contribution to the war was modest, but given the overall population of Taiwan, it was impressive nonetheless. Japanese government statistics claim that Taiwan provided 207,183 soldiers and hundreds of thousands of laborers. Of these, 30,304 died during the war (2,146 soldiers and 28,158 civilian employees).[99]

CONCLUSION

In the twenty-seven years of colonial rule leading up to the outbreak of the Second Sino-Japanese War in 1937, the GGK had strengthened its control over Korean society. However, this power was far from hegemonic. The colonial regime focused on regulating the social, economic, and political nexus of power, but had done little to fashion the Korean people into willing warriors or capable industrial laborers. As the war with China, and later with the Allies, expanded, the central government realized that the Korean population was not prepared for wartime mobilization. To prepare and engage Koreans in the war effort, Japanese authorities moved cautiously, shrouding new policies in propaganda and a veneer of legalism. The Japanese did not move in leaps and bounds to mobilize Koreans. To do so, the Japanese feared, might antagonize Koreans and contribute to resistance. The result was a piecemeal approach to mobilization. The Japanese were not alone in their wartime use of colonial subjects. The GGK and the Imperial Japanese Army had a great amount of European history in African and Asia to use as guidance.

2 | THE KOREAN VOLUNTEER SOLDIER SYSTEMS

The Korean Special Volunteer Soldier System (J: Chōsenjin Tokubetsu Shiganhei Seido) began in 1938, the year after war erupted between Japan and China. Between 1938 and 1943 the Japanese army received more than 800,000 applications for military service, and enlisted 17,664 Korean volunteer soldiers; 6,203 students applied for the Korean Student Special Volunteer Soldier System (J: Chōsenjin Gakuto Tokubetsu Shiganhei Seido) in 1943, and the army drafted 4,385. Another 90,000 submitted applications for the Naval Special Volunteer System (J: Kaigun Tokubetsu Shiganhei Seido), and the navy enlisted 2,000 sailors.[1] Given the large numbers of Koreans who applied for military service, the volunteer systems touched the lives of a great number of Koreans, and the colonial state devoted significant resources to the enforcement of these policies. The purpose, goals, and methods of enforcement of the recruitment systems changed from year to year and system to system, making them useful prisms through which to analyze state-society relations within colonial Korea. In 1944 the volunteer systems were replaced by the compulsory military conscription system.

The use of the word "volunteer" (J: *shiga*; K: *chiwŏn*) in the title of these systems is somewhat of a misnomer. The Japanese word *shigan* can be translated as "volunteer" and "applicant." A more appropriate title would be "Special Applicant Soldier System" because some applications were not voluntarily submitted. However, Japanese authorities clearly implied that the system was volunteer because it was granted in response to the Koreans' volunteer spirit (J: *shigannetsu*) and patriotism.[2]

Korea's military participation in the Asia-Pacific War is vital to understanding what Korean scholars consider the most oppressive years of

43

Japan's colonial enterprise. Studies on the forced mobilization of Korea portray the colonial regime's policies in dark, exploitive terms, emphasizing coercion and exploitation. According to these scholars, all applications for the volunteer soldier systems, excepting a handful from collaborators, were the result of coercion; yet this was not the case. The presence of coercion did not relegate the applicant to the status of victim. Koreans did not passively receive and react to Japan's policies; instead, they actively made choices as agents who controlled their own fates. Furthermore, the introduction of the volunteer system exemplifies the military's piecemeal approach to mobilizing Koreans as soldiers.

POLICY FORMATION

Prior to the volunteer service system in 1938, the Government-General of Korea (GGK) and the Imperial Japanese Army had considered Korean military service. Japanese army officials seriously and carefully considered a Korean draft in the early 1930s.[3] In a two-volume booklet published in 1932, the military police (J: *kempeitai*) addressed Korean conscription. Korean Army officials noted that Koreans had served honorably in the supplemental military and regular police forces, including participation in the suppression of outlaws and nationalist Koreans. According to the booklet, Koreans asked, "While we are one race without distinction, why is it that among the three obligations [the draft, taxes, and education], the draft is something we cannot do?" The answer given was that Korea's impoverished economic conditions, along with their cultural aversion toward military service, hindered Korean soldiering. In other words, the draft was not economically feasible in Korea since too many Korean families would suffer economic hardship if their sons served two years in the army.[4] The issue was temporarily resurrected in April 1934 when Pak Ch'un-gŭm, a socially active Korean residing in Japan, unsuccessfully lobbied the diet to permit Koreans to enlist in the army.[5]

Soon after his appointment as governor-general in 1936, Minami Jirō renewed interest in Korean military service. In January 1937, thirty-three Koreans, led by Pak Hŭi-do (one of the thirty-three signers of the March First Declaration of Independence) and Sin T'ae-ak (a lawyer who graduated from Chūo University), organized a committee to discuss soldiering and to lobby important government and army officials to allow Koreans into the military. They did this so that Koreans would benefit culturally and economically from Japan's tutelage and in time become a more modern people.[6] Minami supported this effort on the grounds that the enlistment of Koreans would strengthen the unification of Japan and Korea (J: *naisen ittai*) and thereby allow Koreans to prove themselves as loyal subjects of the emperor. He also lobbied the Tokyo government, claiming that Koreans demanded this right.[7] The Army Ministry heeded Minami's counsel and in early 1937 asked the Korean Army for its opinion regarding the recruitment of Koreans.

Koiso Kuniaki, commander of the Korean Army, responded in June 1937 to the army's inquiry into Korean military service. He opined that soldiering was possible on a limited scale. His main concern was the Koreans' lack of spiritual and patriotic preparedness for the draft. Specifically, portions of the Korean population lacked patriotism, or, worse still, harbored anti-Japanese sentiments. Koiso claimed that Korean intellectuals supported military service because "it was irrational [for Japan] to demand patriotism without the burden of national defense." He thought that the best way to ensure Korean cooperation was to intensify assimilation policies and highlight the defense of Korea.[8]

Koiso also wrote that assimilation and a military draft would be possible thirty to fifty years in the future, but he expressed concern that even then the draft might not be smoothly implemented. Nevertheless, Koiso suggested that, under the right conditions, this process could be rudimentarily achieved in fifteen to twenty years. As a concrete step toward assimilation and the draft, he recommended a volunteer soldier system for Koreans. He also suggested that the GGK needed to establish an education system in Korea that was equal to the one available for Japanese students, because too few Koreans spoke Japanese or had martial training.

Scholars and Korean popular memory assert that the catalyst for the volunteer system was Japan's war with China.[9] On the surface, the chronology bolsters this belief, because the war broke out in July 1937 and the volunteer system was announced in April 1938. However, the outbreak of the Asia-Pacific War in July 1937 came almost a half year *after* discussion began on the volunteer system, and one month after Koiso submitted his report. Certainly, the war increased the attractiveness of Korean soldiering, but in no way was it a determining factor. It is important to note the timing of events in the context of East Asian international relations: Internal discussions to accept applications for a volunteer system began *before* the outbreak of the war with China, and, more importantly, years before the Japanese army had a recognized shortage of manpower. Japan's deteriorating relations with China and the United States might have loomed in the back of policymakers' minds and influenced the decision to expand military service opportunities to the Koreans. Nevertheless, Japan's military adventurism in China was not one of the acknowledged factors in government documents related to the volunteer system.

Furthermore, throughout 1938 Japan remained confident that the "China Incident" would not last long. In previous conflicts with Chiang Kai-shek's regime, the Chinese usually negotiated a settlement in which the Japanese gained concessions. Japan's leadership expected a quick resolution to the war. It is telling that the volunteer soldier system happened on such a small scale (one thousand men were enlisted the first two years) that it did not improve Japan's fighting ability. Government documents from 1938 and 1939 provide no hint that the military expected several hundred Koreans to make a strategic contribution. Also, the Imperial Japanese Army had large numbers of reservists to remedy troop shortages. The army and the GGK designed the volunteer system to augment Japan's long-term, not immediate, military capabilities and to facilitate the assimilation of Korea.

Proponents of the Korean volunteer system emphasized that the system would benefit Japan in two ways: First, it facilitated the transformation of Koreans into Japanese subjects, and second, Koreans contributed to national defense, even if in a limited manner.[10] On the first point, the assimilation of Koreans, as of 1937, disappointed the colonial regime. Korean ethnic identity and the attending anti-Japanese sentiments remained so deeply entrenched that Japanese government officials did not consider the Korean population culturally or spiritually ready for the draft.[11] The GGK hoped to single out a handful of young men, take them from their villages to training camps, and indoctrinate them with imperial culture, thus replacing the base (Korean) culture with a pure (Japanese) culture.[12]

Colonial officials expected military service to expand the spiritual foundation of the imperialization policies as well as help the Korean public understand Japan's mission in China. This then would replace the young men's parochial and ethnic interests with an emperorcentric national loyalty. Korean recruits would speak Japanese, travel throughout Japan's empire (to give them a cosmopolitan perspective), and develop personal ties to the Japanese nation. Upon returning to their hometowns, the state expected the youths to act as propagandists for the Japanese state. This, in effect, was a way to integrate Korea into the wider Japanese nation and, over time, mentally prepare Koreans for the military draft. This was the method by which Meiji Japan unified as a nation following the feudalistic Tokugawa era, as well as assimilated Hokkaidō and the Ryukyu Islands.[13] The colonial administration anticipated that volunteer soldiers would benefit Japan after their discharge because Korean veterans were expected to travel on lecturing circuits promoting soldiering among younger Koreans, work in schools to develop a younger generation of soldiers, and infuse the Korean populace with a martial spirit.

A second benefit of the volunteer system was that army officials calculated that the volunteer system provided Korea's most capable youth with an opportunity to serve Japan.[14] As noted before, army officials considered the volunteer system a stepping stone, a transition, toward a draft. The army expected the system to accustom Koreans, over several decades, to the expectations similar to those of Japanese citizens and to provide Japan with tens of thousands of recruits. Japan's leaders hoped that Korean soldiers fighting and dying in China might give the Korean populace a feeling that they were bound by blood to Japan. The sacrifice of Korean soldiers would then force Koreans to take a leadership role in Japan's wartime empire.[15]

The volunteer system had another important facet—to give the army time to acclimate Japanese soldiers to the presence of Koreans. Because of cultural differences and widespread prejudices against Koreans within Japanese society, Korean recruits needed to be slowly incorporated into the military to maintain harmony within the Imperial Japanese Army. The Japanese army enlisted a mere four hundred Koreans the first year of the volunteer system, and six hundred the next. The experimental nature of this system shows that the army was in no rush to force military service on the Korean public. Proponents of the system noted that the volunteer system was experimental and could be abandoned without losing face if it failed or proved unpopular.[16]

Support from the Japanese government and Japanese people for the

Korean volunteer soldier system was overwhelming but not unanimous. Opposition to the system was minimal and centered on a perceived lack of loyalty from the Koreans. Many Japanese considered Japan's military to be unique because of its "pure essence," and opponents worried that recruiting Koreans might taint this purity.[17] On a more practical level, internal military and police memos voiced an uneasiness about recruiting Koreans since too few Korean youth were ready for military service. One army memo claimed, "Due to the present conditions of Korean governance, resistance or desperation is active in their subconscious mind."[18] The High Police (J: Tokkō) opined that it was too early to introduce large numbers of Koreans into the army because assimilation was not complete. The police also cautioned that Korean participation in the war might embolden radical Koreans residing in Japan to threaten the public peace in Japan and encourage Koreans everywhere to rebel. The High Police also expressed concerns that Koreans would regard themselves as equals to the Japanese and push for greater privileges.[19] In other words, the enlistment of Koreans posed a potential problem to Japan's political and social domination of Korea because there might follow demands for social and political equality. Yet the police agreed that Koreans should do something to support the nation.

Japanese public opinion was divided on whether Koreans should be required, or even allowed, to serve in the army. Until the war's end, Japanese citizens harbored doubts that Koreans were worthy of soldiering. The Japanese public thought that Korean men were unmasculine, largely because they did not serve in the military, and lacked a cultural foundation to be soldiers.[20] Some colonial officials expressed concerns that Korean customs, especially the Korean diet, were too dissimilar to the Japanese to permit military service. Other Japanese argued that arming Koreans could lead to trouble. This idea is captured in a fictional account in Kajiyama Toshiyuki's "Seeking Life amidst Death." In the story a Japanese boy living in Korea says,

> I clearly saw proof of the insulting discrimination between Japanese and Korean students when we were ordered to present arms by lifting our rifles in salute to the governor-general, up there on his high stage. The rifles that we Japanese students held were genuine weapons, made of shiny black steel; the things held by Korean students were made of wood.... That evening ... when

> I asked [my father] the reason behind our cruel discrimination, my father immediately said, "Don't be a fool! Don't you know those Koreans will cause riots and rise in rebellion as soon as they get their hands on real rifles?"[21]

Anxieties such as these were assuaged by the fact that the army enlisted only four hundred Koreans the first year; for the system to be truly successful for Japan's long-term goals (preparing Koreans for the draft), large numbers of Koreans had to be groomed to serve in the army. This needed to happen slowly at first, and could be expanded, depending on the success of the first soldiers. Furthermore, Korean recruits did not form their own units. Instead, the army integrated them into a number of battalions where Japanese recruits made a majority and in which Korean soldiers could be closely monitored. Yet, despite these efforts to assuage concerns, Japanese distrust of Koreans lingered throughout the war.

The Koreans' low level of Japanese language proficiency was another concern, because bureaucrats equated language skills with the successes and failures of imperialization policies. In the minds of GGK officials, low language proficiency levels were symptomatic of the low levels of education and patriotism among Korean youth. Furthermore, until the end of the war, some Japanese soldiers felt that Koreans were incapable of soldiering because of their simplistic thinking, filthiness, and selfishness.[22] Many bureaucrats felt that Koreans had to exhibit greater levels of loyalty to Japan before the army enlisted large numbers of Koreans. For this to happen, government authorities expected universal compulsory education in Korea prior to the draft. Proponents of the volunteer system conceded that even the most Japanized Korean youths lacked the cultural foundation for enlistment, but argued that these shortcomings could be overcome through special training programs for a handful of Koreans who graduated from elementary school.

The Korean Army Headquarters (J: Chōsengun Shireibu), a branch of the Imperial Japanese Army, argued that the Japanese nation needed to reduce prejudice and discrimination toward Koreans. It also stated that Koreans, after their induction into the army, should be treated uniformly and equally. The army recognized that if discrimination continued, the volunteer system would end in harm rather than benefit.[23]

The debate over the volunteer system also addressed Korean suffrage.

Up until 1938 the government claimed that Koreans were denied suffrage because of the Koreans' low cultural levels and the absence of soldiering by Koreans. But once the volunteer system was introduced, the latter part of this argument became moot. Interestingly, the Korean Army took a progressive stance on this issue and considered the volunteer system a "dash toward gaining enfranchisement."[24] Commander Koiso reasoned that having voting rights would encourage Koreans to cooperate with military service and would assist assimilation. Diet deliberations on the volunteer system also discussed granting suffrage in return for the volunteer system. However, Governor-General Minami quashed this debate because he felt that martial obligations were a moral duty, not a bargaining chip. He declared, "[It] is an error to think that suffrage is a reward for the draft."[25] Minami felt that "about thirty years must elapse" before Koreans would be educated and mature enough for suffrage and representation in the diet.[26] The recruiting section of the Ministry of War (J: Chōboka), in a memo dated January 1938, reasoned that the volunteer system was designed to unify the Korean and Japanese people as well as help the Korean people contribute to national security; it was not intended to lead to voting rights for Koreans.[27] In the end, colonial interests prevailed over altruistic concerns; colonial officials claimed that Korean calls for enfranchisement in exchange for military service profaned the true essence of the draft.[28] Discussion of enfranchisement was postponed due to the worsening war situation in China.

Debate over the volunteer system lasted from June 1937 to February 1938. On February 22, 1938, the GGK announced Imperial Ordinance 95, which established the Korean Special Volunteer Soldier System. This legislation was based on a 1927 revision to the Military Service Law, which permitted special service by specific segments of the populace, which up until that time were Japanese students.[29] The military began accepting applications on April 3, 1938, on the anniversary of the death of the ancient Japanese Emperor Jimmu.

The diet also passed two other volunteer systems. The Naval Special Volunteer Soldier System was the second volunteer system implemented in Korea. On May 12, 1943, the Tokyo government, claiming that the Korean people wished to serve in the navy, announced the Naval Special Volunteer Soldier System and held a mass meeting on May 14 at the Chōsen Shrine in

Seoul. The naval system became law on July 20, 1943, with Imperial Ordinance 108. This system, coupled with the Korean draft, made complete military service available to Koreans. Unfortunately, few primary or secondary sources on the naval volunteer system exist because the state focused its energies on the conscription and student volunteer systems.

The navy implemented their volunteer system five years after the army did theirs. The Imperial Japanese Navy had long denied Koreans the right to naval service based on the belief that Koreans lacked the technical skills and education required to operate technologically advanced equipment. Naval officials also thought that the "peculiar" Korean lifestyle would detract from the efficiency of Japanese sailors on ships.[30] Once the navy decided to recruit Koreans, it claimed that Korean society had improved to the point that a small number could be recruited. However, government documents indicate that the decision to recruit Korean sailors was driven by a growing need for manpower.[31] By mid-1943, Japan's military forces were stretched thin due to wartime losses and limited manpower reserves. Also, the army's announcement of the Korean draft provided the catalyst for the navy's decision, but this belated move profited the navy very little, since much of the fleet was already lost.

A third volunteer system implemented in Korea, in October 1943, was the Korean Student Special Volunteer Soldier System. The student volunteer system was different from the regular volunteer system in that it was designed for a short period (October to December 1943) and targeted students who were twenty years old, as well as recent graduates. In 1942, recent graduates (Korean high school, college, and university students) and student deferments numbered 6,771, of which 1,400 were in Japan (see table 2.1). Under the proposed system, the army would accept applications from October 25 until November 20, 1943, and conduct military exams from December 12 to December 20. The students entered the army without special training on January 20 the following year (the universal enlistment date).[32] In short, students had three months from the system's announcement to their enlistment in the military.

The army accepted the first student applications on October 25, five days after the system's announcement. However, Korean students showed little enthusiasm for the student volunteer system. By November 10, after two weeks of accepting applications, only 200 of the 2,830 qualified students in

Japan had turned in applications. And as of November 12, only 372 of the 6,771 total targeted students and graduates had applied. These low numbers were unsettling to the GGK, which had expected the spontaneous and complete compliance of all students.

TABLE 2.1   Location of Korean Students Who Applied and Were Recruited

Location	Number of Applicants	Number Recruited
In Korea	1,000	959
Home from School	1,529	1,431
In Japan	1,400	719
Early Graduates	1,574	941
Employed	700	335
Total	**6,203**	**4,385**

Source: *Kang Tŏk-sang, Chōsenjin gakuto shujjin,* 370.

Governor-general Koiso Kuniaki and army authorities realized that the enlistment of several thousand Korean student soldiers would not affect the power of the Japanese army or turn the tide of the war. So why did the Japanese government bother to expend valuable resources to recruit Korean students? There are four possible reasons for creating the student volunteer system; the GGK publicly announced one, and the other three can be deduced. Publically, the GGK unconvincingly presented the student volunteer system as a response to the students' "deep desire to seek glory through military service," and the GGK's move to "fulfill the ardent desire of the students who wish to take a position on the front line as shields for the Emperor against the evil Anglo-American brutes."[33] Koiso claimed that Korean students wanted the same benefits as Japanese students and that the student system offered students the freedom of choice.[34]

The three unpublicized (and more likely) purposes of the student soldier system relate to Japan's war needs. First, the Japanese had to force Korean students to contribute to the war for ideological reasons. Japanese students whose deferments were canceled criticized Korean students who remained in school for their unwillingness to serve the Japanese nation. They grumbled that Korean students benefitted from a Japanese education but exhibited no moral obligation to serve Japan.[35] Second, the student volunteer system provided a "soft landing" for the Korean draft, which was to be enacted in April 1944.[36] Student soldiers with advanced Japanese language skills were enlisted to mentor Korean conscripts who would enter military service in December 1944; they were supposed to serve as intermediaries and translators between Japanese soldiers, who spoke no Korean, and Korean conscripts, who might have difficulty speaking Japanese. Thus, the students would bear the burden of handling Korean conscripts who were not prepared for military service.

And a third purpose of the volunteer systems was, in the words of Korean scholar Kang Tŏk-sang, to "bleach the national consciousness of [Korean] students and dye it khaki."[37] Japanese colonial authorities remained mindful, if not fearful, of Korean ethnic nationalism and sought to prevent it from developing into a revolutionary force. The government worried that the implementation of the compulsory conscription system might touch off a national self-awakening in Korea, and that students would lead it.[38] A War Ministry aide-de-camp stated in 1943,

> In general we do not need to worry, but their [student] national subconscious and independent trend of thought still exists as an undercurrent. That is why it is easy for them to be affected by Chinese propaganda, as is a tendency among young intellectuals. It is hard to keep them away from ethnic views that are anti-Japanese. It is easy to use a simpleton, but hard to get students.[39]

The government expected military service to severely weaken students' political influence in the immediate and distant future. Military authorities hoped to force students into the army, where they would develop loyalty to Japan or die.

THE PROPAGANDA CAMPAIGN

Implementation of the volunteer system in 1938 behooved the GGK to win the support of the Korean people for military service. Colonial authorities attempted to do this through propaganda and the colonial education system. Up until the 1930s, Japanese newspapers and journals stressed the racial purity of the Japanese race and, conversely, accentuated Koreans' weaknesses and shortcomings, but from the late 1930s on, colonial organs gradually discontinued these themes in public. The GGK began to downplay negative publicity related to the cultural, social, and ethnic shortcomings of Koreans while promoting propaganda that instilled a sense of esprit de corps between Koreans and Japanese. Most media venues advanced the ideals of oneness of Korea and Japan, the universal brotherhood (J: *isshi dōin;* K: *dōhō*) of Japanese and Koreans, and the benevolence of the emperor who had granted the volunteer systems to Koreans.[40] In retrospect, the colonial regime's efforts to curry favor with the Korean public was largely an effort to ideologically steer Koreans toward assimilation.

The GKK used all available resources to promote the volunteer soldier system to encourage Korean men to apply for military service. The GGK justified the implementation of the volunteer systems to the Korean public by claiming that there had been an increase of peninsular patriotic fervor (J: *hantō aikokunetsu*) and an intensified desire to serve in the military following the Manchurian Incident in 1931 and the outbreak of war with China in 1937. Newspaper reports, journal articles, radio broadcasts, and lectures, often presented by Korean elite, portrayed the volunteer soldier system as critical to the betterment of Korea as well as an example of the unity of Japan and Korea. One publication stated,

> The China Incident was the storm that breathed new life into the Korea that had broken out its old shell. This storm stirred awake the Japanese consciousness that had been sleeping deep within the hearts of our Korean brethren. It gave fire to the mutual sympathy between Mainlanders and Koreans, a sympathy destined by blood. An ardent emotion arose like a surging tide: "Insofar as we are Japanese, we hope to serve as humble shields [for the nation] as members of the glorious Imperial Forces."[41]

This quote highlights the changing tone in colonial discourse, rhetoric, and indoctrination. Government publications began to emphasize pan-Asianism and the blood ties (J: *dōso dōkon*) of the Korean and Japanese peoples that dated back centuries.[42] The GGK claimed that Koreans were worthy of an active role in the Japanese empire and that the volunteer system answered the wish of twenty million Koreans who could now enjoy a newfound sense of being Japanese.[43] The volunteer soldier system was also billed as a once-in-a-lifetime opportunity (J: *issen ichiman no ki*) that should not be missed. One man wrote, "I dream of the time when peninsular youth will gladly die for country and king! Of a glorious day that Koreans become completely Japanese at heart and become prime minister! Will it be after a hundred years or after hundreds of years?"[44]

Colonial sources drew from ancient Korean history to establish a precedence for a time when Koreans held military service in high regard. Young men were told to follow in the footsteps of the *hwarang*, a group of elite young warriors of the Silla dynasty (57 BCE–960 CE), and to revive Korea's martial heritage. For example, literary figure Yi Kwang-su, in the Korean-language journal *Samch'ŏlli*, called on Korean youths to follow the example of Hwang Ch'ang-nang, a seventeen-year-old *hwarang* who volunteered himself to the Silla king to fight and die for the kingdom.[45] One writer ironically reminded Koreans that the Chosŏn dynasty's Yi Sun-sin, an admiral who stymied the Japanese invasions of Korea from 1592 to 1597, was part of Korea's military past.[46] These themes implied that Korean men, whom the Japanese considered effeminate for not serving in the military, could become complete men through soldiering.[47]

Propaganda subtly encouraged young men to apply to serve in the army for economic reasons. Bureaucrats and educators suggested that in the army young men could learn marketable skills to improve future employment opportunities as policemen, firemen, railroad workers, and clerks. The allure of stable employment for young men in colonial Korea cannot be overlooked as an effective recruitment measure. Untold numbers of Korean men, desperate for employment amid the global depression, turned to military careers. Another benefit to joining the army was that employers would give special consideration to Koreans with military experience because they had proven their loyalty to Japan.

Propaganda also targeted the Japanese public to improve ethnic relations and to lessen opposition to the Korean volunteer soldier system. The government emphasized to Japanese citizens that the assimilation of Koreans was of mutual benefit to Korea and Japan. Because of the symbiotic relationship, Japanese authorities encouraged Japanese nationals to treat the Korean people with patience and affection as a way to decrease Japanese historical prejudices against Koreans.[48] The Tokyo and colonial governments replaced more than three decades of negative colonial rhetoric that had emphasized the Koreans' cultural weaknesses with pan-Asian images of brotherhood between the two peoples and portrayals of Koreans as patriotic subjects. Government publications increasingly referred to Korea as "loyal Korea" (J: *dōgi Chōsen*) rather than as merely "the peninsula" (J: *hantō*).

An underlying problem in making Koreans into soldiers was that, up until 1938, colonial schools had taught Koreans that military service was not required or even possible for them. Colonial bureaucrats originally designed the school curriculum in Korea to create pliant, submissive subjects, not military-ready citizens. It did this by indoctrinating young Koreans with Japanese culture, which included belief in the infallibility of the Japanese emperor and that Japan was the leader of Asia. The Korean curriculum lacked martial training, *kendō* classes, and military drills, all of which were available to Japanese schoolchildren. Japan's prewar education policies in its colonies did not produce military-ready men. Furthermore, as of the late 1930s, the education system remained ill-prepared to force Korean youth to become imperial subjects because educational facilities could handle only one-quarter of all school-age children.

The curriculum began to change with the educational reforms of 1938, which intensified assimilation policies in schools and in public life. The GGK reasoned that Korean soldiering was possible if Koreans looked like, talked like, and acted like native Japanese.[49] Schools helped fashion Koreans into Japanese by requiring students to take Japanese names, speak Japanese at school, and recite imperial rescripts—all of which were an assault on Korean culture.[50] The colonial regime encouraged visits to Shintō shrines as a way to change bad Korean habits into good ones and to promote a Japanese consciousness among Koreans.[51] Little room was left for the GGK to approach and mobilize Koreans as Korean subjects.

After 1938 the colonial regime made a concerted effort to weaken the Korean ethnic identity by indoctrinating Korean youth with Japanese ideology. Prior to the outbreak of the war, Japan's assimilation efforts were moderate. The result was that Koreans retained their distinctive ethnicity and were mentally unprepared to accept the divinity of the emperor. Changing the Korean belief system was the essence of the GGK's assimilation policies. One Japanese official wrote that the most important task of colonial education in the late 1930s was to "instill the [Japanese] spirit in Korean recruits." He continued,

But you ask, "How can we instill this spirit?" First, cause them [the Koreans] to accept the emperor as a manifest deity [J: *akitsumi-kami*] and fervently and piously to worship the Emperor as a great god and to believe in the Sun Goddess Amaterasu. So, having a spiritual attitude, we will make them worship [the emperor with] unwavering conviction.... In order to integrate Korean recruits as Japanese soldiers, it is imperative that we conduct spiritual training to instill this spirit in them with regular training.[52]

In conjunction with advocating veneration of the emperor and preparing Korea for future compulsory military service, Minami implemented sweeping educational reforms in 1938 to eliminate the structural differences between the Korean and Japanese educational systems, and, more importantly, to make the Korean educational system compliant with the Military Service Law. Korean schools were changed from "common schools" (J: *futsu gakkō*) to "national schools" (J: *kokumin gakkō*).[53] Minami sent the reforms for preapproval to the Korean Army, indicating that these revisions were related to the army.[54] Minami also announced that by 1946 every village would have an elementary school and that the GGK would implement universal compulsory education. By 1942 his efforts raised attendance rates to 75 percent for boys and 33 percent for girls. The GGK hoped by 1959 that 78 percent of the men of draftable age would be proficient in Japanese.[55]

The GGK and the Education Ministry hoped that the 1938 educational reforms would internalize Japanese culture in Korean youth and transform them into combat-ready soldiers.[56] Compulsory education had two closely connected purposes: to promote the unification of Japan and Korea, and to prevent resistance or heterodoxy (socialism, communism, or Korean nationalism) from infiltrating into Korea. The army presence at Korean schools became widespread in the early 1940s. Some schools provided twelve hours of physical training per week, often under the supervision of army officers. Middle schools provided physical education classes that focused on marching formations in the first year, and hand-to-hand combat and bayonet training in the second year. The third and fourth year curriculums included creeping and crawling, pistol usage, and practical combat skills—but without real weapons.[57] A popular maxim held that entering the school gate was equivalent to entering military service. Pak Kyŏng-sik, a postwar Korean Japanese scholar, pessimistically stated that colonial education and assimilation policies made the Korean youth into cannon fodder (J: *tamayoke*) for the Japanese nation.[58]

THE PUSH FOR APPLICATIONS

The Korean volunteer system implemented in 1938 was similar to the volunteer system used for Japanese men, but with several notable differences: First, it targeted a more demographically diverse population in Korea than in Japan. Second, the Korean volunteer system enlisted a much smaller percentage of applicants than the volunteer system in Japan—in some years, less than three percent. Third, the government employed more coercion to apply on Korean men than on Japanese. And fourth, the qualifications for Koreans excluded a higher percentage of the targeted population. An overview of the six qualifications for volunteer soldiers highlights the first and last points. Korean applicants had to be older than seventeen years (no maximum age was set), more than 160 centimeters tall, mentally sound, free of a criminal record, an elementary school graduate, and economically stable—that is, applicants had to prove that joining the army did not cause economic hardship for their family.[59] Numbers five and six disqualified large numbers of Koreans because Korea was an impoverished agricultural society (in which young men were needed on family farms) with low school attendance rates. In Japan, the volunteer system targeted Japanese teenagers who served for one year prior to their regular conscription. The Japanese volunteer system did not count toward the two-year compulsory term. Also, the minimum height for Japanese volunteers and conscripts was 155 centimeters, 5 centimeters shorter than for Koreans.

The qualifications for the naval volunteer system, which began in 1943, were similar to the regular volunteer system. First, applicants had to be physically fit men between the ages of sixteen and twenty-one who were over 151 centimeters in height—they could be both younger and shorter than applicants for the army. Applicants needed at least an elementary school diploma, an indication that they had had Japanese language training. And third, applicants needed to vocalize a strong desire for military service.[60] Those considered for naval service underwent a background check by the police. Naval volunteers were expected to serve on active duty for five years and spend twelve years and two months in the reserves.

Volunteer soldier propaganda and recruitment efforts targeted unmarried men between the ages of seventeen and twenty, but encouraged applications from men well into their mid-twenties. The average age of the four hundred volunteer soldiers inducted in 1938 was 20.6 years old, but fifty-six were older than twenty-three, and one was twenty-seven. Interestingly, 118 volunteers had wives, and twenty-six had children.[61] A demographic examination of the first 202 volunteer soldiers admitted into training camps in 1938 shows that, geographically, South Chŏlla had the largest number of volunteer soldiers (47), followed by Kangwŏn (28), and North Ch'ungch'ŏng (27). Interestingly, these provinces were among the most rural areas of Korea. Of the 11,365 volunteer soldiers enlisted from 1938 to 1942 only 555 were from Korea's twenty largest cities.[62] The largest occupational groups were farmers (110) and store employees (18). The largely agrarian background of the volunteer soldiers indicates that rural peasants were more likely to volunteer than urban residents. And the highest degree of education for 313 recruits was an elementary school degree (the minimum requirement); fifteen had completed all or some middle school, twenty-five had graduated from higher elementary school (J: *kōtō shōgakko*), and fifty-three had graduated from vocational school.[63]

Applications were due by February 10 each year at the police office in the district where the applicant's family register was located; this required youths living away from home to travel back to their hometowns. Applicants had to submit a personal history, a certificate of address, property and income evaluation forms, a recommendation from the village head or school principal as well as one from their provincial governor, a doctor's verification of the recruit's good physical condition, and an abstract of their family registry. The volunteer also needed permission from the head of household—usually his father—in order to apply. If the parents objected to their son's military service, the colonial regime encouraged officials "to persuade [them] with beautiful anecdotes of bravery and honor by Korean and Japanese soldiers."[64] In actuality, policemen and patriotic unit heads pressured recalcitrant fathers and mothers with random house calls and threats to the family's economic well-being.

The colonial government expected Koreans to welcome the opportunity to serve in the army and prove themselves as loyal subjects. By all indications, the GGK envisioned a large number of applications from Korean men, but applications in the first two years amounted to only 2,954 in 1938 and 12,348 the following year. These low application levels indicate the colonial regime's deliberate, unhurried approach to the volunteer system in the first couple years as well as the apathy of Korean society toward the system. Nevertheless, the GGK sought to increase the number of applications by mobilizing newspapers, literature, lecture circuits, schools, socialites, movies, and semigovernmental organizations to encourage a spirit of volunteerism (J: *shigannetsu*) among Koreans by relating anecdotes, reciting slogans, and highlighting the benefits of being a soldier.

By the early 1940s the number of applications was fewer than the government had expected. At this time, the war in China and worsening diplomatic relations with the United States altered how the colonial regime perceived the volunteer system. In the early forties, officials encouraged young men to apply for military service even if they lacked the proper qualifications. Japanese officials pushed for larger numbers of applications, which, in turn, could be used to justify the implementation of the conscription system as an answer to the Koreans' desires. If too few Koreans applied, the GGK would have no basis to move toward the draft. The GGK attributed the annual increase of applications to the patriotic fervor and high idealism of Korean youths, not to coercion. With hundreds of thousands of applications in hand, the army could, and did, claim that the move toward a Korean military conscription service was a response to Korean desires.

To encourage more applications, the government-controlled media attempted to imbue the Korean populace with loyalty toward the emperor and a desire to serve Japan. Soldiering was publicized as an avenue to glory as well as an honor given to Koreans by the emperor.[65] Government propaganda utilized a paternalistic approach in an effort to coax Koreans to support the system. Printed materials frequently claimed that the Korean people had progressed socially under the guidance of Japan to the point that partial military service was possible. However, it is questionable how much propaganda actually reached Koreans because most newspapers and handbills circulated in the urban areas and were printed in the Japanese language, making them inaccessible to a large numbers of Koreans.[66] Widespread use of the Korean language, no matter the goal, ran counter to assimilation policies.

An important venue of propaganda was literature that glorified service in the army and military values such as honor, valor, courage, and social progress. Two such works were *Success of a Country Bumpkin* (K: *Samdolli ŭi ch'ulse*) and *Volunteer Soldier Iwamoto* (J: *Iwamoto shiganhei*). In *Success of a Country Bumpkin*, a poor ignorant boy from a rural hamlet enlists in the army and serves with distinction on the battlefield, earning a promotion. He returns to his hometown and is welcomed as a hero. The story, told in Korean, is simplistic but modeled the road to success for many of Korea's poorest youth.

Volunteer Soldier Iwamoto, written by Chang Hyŏk-chu (Japanese name Noguchi Minoru), was serialized in the *Mainichi shimbun* from August 24 to September 9, 1943. This fictional tale, published in Japanese, related the life of Iwamoto, a Korean from Japan. Iwamoto applied to serve in the army and enlisted, whereas his friends served Japan by working in a factory. Iwamoto exemplified the ideal of a Korean becoming an imperial citizen and, through his example, helped transform his father's behavior for the better.[67] Chang also wrote *New Beginning* (J: *Atarashii shuppatsu*), a story similar to that of Iwamoto that was serialized in a government-sanctioned journal in 1943. Chang wrote both stories following his conversations with Korean volunteer soldiers in Japan during a three-day visit to a training center. His wartime writings glorified military service and implied that anyone could succeed and find a better life in the army.

Movies were an equally important mode of propaganda. *The Straits of Chosŏn* (K: *Chosŏn haehyŏp*, 1943) and *Volunteer Soldier* (K: *Chiwŏnbyŏng*, 1941) were movies that complemented the GGK's assimilation and militarization efforts. *The Straits of Chosŏn*, with Japanese dialogue, told the story of a young man, Seki, whose father disowned him because he eloped with a girl, Shuku, that his parents disapproved of. Early in the film, Seki visits his uncle and pledges that he has changed because he "realized what is the right thing to do as a man." It is soon revealed that Seki has volunteered for military duty and is preparing to enter a training camp. As the story unfolds, Seki is sent to the front while Shuku works in a factory. The movie juxtaposes the imagery of machine guns on the front lines with sewing machines in the factory on the home front. Shuku gives birth to Seki's son and raises the child without the support of Seki's parents. Furthermore, the story portrays a marriage grounded in sacrifice for the state, as Seki is wounded in battle and Shuku collapses from exhaustion while working in a factory.[68] In the end, the dedication of Seki and Shuku leads to Seki's father having renewed pride in his son, which is followed by his acceptance of Shuku and her baby.

Volunteer Soldier (with Korean dialogue) presented the story of Chun-ho, an ambitious young peasant who has inherited his father's position as supervisor for an absentee landowner. However, Chun-ho longs to be more than a mere farmer. Despite Chun-ho's dedication to his supervisory work, the landowner replaces him after a rival slanders him and convinces the landlord that he is illiterate and incapable. Chun-ho is saddened that he cannot join the military even though the Korean people had, in his mind, been completely assimilated.[69] At this point in the story, Chun-ho learns that the Japanese army has established the volunteer solider system. He excitedly submits his application for service and it is accepted. The landlord learns of Chun-ho's enlistment and realizes that Chun-ho was not the incompetent bumpkin he was led to believe; instead, he was a highly qualified man—after all, only men with the highest qualifications became volunteer soldiers. The landlord pledges to support Chun-ho's mother and sister until Chun-ho returns from war. *The Straits of Chosŏn* and *Volunteer Soldier* convey the message that young men (like Seki and Chun-ho) can restore their manhood, prove their social value, and solve personal problems by joining the military. Chun-ho, for his part, was transformed from a victim of his economic circumstances into a proud soldier marching in formation at a training camp.

The state even capitalized on the death of volunteer soldiers to promote the volunteer system. The story of Yi In-sŏk (figure 2.1), the first Korean volunteer soldier killed in action, was highly publicized and known to all Koreans. Yi, from Okch'ŏn, in North Ch'ungch'ŏng, was killed in Northern China on June 22, 1939, by a hand grenade. The details of his death were recounted in magazines, journals, newspapers, and elementary school classrooms. His father and wife reportedly said that they were honored that In-sŏk gave his life for Japan. The army posthumously awarded him the Order of the Golden Kite 7th Class, promoted him to superior private, and enshrined his spirit in Yasukuni Shrine.[70] The GGK also provided Yi with an extravagant and much-publicized funeral. The GGK promoted Yi's sacrifice to establish a blood tie between Korea and Japan. Yi's story was also used to beautify and glamorize death as part of Korea's Japanized culture.[71]

FIG 2.1
Volunteer soldier Yi In-sŏk
was the first Korean casualty
of the Asia-Pacific War.

Japanese writer Ōmura Kenzō cited other accounts of Korean combat casualties. Ōmura traveled throughout Northern China collecting anecdotes about Korean volunteers in the Japanese army that he published in the Japanese-language *Fighting Peninsular Soldiers* (J: *Tatakō hantō shiganhei*). Like Yi In-sŏk, Chang Song-ju served in Northern China and got pinned down when his unit came under heavy fire from Chinese troops. In an attempt to save his unit, Chang heroically charged the enemy but was gunned down in the process.[72] Ōmura glorified Chang and other Korean soldiers as heroes and capable warriors who should be emulated by other Korean youth.

Lecture circuits and symposia were yet another front of propaganda. Lecture circuits often included national and local elites, as well as active-duty volunteer soldiers. Korean officers who had joined the Japanese military before the implementation of the volunteer system traveled on lecture circuits to encourage youths to apply.[73] Volunteer soldiers returning from training camps and the battlefield traveled on lecture circuits that visited schools and villages. Adorned in their dress uniforms, Korean soldiers gave pep talks that glamorized the military life, encouraged young men to apply, and advised parents that their sons should volunteer. Through these lectures, boys became enamored with the veterans' crisp new uniforms and shiny leather boots. One man, for example, applied because he envied the popularity of soldiers who wore clean uniforms and traveled on lecture circuits as folk heroes respected by Koreans and Japanese alike. He applied, but the army rejected his application; he ended up working as a contract laborer for the military.[74]

At these meetings, the audience listened to speeches, sang songs, watched movies, and repeated slogans, all of which made the Koreans in attendance participants in government propaganda. On April 13, 1939, Major (later Colonel) Kim Sŏg-wŏn, famous for pursuing Kim Il-sŏng's guerilla band, gave a two-hour speech to a filled auditorium about his experiences on the battlefront in China.[75] Major Kim was a famous Korean officer who made frequent rounds on the lecture circuit. Kim had had astounding successes leading Japanese troops into battle in China at the outbreak of World War II in 1937. In fact, Emperor Hirohito personally decorated Kim for his bravery, and he was warmly received by audiences in Korea.[76] Throughout Korea, the Japanese army propagandized Kim as a hero in order to recruit Koreans for military service.[77] More significantly, these lectures helped the GGK reach the rural areas of Korea, where most Koreans lived.

One of the largest lectures was held on October 30, 1943. The GGK held a rally attended by 30,000 elementary and middle school students in Seoul. The speakers included Governor-General Koiso Kuniaki, Korean Army commander Itagaki Seishirō, and student leaders. The star lineup of officials gave speeches that called on students to joyfully and boldly enter the military. Koiso beseeched students to be "shields for the emperor," and student speakers encouraged their peers to seize this "once-in-a-lifetime opportunity [J: senzai-ichigū no ki] with a smile" and go to war as if their life was "as light as a feather."[78]

The GGK enlisted the assistance of Korean elites, scholars, and anyone of social repute to present the volunteer system as a Korean undertaking.

The Korean elite, as mouthpieces of the state, gave a tinge of legitimacy to the volunteer soldier system that enabled propaganda to reach larger numbers and helped deflect criticism from the regime. Elites published articles and poems that encouraged youths to apply for the military or labor corps. Literary figures such as Yi Kwang-su were important in promoting the volunteer system. Popular poets wrote poems attempting to strike an emotional chord with their countrymen. Mo Yun-suk, a renowned poet, wrote,

> The nation is more important than your mother,
> The nation is more important than family,
> The nation, which is more important than life,
> Is beckoning you to come, so go,
> Go for your fatherland, for your Korean brethren.[79]

The defense of Korea and Asia from Anglo-American expansion was a common theme of their poems. In a poem titled "I also will go" (K: *Na tokagessŭmnida*), Kim P'al-bong wrote,

> Mother, Father,
> I too will go volunteer.
> . . . .
> My hot blood was passed from generation to generation;
> This blood is Korean and Japanese blood,
> Is it not all Asian blood?
> . . . .
> The nation urgently calls for us.
> Whatever happens, put aside everything
> because we must win the Great East Asian War!
>
> Life is only once, death is only once.
> Not twice, so we must use it preciously.
> If we use this blood vainly
> It will be a hundred-generation humiliation.[80]

In response, the fictive mother urged her son to go fight for Japan, since he was now Japanese. She told her son not to be concerned about dying as a soldier, since it was the only way to live eternally. An important theme of this poem, as well as others, is pan-Asianism. Japan's conflict with China was presented as an effort to save China and Asia from Western imperial powers. By framing the war in racial terms, the GGK hoped that the Koreans would have a personal stake in the war to save Korea and Asia. The effects of such propaganda and indoctrination is difficult to assess, but accounts of volunteer soldiers attributing their willingness to serve to a belief that they were Japanese indicates that these methods had some success.[81] The exaggerated propaganda of the *Keijō nippō*, the largest newspaper in Seoul (Keijō), with a circulation of 62,000 copies, appears to have succeeded in changing public opinion related to the volunteer soldier system.[82] A museum exhibit that opened in 1940 displayed military materials and weapons as a way to promote the volunteer system. According to the *Keijō nippō*, tens of thousands of people viewed the exhibit, and some even broke down in tears.[83] The colonial regime endeavored, through elites, schools, museums, and media, to create a social environment that favored military service.

As part of the media blitz to recruit Korean students between November 4, 1943, and January 23, 1944, the *Keijō nippō* and *Maeil sinbo* published seventy-three articles by elites, including scholar Ch'oe Nam-sŏn, former nationalist Yun Ch'i-ho, businessman Kim Yŏn-su, and members of the Korean royal family. Author Yi Kwang-su, for example, wrote, "You Korean soldiers are called to a holy war. Did you apply? Did you apply? Why? Because of your parents? There is no duty without loyalty. There are no parents without a country."[84] In another article, educator Kim Sŏng-su bemoaned that Korea's historical aversion to martial duty accounted for Korean reluctance to volunteer for the army and encouraged the abandonment of this tradition.[85] Kim's condescending attitude toward Korean culture is noteworthy, but was common among elites. He is credited with writing the following:

> With the great works of the conscription system underway, the correlation between "soldiers" and "Koreans" has truly deepened to a heartening degree. Until now, Koreans have been stuck in existing tradition, and [they] have been excessively narrow-minded toward the conscription system. I think this is a shortcoming of all Korean compatriots. Koreans hereafter must fling off their selfish thoughts and ideas and rally to patriotic thoughts and concepts grounded in morality. This is literally [a time of] war. What a glorious [sight]

you are.... Your victory is not only the parent that will give birth to a new
Korea; it is also the only way to preserve peace in East Asia.[86]

The most noteworthy event involving Korean elites came in mid-
November 1943, when Ch'oe Nam-sŏn, Yi Kwang-su, Kim Yŏn-su, and
eight other prominent figures traveled to Tokyo to encourage Korean students to volunteer. At Waseda University, Yi Kwang-su urged Korean and
Taiwanese university students not miss this opportunity to volunteer. He
called on them to "go and fight the Anglo-American enemy and bring glory
to the nation" and to resume their studies after the war.[87] However, among
themselves, these students expressed dismay that a man of Yi's nationalist
credentials would actively promote Japan's militarist agenda. The students
concluded that Yi was cooperating with the colonial regime to escape
imprisonment. Furthermore, they doubted the sincerity of Yi and the other
elites because of rumors that the sons of Yi Kwang-su and Ch'oe Nam-sŏn
refused to submit a applications.[88]

Korean elites were under tremendous pressure to cooperate with mobilization efforts.[89] Korean businessmen, such as Kim Yŏn-su (Kim Sŏng-su's
brother), cooperated in order to protect their social standing and financial
well-being, which depended on Japanese capital. No simple explanation
summarizes the motives of all elites, but Koreans who cooperated with
the Japanese earned a place within the Japanese nexus of power. Few elites
remained above the taint of cooperating with the colonial regime as they
became increasingly co-opted into the lower levels of Japanese social and
economic networks. After thirty years of colonial rule, numerous Koreans
had developed ties to the colonial regime and assumed that Korea would
remain Japan's colony for many decades. Koreans of all social strata lived
according to realpolitik. Of course, some banked their social status and
economic standing on Japan winning the war. At one extreme was Pak
Ch'un-gŭm, a Korean candidate for political office in Japan and long-time
proponent of Korean military service. He wrote, "Do not let Koreans be
labeled by the Japanese as being afraid to die for the nation. People die only
once, and let's make that death meaningful."[90] Pak's son, who was in his
third year of law school, became a student volunteer soldier. Pak's wife said
that offering their son to the nation was a parent's right and duty. She went
so far as to claim that it was a family dream.[91]

The GGK pushed for the sons of the elite, such as Pak, to travel on the lecture circuits in an effort to provide Korean leadership for Japan's policies. The colonial bureaucracy placed greater value on applications from upper-class families because of the hierarchal nature of Korean society. The rationale was to have the sons of Korean elites lead by example and to place them at the forefront of the imperialization policies. One publication stated in 1941, "It is very important that influential people's sons enter the military in order to expand the volunteer soldier system in all ways."[92] However, very few Korean elites urged their sons to volunteer. Traditional Korean aversion to soldiering remained firmly entrenched among the elites, who often used their connections to help family members evade martial obligations.

The wartime media subliminally presented military service as a way for Korean men to join the modern world. The message delivered in the movies and in other propaganda was fascist in nature: it promoted imperialist expansion, nation above individual, and was militaristic. Yet Korean propaganda generally lacked the rhetoric of racial purity found in Japan. Wartime photographs showed young healthy Korean men in military uniform standing with their families dressed in the traditional Korean *hanbok*. The message was that the son, brother, and husband who joined the military would become a "New Man" who belonged to the modern world as well as a new generation of assimilated Koreans; this was in contrast to the traditional family system that symbolized the weak, effeminate Korean society.[93]

Another source of government propaganda was semigovernmental and religious associations. As part of the GGK's corporatist approach, these groups encouraged the Korean population to participate in mobilization efforts. The most powerful of these organizations was the Chōsen League and its local branches, the patriotic units. Leaders of these local groups visited the homes of prospective applicants, multiple times if needed, and recited the benefits of serving Japan. If a youth proved recalcitrant, these groups demanded compliance, and if that failed, threatened bureaucratic pressure. Among the Korean upper classes, the Green Flag League (K: Nokki Yŏnmaeng; J: Midori Hata) was a popular association that urged elites to participate in public lectures, visit the homes of recalcitrant students, write newspaper and journal articles, and perform other tasks for the state.

The inclusion of elites in the mobilization process was a priority of the colonial regime. A case study can be made of Yun Ch'i-ho's involvement in the semiofficial Special Volunteer Soldier Support Association (J:

Tokubetsu Shiganhei Kōenkai). The GGK and Korean elites, such as Pak Hŭng-sik, founded this association in January 1939 and appointed Yun, a former Korean nationalist figure, as its president to create the appearance that Koreans headed the organization. Yun's diary indicates that this was an unwelcome appointment; he sarcastically wrote, "As there was no pay for the nominal president, they were generous enough to elect me for the position."[94] This association helped pay for costs associated with the application process, gave luncheons, and hosted send-off parties for volunteer soldiers, as well as collected donations for the volunteer soldier system. Half of the collections were earmarked for the police, who coerced applications from many young men. Yun, for his part, became caught up in the euphoria of pan-Asianism and apparently thought that cooperation was best for Korea's national development.

Additional support for the volunteer system came from religious groups. Renowned monk Pak Tae-ryun, famed for assisting in the educational advancement of Koreans, offered money in support of the Japanese troops in 1938, as well as one thousand days of prayer.[95] Monks at T'aegosa, a Japanese government-supported Buddhist temple, held a commemorative ceremony for the volunteer system. T'aegosa Temple offered Japanese-language courses for recruits to ease their transition into military life. Several monks even submitted volunteer soldier applications. Other religions promoted the volunteer system; one interfaith committee, with representatives from the Christian, Ch'ŏndogyo, and Tenrikyō faiths, traveled throughout the peninsula to discuss problems related to the volunteer system and offered suggestions for correcting them. This small sample shows the colonial government's ability to co-opt religious organizations as mouthpieces of the state.[96]

The GGK realized that the Korean population, as a whole, lacked the educational, economic, and physical preparedness to serve in the army. To remedy these shortcomings, the Korean Army recommended that small cohorts of Korean men serve in the military for several decades as a way to militarize Korean society. The Korean Special Volunteer Soldier System exemplifies the colonial regime's careful mobilization of Koreans. The system began with the long-term goal of facilitating the assimilation of Koreans and eventually moving to a conscription system. However, as the war with China worsened and Japan's international relations with the United States soured, the purposes and methods of implementation of this system changed. Namely, the GGK pushed for more applications and intensified its efforts to make the Korean people loyal subjects of the Japanese emperor.

THE EXAMINATION PROCESS

After youths submitted an application, they then underwent written and oral examinations. Army examiners looked for three mental qualities in applicants: a "thorough inoculation with the national essence"; possession of a martial spirit of allegiance, courtesy, bravery, and faith; and a willingness to uphold the reputation of the army.[97] Japanese language comprehension was critical to all three. Colonial authorities believed that if a Korean did not understand Japanese, he was not qualified for military service.[98] The examination process shows the Japanese army's careful, gradual approach with the volunteer system; it recognized that most applicants lacked proper qualifications and that testing was needed to separate the worthy and willing from the unqualified.

Oral examiners were especially keen to ask the applicants to explain their motives for wanting to join the army. The military remained wary of enlisting large numbers of Koreans out of a concern that resistance and nationalist desperation remained latent in the subconscious minds of most Koreans. Army officials feared that Korean socialists or sympathizers of the independence movement might infiltrate the armed forces and rabble-rouse or defect and join the war against Japan. The Korean Army conducted background checks of applicants to weed out possible malcontents, bad elements (J: *bunshi*), and individuals whose families had connections with the independence movements.[99]

Applicants also underwent a physical exam, which included an X-ray and an eye exam, and were classified according to their height and general physical condition.[100] Many recruits who met the height requirement were subsequently disqualified due to diseases such as tuberculosis or conditions caused by malnutrition, again indicating the shortcomings of the GGK's prewar social policies. Yet even men who were classified as fit for active duty lacked the martial background Japanese boys received in elementary school; this required new recruits to undergo special training.

The army intended that the volunteer system would lay the groundwork for the draft (whether it be in the distant or near future), thus, army officials sought out the best available recruits. It is logical that recruiters selected those who could best serve Japan. As table 2.2 shows, the number of applications was far greater than the number of men to be enlisted, which meant that the army could enlist those best qualified and most willing to join. Japan maintained strict moral and educational qualifications to prevent unqualified men from entering the military. Applicants who had been forced to apply were usually weeded out during the long grueling examination process and background check. The army did not loosen its standards to enlist tens of thousands more Korean "volunteer" soldiers.

TABLE 2.2   Korean Volunteer Soldiers: Applications and Enlistments

Year	Applications	Enlisted	Deployment
1938	2,946	406	Korean Army
1939	12,348	613	Korean Army
1940	84,443	3,060	Korean & Kwantung Armies
1941	144,743	3,208	Korean & Kwantung Armies
1942	254,273	4,077	Korean, Kwantung, & Northern Armies
1943	303,294	6,300	To all armies
Total	802,047	17,664	

Source: Hanil Munje Yŏnguwŏn, *Ppaeakkin choguk kkŭllyŏgan*, 79; and Pak Kyŏng-sik, *Nihon teikoku shugi*, 28.

As table 2.2 shows, the army rejected hundreds of thousands of volunteers. In 1938 the army accepted one recruit for every 7.36 applications, in 1939 one in 20.58, and by 1943 one per 48.25. The cumulative number of applications from 1938 to 1943 reached 808,779, and the number of volunteer soldiers totaled 17,664. It is curious that the army did not enlist more Koreans in 1943 after the government announced the Korean draft. A likely explanation is that the army lacked the training facilities for larger numbers of Korean recruits. Statistics for the naval volunteer system show that Koreans submitted 45,000 applications in 1943, and the same amount in 1944, which was quite modest compared to 303,000 for the army volunteer system in 1943.

Table 2.2 is a useful tool for calculating the extent of the volunteer system in Korea. In 1937 there were 170,000 men aged twenty years old, and the population of men between nineteen and twenty-two was approximately

700,000. Colonial authorities encouraged men older than twenty-two to apply, significantly increasing the target population. As the statistics show, in 1938 only a small fraction (.004 percent) of eligible men applied. In 1943 less than half (43 percent) of the targeted population applied, in spite of bureaucratic coercion, propaganda, and enticements. These numbers, while impressive, were still not as high as the colonial regime wanted. There are several possible explanations for why more men did not apply or were not pressured to apply: There were men whose height, education, or health did not meet minimum standards, and they were not asked to apply; some men were impervious to GGK pressure because of their poverty or economic isolation; and some effectively resisted government calls for compliance. While the increase in the number of submissions was remarkable, the widespread evasion of submitting applications indicates resistance to this policy, as well as the inability of the volunteer system to legally force Koreans to submit them.

The application system for Koreans residing in Japan was slightly different because the GGK played almost no role in the process. Instead, the Tokyo government relied on the police and on auxiliary organizations, such as the Mutual Assistance Society (J: Kyōwakai), to encourage men to apply. The volunteer system in Japan had lower applicant percentages from Korean youth than that on the peninsula. Most Koreans in Japan worked full-time in mines and factories, so the government did not push them to apply. Also, Koreans in Japan had to travel back to their hometown in Korea to submit applications, to interview, to train, and so forth. Individuals had to make up to five trips to and from Korea at their own expense throughout the process.[101] This was an expensive feat that few could afford. Eventually, the government opened an examination center in Osaka in 1942 to alleviate the expenses for Korean volunteers.[102] Still, travel within Japan remained a financial burden for applicants.

Even though thousands of Korean men applied for the army, few of them had the linguistic training, cultural understanding, or martial skills to enter the army directly, something that could not be ignored.[103] Some bureaucrats reasoned that a short, intensive training period would compensate for these shortcomings. Shiobara Tokisaburō, head of the Education Affairs Bureau, stated,

The preparation [of Koreans] as imperial subjects has not reached a point where we are comfortable that all can do military service. Some young men have the self-realization as Japanese where they are practically equal to their Japanese counterparts. With a short period of training they may reach that state for which we have hoped. If we select the best qualified men, we can train them to be soldiers.[104]

Shiobara, as well as other bureaucrats, considered the assimilation policies a qualified success. They felt that the army should target a handful of young men who were the most Japanized and provide them with intensive training before they entered the military. The Korean Army, in agreement, stated that Korean soldiers needed to complete preparatory training "in order to cultivate within them the right temperament to be noble and sacred soldiers."[105] With training, the GGK hoped that volunteer soldiers could smoothly integrate into the army. This led to the establishment of training centers throughout the Korean Peninsula.

Each year, half of the volunteer soldiers entered one of three training camps (J: *gunmu gunrensho*) on April 1, and the other half on October 1.[106] Up until 1941 the training period lasted six months, but from 1942 to 1943 recruits underwent only four months of training to allow for more recruits to be trained. Training lasted six to seven hours per day and emphasized Japanese language, ethics, morals, math, and basic military drills. It also included a heavy dose of manual labor, such as helping with reforestation efforts. Camp life was Spartan, particularly for Korean youths, who had little prior military training at school. Recruits were unprepared for the regimented lifestyle. Japanese personnel at the training camp were strict, if not overbearing, toward Korean trainees. The emotional and physical demands rankled many Koreans. One trainer made the Korean cadets clean their shoes with their tongues and frequently slapped them.[107] One soldier, in 1941, could not bear the rigors of camp training and committed suicide by jumping in front of a train; the Education Affairs Bureau reported that the cadet's weak will caused the suicide.[108]

Training for Korean sailors took place at Chinhae and lasted six months. Naval training emphasized the practical skills needed for service. Midshipmen woke up at 5:30 am to train for life at sea. They learned special naval measurements and terminology and underwent physical training (such as swimming). Training focused on cultivating an imperial spirit in their hearts, bodies, and actions. Additionally, trainers taught Japanese history and customs. In other words, camps offered an intensive period of indoctrination to help Koreans fit in with Japanese recruits. Oral histories

FIG 2.2 The cover of a soldier's handbook (J: *Guntai techō*).

indicate that the naval training camp curriculum offered nothing of practical value. Im Kwang-ho, a former sailor, stated that the Chinhae training camp offered no serious training in weapons or fighting. Instead, cadets performed labor duties such as digging bomb shelters. To make matters worse, Im reminisced, Koreans suffered discrimination from Japanese drillmasters.[109]

WHY MEN APPLIED

The national historical paradigm portrays Korean applicants for military service as victims of the iron-fisted colonial regime. As the war grew worse for the Japanese, the numbers of applications the Japanese extracted from Korean men increased exponentially from year to year. In 1938 Koreans submitted 2,946 applications, but the number more than quadrupled to

12,348 in 1939. What accounts for this increase? There is little evidence that the GGK resorted to widespread coercion those first two years. Low numbers of volunteers in 1938 and 1939 suggests that there was a lack of interest among Korean youths to offer their lives to Japan, as well as a lack of urgency within the GGK because the program was designed to be a long-term project, with early applications likely submitted by genuine volunteers.

From 1940 onward the colonial regime exerted more pressure on Korean men to apply for military service. In 1940 the number of submissions increased sixfold to 84,443, and in 1941 reached 144,743. Japan's attack on Pearl Harbor in December 1941 altered how the army and the colonial regime looked at the volunteer system. Thereafter, the Tokyo and colonial governments began to lay the foundation for a compulsory Korean draft by pushing for more volunteers. In 1942 the army accepted 254,273 applications, and in 1943 accepted another 303,294. This increase was partially encouraged by the army to create the perception that the Koreans supported a conscription system.

Many local officials played a numbers game in which they spuriously inflated the number of applications so that their school or village appeared to be in compliance with government policies. Scores of officials drummed up a false sense of support for military service through dubious methods without regard to the legitimacy of the submission. Former soldier Kim Haeng-jin, for example, recalled that the police wanted one person from his school to submit an application. There were four people in his class, so they drew straws: He lost and had to apply.[110] Many young men were volunteered into the army by educators and police who applied for them, sometimes without their knowledge. Im Yŏng-ung reminisced that his village officials aspired to collect thirty applications, but fell short. City officials approached Im, who was thirty-five years old (too old to be a soldier) and asked if they could "borrow his name" to meet the village goal. He consented, and nothing came of his application.[111] In situations such as this, bureaucrats merely hoped to meet a statistical goal rather than collect legitimate volunteers. It is impossible to know the pervasiveness of this practice.

The meteoric rise in the number of applications from 1941 to 1943 can be attributed to a combination of indoctrination and a heavy dose of persuasion administered in varying degrees of acrimony and kindness. Government organs, especially the police, school authorities, and patriotic units, promoted a spirit of "volunteerism" among Koreans.[112] Local and national authorities found ways to encourage and extract a applications from the unwilling. Specifically, if a young man did not desire to volunteer, officials found pressure points (family, school, and income) to compel him.

By 1943 the GGK more frequently resorted to coercion and other questionable methods to collect applications. In one instance, the police told a student to affix his seal to a blank sheet of paper that they claimed was used to collect statistics on foreign-born students. Later, that blank sheet metamorphosed into an application for military service. In another case, Chŏng Ki-yŏng, a university student writing his thesis, attended a recruitment rally in Seoul but refused to submit an application. Soon after, the police visited his home and told his parents that if he did not apply, the government would ruin the family business. He duly applied but ran off and hid at a friend's home. However, a Japanese family friend tracked him down and turned him in to the police.[113] In another instance, students at a school were intimidated into applying by a military trainer who brandished a sword.[114]

In response to the announcement of the student volunteer system, colonial bureaucrats expected a spontaneous outpouring of loyalty by all students. However, the students' tepid response indicated a disconnection between government propaganda and reality. The regime stood to lose face over the low turnout because Governor-General Koiso had claimed that the student volunteer system was the students' desire. Kondo Hideo, a school inspector for the GGK, was disgusted with the inadequate number of submissions and wrote, "If we do not get peninsular students to immediately leap into action, it will not only be a shame for a single school, but for all. It will [poorly] reflect on their honor. If we do not get them into action now, my fifteen years [in Korea] will have been wasted and I will commit suicide as an apology [to the emperor]."[115] Governor-General Koiso was equally indignant. He threatened, "Among the peninsular students, it seems there are those who misunderstand the meaning of 'volunteer soldier' and it seems there are those who do not want to volunteer themselves.... I regret that I have to force the Koreans to alter their opinions."[116] This quote exemplifies the hollowness of the term "volunteer." By 1943 the Japanese regime intensified its use of social and economic weapons to patronize, shame, and coerce Koreans into submitting applications. Even then, it did not get complete compliance.

The colonial bureaucracy recognized that coercion was at the root of many applications and could not ignore the potential backlash of discontent. The police closely monitored Korean public opinion and decisively acted to prevent resistance or anything that might negatively affect the volunteer program. High Police sources noted that roughly half of the Korean applicants were apathetic toward the volunteer system because they had been bullied to apply for service.[117] A 1941 government survey (see table 2.3) estimated that one-third of all applicants were true volunteers, while 55 percent had been coerced in one way or another.

TABLE 2.3 Motivations for Submitting a Volunteer Soldier Application, 1941

Age	True Volunteers	Coerced Application	Other	Total
17	5,673 (33.5)	9,355 (55.2)	1,915 (11.3)	16,943
18	6,943 (34.6)	11,089 (58.2)	2,012 (10.6)	20,044
19	7,771 (35.0)	12,117 (54.6)	2,318 (10.4)	22,206
20	7,591 (35.2)	11,844 (55.0)	2,125 (9.8)	21,560
21	6,486 (34.3)	10,704 (56.5)	1,742 (9.2)	18,932
22	5,357 (33.7)	8,722 (55.9)	1,610 (10.3)	15,689
23	3,965 (28.2)	6,682 (61.4)	1,132 (10.4)	11,779
24	2,694 (33.0)	4,347 (53.1)	1,146 (13.9)	8,187
25+	3,704 (38.2)	4,812 (49.6)	1,190 (12.2)	9,706
Total	**50,184 (34.6)**	**79,672 (55.0)**	**15,190 (10.4)**	**145,046**

Source: *Chōsen Sōtokufu Teikoku Gikai setsumei shiryō*, Diet 79, December 1941, 104; in ICCCSC 22, 231. The standard used to determine the willingness of the recruits was not provided, nor is "Other" defined in the document. The number in parenthesis is the percentage value.

Examiners likely rejected unwilling applicants in favor of those who exuded patriotism and a desire to serve. If a man wanted the army to accept his application, he needed to exhibit an eagerness to join the army. It would have been illogical for the army to accept from the 55 percent who admitted that they had been coerced to apply. In 1941 there were 145,046 submissions, but the army enlisted only 3,208 men. Recruiters would have selected from the 50,184 "true volunteers" who expressed patriotism to Japan and whose background reflected a pro-Japanese mentality rather than from the 79,672 who had been forced.

Koreans who exhibited an eagerness to serve could have been loyal patriots or economic opportunists. Some applicants were sincere Japanese patriots who believed in Japan's propaganda of pan-Asianism and the East Asian Co-Prosperity Sphere, and felt that Japan had Asia's best interest at heart. Others accepted the imperial ideology taught by their parents or educators, and military service was a rite of passage for all Japanese men. Some Korean men were drawn to joining the army as a way to attain manhood or to earn a living to contribute to their family's well-being.[118]

Early in the Sino-Japanese War and soon after Pearl Harbor, the Japanese military enjoyed a series of victories that created a nationalistic euphoria that young Korean men wanted to be a part of, and submitting an application was an easy outlet.[119] One unnamed Korean said, "Because we are also Japanese, we want the glory as soldiers to be the shield of the emperor."[120] Matsubara Takanobu, a Korean law school graduate, said that he jumped for joy when he was inducted into the army. He had failed the physical previously, but with regular exercise he eventually met the minimum standards.[121] Another veteran, Wŏn Cho-jang, stated in a postwar interview that he did not doubt the sincerity of the government propaganda and wanted to fight for the emperor and his country (Japan) despite the protests of his parents and wife.[122] At least one patriotic applicant reportedly committed suicide when the military rejected his application. These cases show the effectiveness of Japanese indoctrination as well as the sincerity of some of the applicants. They also show that not all applications were the result of coercion. Korean independence was not within the foreseeable future as of 1941, so some applicants pursued the best available career option.

An unknown number of "true volunteers" had ulterior motives, namely to assist the long-term independence of Korea. In other words, Koreans used the volunteer system to resist Japan, both individually and ethnically. One volunteer stated, "At the oral examination … one Japanese officer inquired about my motives for joining the Japanese army. I replied that I wanted to learn how to die for the state—by state, I meant the Korean nation. But the Japanese officer might have interpreted this as the state of Japan."[123] A 1943 Manchukuo newspaper article, written by an unidentified Korean, expressed this motive: "I am hoping to apply for the volunteer soldier system for Korean independence. Many Koreans do not know how to use a weapon, so I will learn how to use one and use it for Korean independence."[124] This was precisely what the Japanese regime feared most: it was training enemies of the state.

The High Police realized that scores of Koreans volunteered for personal economic and social reasons. Many Koreans had given up on Korean independence and began to seek a better life, even if it meant cooperating with the colonial government. Koreans, being at the bottom of the colonial hierarchy, viewed military service as the quickest and surest way to economic and social advancement.[125] Propaganda highlighted opportunities for day laborers and farmers.[126] Untold numbers of applicants sought to escape poverty and starvation through military service. Nearly 44 percent of applicants in 1941 had assets (including land) totaling less than 1,000 yen.[127] Poverty was a powerful push factor. In the army, men ate regularly, received a stable income, and learned marketable job skills such as how to operate telegraph equipment, drive trucks, and speak fluent Japanese; these skills, and a military record, provided occupational opportunities for veterans that were significantly better than those available to the average Korean.[128] Men chose soldiering over remaining on the farm where they confronted the doldrums of periodic drought and famine.

Men also attempted to join the military to help their families. The colonial regime provided privileges to families with sons in the army. Japanese officials offered soldier's families social respect and material benefits that afforded better social standing. Soldiers' fathers received small gifts (cigarettes and stamps), and the family suffered less bureaucratic discrimination. Such incentives, while seemingly minor, were sufficient for some rural families on the verge of starvation to encourage their sons to enlist. Neighborhood associations and city offices orchestrated social networks to host ceremonies to honor soldiers, and, in some instances, cheered applicants who were inducted into the army. The army even provided these families with banners to hang outside their homes as a token of respect. Such banners represented the glory, pride, and social equality of these families.[129]

A number of submissions included a blood oath, which army authorities considered the most significant sign of loyalty to the Japanese state; these blood oaths also indicate a blurring of Korean ethnic consciousness among the applicants. Ōno Rokuichirō, vice-governor-general of Korea under Governor-General Minami, interpreted these pledges as the unqualified willingness of *all* Koreans to serve in the army. In a postwar interview, Ōno rhetorically asked of those who turned in blood pledges, "Wouldn't it have been unfair not to let Koreans participate in [Japan's] national defense?"[130] By February 1941 the military had received 293 blood pledges from Koreans seeking admittance to the volunteer soldier program. An Sŭng-ch'an wrote in a blood pledge, "I absolutely want to become a soldier,"[131] and future ruler of Korea Pak Chung-hee wrote, "I am both physically and spiritually ready to be a Japanese subject and am willing to give my life for the emperor."[132] *Morning Light* (K: *Chogwang*), a Korean-language journal from the colonial era, claimed that there was an explosion of blood applications after the naval volunteer system was announced.[133] Another wrote, "I want to rise up and take a gun at the battle front and becoming a great soldier to serve for the benefit of the nation in the hour of the fatherland's peril."[134] A room in the Seoul training center displayed a scroll some six feet long, with large red characters written in blood by the 1938 class. In this pledge, the authors promised that they would go into battle and die for the emperor.[135]

Blood pledges by Korean volunteers are problematic for scholars who portray applicants as victims of either exploitation or indoctrination. Many Korean scholars claim that *every* submission was a result of compulsion, intimidation, or badgering. Korean scholars, as well as many former applicants, charge that the Japanese education system "brainwashed" sincere applicants, especially those who turned in blood pledges.[136] Such black-and-white portrayals are too limited for historical analysis because they ignore agency. Koreans reacted to the volunteer systems with a full range of activities that included the extremes of both collaboration and violent resistance—and everything in between. It is difficult, however, to determine the motives of individuals, because few felt free to express an honest opinion during the colonial era (with the social environment that the Japanese had engineered) or after Korean independence (in which Korean nationalism discriminated against pro-Japanese proclamations). Few Koreans in the postwar era dared to admit that Japan's assimilation policies were successful and that the Japanese identity began to slowly take root among youth and blur the Korean national consciousness.

The motives of many submissions are not clear. In 1943, 894 Koreans from ten prefectures in Japan applied to join the army. Of this number, 732 showed up for the oral and physical examinations, and 470 passed. Of the 732 that were examined, 595 stated that they wanted to "take the lead" and "set an example" for others. Another 120 said that they were following the advice of others. The meaning of "taking the lead" is not clear. It can be interpreted as showing an assertiveness and eagerness to prove to the Japanese that Koreans were deserving of political equality. In essence, they wanted to prove to the Japanese people that Koreans were capable soldiers. This is an example of Korean ethnic pride, in which "taking the lead" was an effort to counteract social discrimination.[137]

As table 2.3 shows, the regime recognized that the majority of applicants (55 percent in 1941) were "made to volunteer." This percentage likely increased in 1942 and 1943. The colonial regime used coercion for all volunteer systems (including the naval and student) to increase the number of submissions to fabricate the perception that Koreans supported military service. The army solicited assistance from policemen, patriotic unit heads, educators, and city officials to threaten family livelihood, make home visits, and even badger families to pressure young men to apply. Yi Kong-sŏk of Cheju Island, for example, felt pressured by police and educators to apply for service in either the army or the navy. He eventually applied and was accepted into the navy after he passed a physical.[138] And Sŏn T'ae-su entered service as a naval volunteer when he and twenty of his classmates were asked by their teachers to go on a field trip to the Chinhae naval training center. Once there, they were pressed into volunteering and completing the four-month training.[139] The GGK used all kinds of tricks and stratagem to get men to apply; nothing was sacred, especially after the Korean draft announcement in May 1942. Thereafter, larger numbers of submissions were critical so that the GGK could claim that Koreans supported the draft.

The student volunteer system exemplifies how the colonial regime (under the strains of war) used its coercive mechanisms by creating, altering, and ignoring laws at its convenience. On September 21, 1943, the Tokyo government announced the suspension of student deferments for Japanese men in nonscientific fields. This forced around 130,000 Japanese students into the military.[140] However, Korean student deferments remained untouched because Koreans were not Japanese citizens. Furthermore, the deferments exempted Korean students from the Korean draft that was enacted in August 1943. Governor-General Koiso Kuniaki closed this loophole on October 20, 1943, when he suspended Korean student deferments in nontechnical fields by introducing the Korean Student Special Volunteer Soldier System. This measure, aimed solely at Korean students, "bestowed upon" them an opportunity to apply for service in the army.

The student soldier system was a last-minute measure that was sloppily implemented because government officials were focused on the military draft and labor mobilization. Little thought had been devoted to the 6,771 students on deferment. An examination of this system also highlights the complex nature of Koreans' actions in compliance with and in resistance to Japan's mobilization policies. During peacetime, the army would have rejected most Korean students as ideologically bad elements, but the war necessitated that capable men join the military, whether they were willing or forced, Japanese or Korean.

The application process for the Korean Student Special Volunteer Soldier System was similar to that of the regular volunteer system, except that in the student volunteer system schools played a more central role. Governor-General Koiso delegated to educators the responsibility of encouraging students to apply in order to maintain the fiction that the process was voluntary. He knew that educators had authority over students and could use that authority to pressure students to apply. Educators distributed applications to students and touted the long-term economic and social advantages of military service.[141] One such advantage, educators claimed, was that it would help reduce discrimination against Koreans because they would had proven their loyalty to the state.

Principals successfully inspired their students to apply. One such principal, technical school principal Matsuda Michiyoshi, had three students who served Japan with distinction. One student, Natsuyama Masayoshi (Korean name Ha Mun-hwa) submitted the first student volunteer soldier application. He traveled on the lecture circuit and participated in symposiums, encouraging other students to follow his lead. His mother also spoke publicly in favor of the military service, telling other mothers, "It is happiness to bear children and give them to the nation."[142] After the war, Natsuyama was accused of collaboration, but he defended his actions on the grounds that principal Matsuda enrolled him in school on the condition that he must serve in the military should the need arise. Whether this was true or not, Natsuyama's case exemplifies the effectiveness of principals in shepherding students into the army.

Another of Matsuda's students, Takehira Tadao, was the first student soldier to offer a blood pledge with his application. On November 2, 1943, he submitted a two-page letter, written in blood, that said, "I will try to live forever in righteousness, working with a heartfelt effort without regard for myself."[143] He ascribed his motivation for applying to the emperor's benevolence and to Matsuda's guidance. The third of Matsuda's students to serve, Second Lieutenant Kawata Seiji, gained fame as a *tokkōtai* (i.e., *kamikaze*) pilot by crashing his fighter plane into a B-29 bomber on May 29, 1945, over Mimaesaki on Shikoku. Matsuda stated that Korea should be proud that Kawata had shown such valor. These three students' stories attest to the complex nature of Korean activities during the war and suggest that the student volunteer system cannot be painted in purely coercive terms.

Korean student volunteer soldiers submitted applications for a more limited range of reasons than did applicants for the regular volunteer system. Very few, if any, students sought economic or social advantage through military service. Most student submissions were the result of government pressure. A large number of students had extended their studies to avoid military service. Oral histories indicate that one similarity between the regular volunteer and student volunteer systems is that applicants to both were motivated by trying to save their families from government harassment. Unlike applicants to the regular volunteer system, student soldiers did not attend special training camps. Instead, they entered the military directly on January 20, 1944. The government reasoned that students had had sufficient academic training in Japanese culture and language.

Once the deadline (December 19, 1943) passed, 6,203 of 6,771 students had applied, and 4,385 entered the military, an enlistment rate of nearly 70 percent. This number included 700 applications (335 enlisted) from recent graduates.[144] Those who did not enlist usually changed majors or found work in conscripted industries. This contrasts with the volunteer system in 1943, in which 47 out of 48 applications were rejected. The colonial bureaucracy exerted a tremendous amount of social and political pressure on a small group in an effort to secure compliance. They revised laws without much forethought and then brought to bear their massive state power to force less than 7,000 students and recent graduates to apply for military service. This system provides the best example of the GGK's naked bureaucratic power in action.

NONCOOPERATION AND THE VOLUNTEER SYSTEM

To secure applications, the colonial regime exerted tremendous pressure on youths and their families, especially after the attack on Pearl Harbor.

Despite this coercion, thousands of Korean men and their families chose not to apply. This choice took courage, considering the power of the colonial regime in the everyday life of Koreans. The odds of being enlisted were quite small, so most men simply acquiesced to state demands. However, many young men did not want to take the chance that they might be enlisted and refused to submit an application.

Open resistance to the volunteer system was negligible because most applicants were asked only to complete an application and to undergo an examination. In fact, government records indicate there was only one group conspiracy against the volunteer system. In 1939 two communist Korean men, Pang Yong-p'il and Yu Ryu-rok, were caught attempting to infiltrate semigovernmental organizations and destroy the volunteer system from within. These men, who had Comintern backing, claimed that if their plot had not been exposed, they could have organized a commune of 2,000 Koreans, recruited soldiers as communists, and possibly undermined the volunteer soldier system.[145] However, potentially violent confrontations such as this were rare.

Resistance to the volunteer system had many causes, particularly personal reasons and dissatisfaction with Japanese policies. The most prevalent personal reasons for not wanting to submit an application included fear of death, not wanting the burden of military service, and a deep sense of familial responsibility. Not all dissatisfaction with Japanese policies can be classified as nationalism, but much of it included the forcible collection of applications, discrimination against Koreans, and resentment over disenfranchisement.[146] A 1939 police study found a variety of ethnic-based reasons for opposition. An unnamed Korean student in Japan stated, "I have an opinion of strong opposition because the volunteer soldiers' application system is highly contradictory. The motivation for most submissions was frequently to end the constant bureaucratic solicitation."[147] An unidentified Korean officer stated that "there are glaring contradictions in the volunteer soldier system." He noted that the police forcibly collected applications, and that, on the whole, there was little volunteering.[148] Another Korean stated, "Koreans cannot support military service under the current system of discrimination." These opinions contributed to police doubts that most Koreans were willing to risk their lives for Japan. The police correctly assessed Korean public opinion as being tepid toward military service, but continued to hope that heavy doses of indoctrination would effect change.

Noncooperation with the volunteer system was especially strong among the upper classes, much to the surprise of the GGK. The colonial bureaucracy expected upper-class and educated youths to be pro-Japanese and willing participants in the volunteer program because their families benefitted most from the colonization of Korea. However, upper-class Koreans had long deigned military service to be beneath their station because they were traditionally exempted from military obligations. Governor-General Minami Jirō, speaking of those who debased martial duty, said, "There are many who truly do not comprehend the importance of soldiering. This is due to the influence of Chinese culture … which thought 'soldiers are things to be despised.'"[149] A 1943 conference noted, "There is a very small number of people whose way of thinking is completely against the Imperial will. In truth, this is among the intellectuals and students."[150] On the other end of the social ladder, the lower classes applied in greater numbers because they had fewer political and economic resources to evade recruiters and had more socioeconomic benefits to gain by joining the military.

The most common form of resistance to the volunteer soldier system was to not apply. There were several ways an individual could do this. A common method was for the father not to affix his seal to the application. If a father refused to approve his son's submission, the police pressured the father with frequent visits at home and work. In some instances the police pressured youths through daily visits or the groundless arrest of family members. Im Mun-ok, from South Chŏlla, stated that he tried to avoid volunteering by telling local authorities that his father refused to give permission for him to apply. In response, the police visited his family every day to persuade his father to approve Im's application, but his father refused, saying that his son was needed on the farm. Over the course of several months, the village head, the county head, and the provincial governor visited the family's home to argue that becoming a volunteer soldier would help their son's future. In the end, Im's parents acquiesced when the local authorities threatened to cut off the family's food rations.[151] Many youths caved to this sort of pressure. Chang Chun-ha, for example, applied to become a student soldier, hoping that his family would receive better treatment from the police. His father was a Christian minister who refused to recognize the Japanese emperor as a divine figure (J: *kami*), which led to friction with government officials.[152]

Students had several methods at their disposal to avoid compliance; some dropped out of elementary school or got expelled, because volunteer soldiers were required to have an elementary school diploma. In Kangwŏn, for example, seven students quit school to avoid government pressure—one of whom was forced to withdraw by his father. Others continued their studies at higher levels or returned to school to qualify for a student exemption. As of late 1943, nearly seven thousand students qualified for student exemptions and successfully avoided the volunteer system as well as the draft; however, in 1943 students were targeted by the student volunteer system. Hundreds of students changed their majors to science and medicine (which continued to be deferred from conscription), found work in industries designated as essential to the war effort, or simply refused to submit an application. As with the regular volunteer system, numerous Korean students absconded without informing authorities of their destination.[153]

To increase the number of submissions among students, the government simplified the burdensome volunteer process. In a change from regular volunteer soldier practice, students could submit their materials at the nearest military district office, regardless of their permanent residence. Students could even submit incomplete packets, or just announce their intention to apply, and turn in the required materials later. Parents could stamp their son's application even if the son had run away, thereby making the army the student's legal guardian. The GGK even permitted student submissions without the head-of-house's official stamp, which previously would have invalidated the application. The seal was still required, but the police assumed responsibility of making sure the head-of-house would affix his seal. Some colonial officials encouraged students to apply even if their parents objected. One school advised, "If your parents oppose you applying, discard them [J: *suteru*]."[154] This is in contrast to the earlier use of flowery anecdotes to win parents' support.

In this atmosphere of increased pressure on students to apply, the dean of Keijō University's law department, Naitō Kichinosuke, stated that "thinking 'Should I volunteer or not' is a basic mistake," because the choice should be made automatically.[155] In a similar tone, Nagaya Kōsaku, head of the Korean Army Information Department, wrote, "The meaning of 'volunteer' [J: *shigan*] has been interpreted at each person's discretion. These days it should be seen as giving one's self to a summons."[156] These two quotes highlight the increasingly impatient and belligerent attitude of bureaucrats toward students who had not complied.

Korean students formed the most intellectually and ethnically empowered group that the Japanese attempted to mobilize. They had suffered discrimination and ostracism in schools and on the job market in Japan and in Korea. Korean students had met scores of Japanese with less education and skills than themselves, thus boosting their ethnic pride. These experiences forced upon them a sense of being Korean. Such ethnic sentiments remained deeply rooted in these students and could not be removed by propaganda or assimilation. As a result, Korean student soldiers developed a deeper political consciousness than the general population and offered more resistance than any other group of Koreans.

The methods of resistance tended to be simple and nonviolent. Many applicants disappeared after submitting an application, hiding with relatives, moving to another city without notifying authorities, or fleeing to Manchuria. This was possible because the Korean family registry system, which contained the names and addresses of all Koreans (see chapter 5), was in disarray. GGK sources noted that those with a middle school education were more likely to not apply or to desert after doing so.[157] Well-to-do Koreans either sent their sons into hiding or encouraged them to continue their education and receive an educational deferment. Men also hindered their chances of having their application selected by intentionally speaking poor Japanese or by attributing their submission to coercion. These tactics reveal the nature and extent of resistance, as well as the cracks in state hegemony.

Large numbers of students attempted to avoid applying by procrastinating until the November deadline passed, but the GGK then announced that late applications would be accepted at police offices until December 19, 1943, the day before the oral and physical examinations ended. The GGK emptily claimed, again, this was in accordance with the students' desires. Bureaucratic coercion became increasingly blatant, giving students and recent graduates less room to decide the matter for themselves. The bureaucracy treated nonvolunteers like traitors, and labeled them as such. The government terminated the enrollment of students and forced them to apply for military service or to find work. The police dealt with any hint of nationalist or socialist resistance through surveillance, preemptive arrests, questioning, imprisonment, and torture. A number of incorrigible students were even sent to ideological camps that lasted two weeks. After this, they were forced into heavy labor at mines and in factories.[158]

Rumors also contributed to the unpopularity of the volunteer soldier systems. In 1939 the war became more real for Koreans when Japan and the Soviet Union clashed in the Nomonhan Incident. In July 1939 a Korean spread a rumor that Japanese soldiers were losing battle after battle to the Soviets. In early August 1939 another rumor spread throughout South Chŏlla when a Korean claiming to be a runaway soldier spread stories that Japan had lost so many men in battle with Soviet troops that the Japanese left their war dead lying on the battlefield like dogs.[159] A rumor in North Kyŏngsang stated that the droughts afflicting Korea that year were heaven's punishment for the war dead, and that if the war did not stop, the harvest would be half the normal yield; another claimed that the Japanese army feared a growing Korean presence in the military, so Korean soldiers were being placed on the front lines to die in battle.[160] Rumors such as these contributed to Korean hesitancy to apply for military service because men did not want to join the military only to die.

From 1940 on resentment began to swell against the volunteer system, and some vocalized their discontent. Korean Army authorities and applicants received threatening letters from angry Koreans. One letter, sent by Yu Chae-hyŏk, a resident of Seoul, stated that the Japanese had taken advantage of Yi In-sŏk's family hardship and forced him to die for Japan. Yu's letter, sent to an applicant, told the receiver, "I cannot be impressed with anyone who volunteers for Japan. You who volunteer contribute to the colonization of Korea." It concluded, "I hope you die in North China."[161] In response to these letters, the military police arrested the sender. The standard punishment for this type of crime was ten months in prison.

VOLUNTEER SOLDIERS IN THE MILITARY

The first group of 202 Korean volunteer soldiers entered the army on June 15, 1938, and a second group on December 10. Other than a handful of highly publicized cases, such as that of Yi In-sŏk, there is little information on Korean volunteer soldiers' activities within the army. Upon graduating from the training centers, the recruits, if deemed worthy, were placed on active duty; if not, they were assigned to the First Reserve. The military assigned roughly half of the Korean volunteer soldiers to the reserves, essentially returning them to civilian life, but with the prerogative to call them up for active duty at a later date. Reserves were likely activated for war in 1944 or 1945, but information on this is sparse.[162] Those in the reserves could be called up for one month a year for the next fifteen years. They were expected to help the army with the application and recruitment process, as well as provide auxiliary assistance in training camps.

Among the first four hundred volunteer soldiers, 350 were assigned to transport units, and twenty each to transport and infantry units.[163] Volunteer soldiers enlisted for two years, but once their duty was up, the army often extended their deployment each year until the war ended, so they blended statistically with Korean conscripts. For this reason, discussion of the wartime experiences of Korean volunteer soldiers is discussed in the next chapter.

On October 1, 1943, the first cohort of one thousand naval recruits entered Chinhae training camp, which had been established specifically to train Korean sailors. A second cohort of one thousand entered in April 1944.[164] A third cohort of two thousand volunteers was scheduled to enter Chinhae in October 1944, but the training program was eliminated in May 1944. The small number of sailors recruited through the naval volunteer system has contributed to the scholastic neglect of this subject. In June 1944 the first Korean volunteer sailors went to war. They performed duties as sailors, maintenance workers, machinists, construction workers, engineers, and paymasters.[165] Only a handful of Korean sailors died, because the navy was largely disabled by the time Korean sailors were enlisted. The naval volunteer system was superseded by the conscription system in 1944. In both 1944 and 1945, ten thousand naval recruits were sent straight into the navy without training under the conscription system.

The Korean Special Volunteer Soldier System was abolished on April 20, 1944, in favor of compulsory military service with legal mechanisms to force Koreans into the military. The volunteer system served as an important transitory step in the colonial regime's efforts to militarize and assimilate Korean society, a step taken much sooner than expected. The system co-opted a handful of Korean men and put them at the forefront of Japan's regional empire, where they sweated, bled, and died as Japanese soldiers for the Japanese emperor.

CONCLUSION

It is curious that Japan diverted a significant amount of economic, social, and political resources to recruit 17,664 men under the regular volunteer system, less than 5,000 via the student volunteer system, and 2,000 through the naval volunteer system. At no point did these volunteer soldier systems improve or provide Japan any military or political advantage. Koreans provided no new intelligence, did not instill the military with a new fighting spirit, and did not strategically strengthen the military. Thus, the most plausible explanation for these volunteer systems is that they were an ideological step toward the Japanization of the Korean population and part of long- and short-term efforts to implement a draft system in Korea.

An examination of these three volunteer programs highlights several themes. First, the Japanese government established and initially abided by a legal framework for the mobilization of Koreans as volunteer soldiers. Early on, the Japanese army recognized that Koreans were not educationally, socially, or ideologically ready for war. The Korean Special Volunteer Soldier System, as originally conceived by the army and GGK, was to last at least thirty years and then be replaced by a conscription system. However, Japan's attack on Pearl Harbor obviated this timeline and perverted the purpose of the volunteer system. Thus, the colonial regime set aside the original plan to go slow and increasingly relied on coercion to secure applications for propagandistic purposes that would justify the implementation of the conscription system. The Korean Student Special Volunteer Soldier System had slightly different purposes and implementation processes than the regular volunteer system, targeted a small group of students, and lasted only two months. The colonial regime focused on coaxing and coercing 6,771 students and recent graduates to apply for military service or find work in strategic industries. The GGK implemented the student volunteer system to provide a soft landing for Korean draftees and to close a legal loophole in the draft laws. The GGK exhibited its full might with the student volunteer system by altering laws at will and squeezing the social, economic, and psychological pressure points of students to force their compliance.

A second theme is that Koreans were not uniformly deprived of their decision-making ability during the volunteer system. They chose between compliance, collaboration, and resistance (sometimes choosing all three at once). There were true volunteers who sought economic betterment or, in rare cases, exhibited patriotism toward Japan. Koreans used the volunteer systems to their advantage or resisted using a variety of methods. The supposedly powerless Koreans had multiple voices throughout the volunteer systems. The colonial regime had an impressive amount of power and used it in an authoritarian manner, but the regime failed to gain the complete compliance of the Koreans who remained suspicious of the colonial regime. Without Korean cooperation, the GGK had little choice but to rely on coercion.

The third theme is the GGK's lack of hegemony over Korean society. Koreans eluded and frustrated the will of the colonial regime, successfully challenging the ideology of the Japanese state. Tens of thousands of youths and their families refused to comply with government demands, did not appear for military exams, and dropped out of school to disqualify themselves from service. Others simply vanished before or after submitting an application. The government controlled the financial, social, and political networks of power and used them to mobilize Korean manpower for war. Indeed, the coercive capability of the colonial regime was impressive by international standards. However, despite all that power, the GGK lacked the legal means to force Koreans to volunteer. The portrayal of the GGK as holding absolute power over Korea needs to be replaced by a more textured and nuanced picture.

3 | THE KOREAN CONSCRIPTION SYSTEM

In the months following Japan's attack on Pearl Harbor, the Japanese
military invaded and occupied territories in Southeast Asia and the Pacific.
These conquests added large numbers of fatalities to the tens of thousands
of soldiers already lost in the Sino-Japanese War that began in July 1937.
Japan's human resources were stretched thin across thousands of miles of
front lines. The Japanese military needed additional troops, so it called up
men from the reserves and lowered the conscription age from twenty years
old to nineteen and then to seventeen. Military officials realized that the
Japanese population alone could not defend these newly conquered territories. In short, Japan faced a shortage of soldiers and needed colonial Korean
and Taiwanese manpower to serve as soldiers and laborers.[1] A military
conscription system was best suited for the recruitment of large numbers
of colonial Korean men.

The military expected the volunteer soldier system, initiated in 1938,
to recruit and indoctrinate a small coterie of Koreans who were to form a
foundation for the long-term assimilation of Korea. The volunteer soldier
system was expected to last at least thirty years before the enactment of
a conscription system. However, war with the United States commenced
only three and a half years after the enactment of the volunteer system.
Too little time had passed to prepare Korean society for the draft or to
acclimate the Japanese army to large numbers of ethnic Korean soldiers,
yet wartime realities necessitated a conscription system to mobilize tens of
thousands of Koreans for service in the army. To this end, on May 9, 1942,
six months after the attack on Pearl Harbor, the Government-General of
Korea (GGK) announced that the Korean military draft would be enacted

on August 1, 1943, and that the first cohort of Koreans would enter the army in December 1944.

Japan's enactment of the military draft in Korea was a titanic undertaking. The Tokyo and colonial governments diverted vast amounts of manpower and finances from the war effort to revise laws and clear bureaucratic red tape as well as to force Korean youths to take military exams, and to train those youth and to send them off to war. Consideration of this development raises a number of questions: Why did Japan wait thirty months after the announcement of the draft to enlist the first Korean conscript? What concerns did Japanese authorities have about conscripting Koreans? How did the army implement the draft in Korea? Did the military alter its enlistment policies to account for the cultural differences of Koreans? What choices did the Koreans have in response to this sudden state demand? In what ways did Koreans resist the conscription system? And how did the colonial regime handle resistance?

JAPAN'S DECISION TO DRAFT KOREANS

Military and GGK documents stated that, as of 1938, the Korean people were not economically, culturally, or spiritually prepared for military service. Governor-General Minami Jirō asserted in 1939 that Japan could "scarcely expect to attain our objective [assimilation] until a new generation, educated and trained from childhood in Japanese schools, Japanese ideology and Japanese ways ... has reached maturity and replaced those Koreans who still recall the days prior to annexation."[2] In other words, the assimilation of Koreans, a precursor to the conscription system, was not considered possible for decades. Yet the draft was announced three years after Minami spoke these words.

Impetus for the draft came from two army generals: Prime Minister Tōjō Hideki, who served concurrently as army minister, and Governor-General of Korea Minami Jirō.[3] They requested that the army study the potential military contribution of Koreans. An army document dated January 20, 1942, estimated that Korea could supply 200,000 soldiers by 1946 and upwards of 400,000 thereafter.[4] The army introduced this issue to the diet, and it was briefly discussed on February 4, 1942.[5] In March 1942, Minami went to Tokyo to discuss the Korean conscription system with Premier

Tōjō Hideki and army officials. At this meeting, they agreed to extend the Military Service Law to Korea. After Minami returned to Korea, he did not forewarn the colonial bureaucracy of the upcoming draft announcement. On May 1, 1942, the Tōjō cabinet sent the Korean Army (Chōsen-gun) a copy of the draft announcement, and the Korean Army accepted the draft without revisions. On May 8, 1942, the Tōjō cabinet voted to draft twenty-year-old Korean men beginning December 1944, more than two-and-a-half years later. The GGK and the Tokyo government announced this decision the next day. The Board of Information released a statement that read,

> Following the outbreak of the China Emergency, there had arisen the tendency for the unification of Nippon [Japan] Proper and Chōsen [Korea]. With the recent outbreak of the Greater East Asia War as the turning point, the patriotism of the [Koreans] on the home front has become heightened.
>
> In consideration of these facts, it was decided at the Cabinet meeting to make preparations for the enforcement of the military conscription system among the [Koreans].[6]

The Japanese government publically provided a number of reasons for the Korean draft, and internal memos offer insight into the thinking of Japanese bureaucrats. A confidential letter to prefectural police in Japan, dated July 15, 1942, outlined five reasons for the draft: to show universal benevolence (J: *dōjin*) to all imperial subjects; to stimulate a spirit of loyalty in Koreans so they could enjoy unparalleled glory; to instruct Koreans that they were the arms and legs of the emperor; to give Koreans comparable rights and duties as Japanese; and to accelerate the assimilation of Koreans.[7] None of these indicated Japan's wartime needs. While mention of Koreans as the "arms and legs" of the emperor hinted at Japan's manpower needs, Japanese officials rarely acknowledged in government documents that the army needed Korean manpower.

The timing of the draft announcement surprised colonial bureaucrats, the Korean public, and the Japanese citizenry. Japanese officials and the Korean public had expected compulsory education, which was to begin in 1946, to precede the draft. For many people, the draft was a premature realization of a key responsibility (or burden, depending on one's view) of citizenship. Tanaka Takeo, vice-governor-general from May 1942 to July

1944, stated in a postwar interview that he and other bureaucrats thought the system could not be introduced in the near future because the economic and social conditions in Korea were unfavorable for the draft. Tanaka estimated that Korea needed another twenty to thirty years before economic and social conditions were right for large numbers of Koreans to serve in the military.[8]

Members of the diet also thought that Koreans were culturally and educationally unprepared for soldiering. Basically, as of 1942, too few Koreans spoke Japanese, too few had an elementary-level education, and too many qualified for an economic hardship exemption. Such conditions were similar to those of the Meiji government in the early 1870s. Curiously, in 1945 Minami Jirō, as former governor-general of Korea, wrote that the draft had been implemented too early. Specifically, he opined in a labor publication,

> In retrospect, today's actualization of the enforcement of the draft system is the fruit of thirty-four years of [Japanese] rule of Korea. Educational improvements; the expansion of economic production, transportation, and communication; and the elevation of cultural standards are all manifested as support for the central government and the united efforts of the people and government.... *However, the preparations were not sufficient for the enforcement of the draft system.* Rural villages that are a supply source of strong soldiers should be rebuilt through agricultural prosperity. [The Government-General] should aim to improve the moral and mental training [of Koreans] through promoting education. Furthermore, expansion of the Japanese language is an absolute necessity. Thus, a more important thing is to clarify the consciousness of our Korean brethren as Imperial subjects.[9]

This is a curious admission of Korean unpreparedness, especially considering that three years previously Minami had been instrumental in the implementation of the draft. Colonial era statistics support Minami's premise that Koreans were not ready for the draft. The military hoped to compensate for the remaining shortcomings during the thirty-month delay. This "move slow" approach allowed the GGK time to rectify a host of problems. After all, the conscription system could have been implemented in December 1942 and targeted a wider age group. In other words, Korean capabilities (both positive and negative) shaped the mobilization policies, propaganda efforts, and educational policies of the GGK. The colonial regime eschewed the use of overt power in an effort to win support from and to develop Korean human resources.

One of the GGK's first priorities before the draft was to initiate an intensive propaganda campaign to win the approval of the Korean public. The GGK publically claimed that the large number of volunteer soldier applications represented widespread Korean support for military service.[10] This was then parlayed into the perception that all Koreans backed Japan's policies. In a combination of propaganda and denial of reality, the Government-General announced that Koreans met the announcement of the military draft with the natural and "spontaneous delight of twenty-four million [Korean] people to completely transform the peninsula into the arousal of songs of delight and crucibles of deep emotion."[11]

As part of the propaganda effort, Governor-General Minami publically reported that the Japanese government had implemented the draft for four reasons: to fulfill a crucial step toward assimilation (J: *naisen ittai*); to respond to four years of favorable results from the volunteer soldier system; to answer the surging desire of Koreans to participate in the war effort; and to assure Koreans a leadership position in the Japan's wartime empire, euphemistically called the Greater East Asian Co-Prosperity Sphere.[12] Minami also noted that the draft system would enrich Korea's economy and reduce the bureaucratic differentiation between Koreans and Japanese. The colonial regime never publically admitted that the draft was implemented in response to a manpower shortage.

Pro-Japanese Koreans and groups such as the Green Flag League (J: Midori Hata; K: Nokki Yŏnmaeng) excitedly welcomed news of the draft.[13] Within days after the announcement, elements within the Chōsen League telegraphed letters of thanks to the prime minister and the ministers of the army, navy, and colonial affairs. One source claimed that "telegrams of appreciation made mountains on the desks of the government-general and the Korean Army."[14] The colonial media emphasized the excited response of a handful of Koreans and extrapolated it to mean that all Koreans supported the draft.

The English-language *Japan Times and Advertiser* endorsed the draft by claiming that conscription exemplified "the self-motivated effort on the part of the people of Chosen [sic] to train themselves to become model subjects of His Majesty the Emperor of Japan." It boldly asserted that the Koreans' growing support for assimilation and the draft were "but another evidence of the brilliant success of Japan's administration in the peninsula."[15] Minami Jirō declared, "I know for certain that the young men of Chosen will make very good soldiers.... As far as I know, [Korean] youths stand comparison [sic] with Japanese young men in every respect, especially in intellectual strength."[16]

The GGK manipulated the public sphere to ensure that only opinions supportive of Japan's policies were publicized; no criticism or questioning of the draft was allowed. The colonial regime encouraged the Korean elite to engage in a public discourse about the benefits and blessings of military service. Essentially, the Korean elite were coopted into government propaganda efforts. Support for the draft was voiced by members of the Korean business class, the academic community, and other sectors, as well as from scattered elements of the lower class. Colonial authorities maintained ties with Korean elites for ornamental claims of building legitimacy among the Korean population as well as to prevent elite leadership from joining the Korean nationalist movement.

The draft announcement caught the Korean public off guard because it had not expected the draft so soon. By and large, the Korean response was begrudging acquiescence and resignation to a fiat accompli. There was no major rebellion, nor was there an outpouring of cheer in Korea (other than that orchestrated by bureaucrats). It is also not clear whether the GGK comprehended the disconnect between the elite class's support for the draft and the average Korean's reluctance to serve. Open opposition to the draft was imprudent, so Koreans who disagreed kept their true opinions to themselves.

The Japanese, for their part, were of two minds regarding the draft. Ethnic prejudice permeated Japan's acceptance of Koreans as soldiers. On the one hand, they supported Korean military conscription so that Koreans could suffer population losses comparable to those of the Japanese. For example, an unnamed Japanese person said, "If only Japanese die in large numbers, then ethnic Koreans will survive in [greater] numbers, so we should send Koreans to war." Another reasoned, "It is not appropriate to carry out this war only at the expense of the Yamato [Japanese] people because it leaves Koreans [unaffected]. They, together with their formidable power to reproduce themselves, will pose a serious threat in the future."[17]

The Japanese public also was concerned over the declining quality of the Japanese army, which was losing seasoned soldiers in combat. Many Japanese citizens hoped to slow these losses by sending Koreans to the front lines as cannon fodder. They thought that if the Koreans were remodeled into imperial citizens who served and died for the emperor, then the Japanese youth on the war front would be less worried about the home front and better able to focus on the war.[18] Shitamura Hiroshi, a councilor of the House of Peers, felt that Japan needed to mobilize colonial subjects to compensate for Japan's demographic shortcomings compared to Western nations, such as shorter life spans and lower birth rates.[19]

On the other hand, not all Japanese favored the Korean draft. Some considered Koreans unreliable and unworthy of military service. Koreans were accused of placing family duties ahead of civic duties, and this made them bad candidates for soldiering.[20] The Japanese expressed concern that Korean soldiers might surrender to the enemy at the first opportunity or use the Korean language on the battlefield to plan and commit open treason. Another worry was that Koreans planned to desert and strengthen the independence movement. One anonymous Japanese stated that the Koreans "are stabbing us in the breast like a treacherous friend [literally, "a bug in a lion's body"]. No doubt there have been many spies up to today and ... after this, it will be more pronounced."[21]

This xenophobic thinking by some Japanese epitomizes their lingering distrust of Koreans. The arguments for both the support of and the opposition to Korean conscription were impregnated with prejudice. Expectations that Koreans should serve and die for their colonial overlord are examples of the failure of assimilation policies to persuade Japanese citizens to accept Koreans as equals.[22] The Tokyo government sought to alleviate Japanese citizens' concerns over Korean loyalty during the thirty months between the draft announcement in May 1942 and the enlistment of Koreans in December 1944.

PREPARATION FOR CONSCRIPTION

Colonial bureaucrats and army officials agreed among themselves that Korean men were not adequately prepared for military service when the draft was announced in 1942. The army considered Korean men linguistically, educationally, and culturally unprepared for military service in 1938, and the GGK had done little to rectify these shortcomings by 1942, despite public claims otherwise. The Japanese government needed to delay the implementation of the draft to shore up the loyalties of young men, provide martial training for recruits, revise laws, and straighten out family registries. Even more telling, the army and colonial administration were equally unprepared to send out draft notices or conduct military exams. The GGK needed thirty months to correct the above problems, a considerable amount of time considering Japan was at war. The three most important issues that Japan had to address in the two and a half years of preparation for the draft were propaganda, educational training, and administrative reform.

Colonial authorities did not, and could not, admit that the draft was the result of Japan's worsening fortunes because doing so would have been a loss of face and would have weakened the regime's mental dominion over the Koreans; they were concerned that any sign of weakness on Japan's part might increase Korean noncooperation or, worse yet, contribute to Korean ethnic nationalism. The Japanese lacked the manpower and resources to subdue a wartime Korean rebellion similar to the March First Independence Movement. The colonial regime realized that outright coercion had failed in the 1910s and had, in fact, contributed significantly to the outbreak of the March First demonstrations. The best option available to the GGK was to try to win the cooperation of Koreans. To this end, an intensive propaganda campaign and stricter assimilation policies followed the announcement of the draft. The outbreak of war with the United States effected a significant change in the colonial regime's treatment of its colonial subjects. Koreans, previously second-class subjects, gained key rights and responsibilities previously limited to citizens. This alteration in policies and propaganda entailed nothing less than an ideological shift by the Japanese nation, because this extended the parameters of the Yamato spirit to include Koreans as part of Japan's uniqueness.

Wartime propaganda played on Koreans' emotions and logic to spur them to action and to make them believe that they had something at stake in the war.[23] The colonial regime used newspapers, journals, educators, social elites, radio, youth associations, movies, and lecture circuits to inform men of their new military obligations as well as to win their family's support for the draft. The calls to duty poured forth as the GGK introduced slogans such as "One cannot gain glory without military service" and made claims that Koreans could "become the right hand of the emperor," a "shield of the Emperor," and a "soldier in a holy war" against the Anglo-American enemy. Japanese authorities paternalistically claimed that the conscription system was a gift from the emperor that was the embodiment and culmination of Japan's assimilation ideology. This propaganda was done in conjunction with other facets of mobilization to create a social environment that made it acceptable, if not obligatory, for men.

Colonial authorities disseminated propaganda to weaken women's social intransigence and cultural aversion to the conscription system. Many mothers and wives equated military service with the imminent death of their sons and encouraged their sons to desert. A survey taken in Seoul in late 1942 found that 58 percent (354 of 615) mothers surveyed and 68 percent (78 of 115) wives opposed soldiering by their sons or husbands. This was far higher than the 8 percent of fathers (52 of 637) and 0.07 percent of brothers (4 of 537) who opposed a family member entering military service.[24] Many women remained outside of the colonial regime's nexus of power because they had little contact or affiliation with the colonial state. Mothers of draft-eligible men grew up in an era (likely between 1900 and 1920) in which few girls attended school, a critical point of contact between the GGK and women, and few had opportunities to learn Japanese. Thus, the state had a difficult time indoctrinating them. The colonial regime countered resistance with a strong propaganda effort that focused on mothers through women's magazines and semigovernmental organizations. Bureaucrats sought to assuage women's fears of military service so that mothers and wives would willingly send their sons and husbands off to war. The regime claimed that in Korea, new "soldiers" were born into families with "soldier fathers and soldier mothers."[25]

The GGK also adapted Confucian ideals to win over recruits' mothers. One government-run, Japanese-language journal encouraged mothers to provide the best environment for their sons in order to support them to become great men, just like the mother of the Chinese sage Mencius, who moved her son three times.[26] Kim Hwal-lan (Helen Kim), the first Korean woman to receive a doctorate (from Columbia University in 1931), gave speeches and wrote articles persuading mothers and wives to support the draft. She used her position as principal of the Ehwa Women's School to inspire women to encourage their sons, husbands, and brothers to enter the army. She praised the military draft, saying, "Finally we receive the military conscription system for which we long awaited."[27]

Ch'oe Chŏng-hŭi, a female literary figure, publically supported the draft through her literature. In "The Wild Chrysanthemum," published in 1942, she tells the story of a single mother who takes her ten-year-old son to visit a volunteer soldier training camp just after the announcement of the draft. In the story, the mother senses that she must teach her son to develop a martial spirit because "a military man without a spirit is the same as being human without a soul." At the training camp, the instructor states that it is common for women to oppose military service, but that those "ignorant mothers see only their own blind love and cannot even grasp anything beyond it—nothing of the great, shining future beyond"; he adds that mothers who do not support their soldier sons "are killing their children with their own hands." The story concludes with the son announcing his desire to give his life to the state; he tells his mother not to show sorrow should he die.[28] This story set the parameters for a model Korean mother that readers should follow when raising their sons. The mother in this story was idealized because she had internalized the imperial ideology and had integrated her son into the state family, which was headed by the emperor.

Koreans actively engaged in the spread of propaganda, the enforcement of polices, and all other aspects of mobilization. The colonial regime secured the backing of many former Korean nationalist leaders so that the draft implementation was presented as a Korean affair. Elite backing of Japan's mobilization efforts effectively decapitated resistance at a national level and, more importantly, gave Japanese propaganda a Korean face. The employment of Korean elites and bureaucrats at the forefront of propaganda and policy implementation campaigns was critical to their success. This Machiavellian move gave Koreans the odious tasks of implementing unpopular policies; this use of Korean elite also weakened the Korean independence movement within Korea. Korean patriotic unit (J: *aikokuhan*) heads, Korean policemen, and Korean educators resorted to exhortations, pleadings, arrests, beatings, and persistent hounding of potential recruits to ensure compliance. For example, Ch'oe Rin, a key figure in the March First Independence Movement (1919), wrote that "every single person must become a great imperial subject of Japan. Without our complete cooperation with Japan, the Great East Asian War would be difficult." He continued, "What is the meaning of loyalty? It is to devote and give everything to the nation."[29] And Ch'oe Nam-sŏn, who drafted the Korean Declaration of Independence in the March First Independence Movement, wrote in the *Maeil sinbo*, a Korean-language newspaper, "The purpose of this war is to guide an imbalanced and unfair world to the righteous way and give an opportunity to all those who are controlled by others [Westerners] to achieve independence and to gloriously live together. Therefore, the only way to explain this war is as a holy war."[30] As these quotes show, former nationalist leaders publically supported assimilation and the brotherhood of Japanese and Koreans. The colonial government did not tolerate voices of dissent.

Other educated Koreans wrote books and journal articles in support of the draft system. In 1944 Kang Ch'ang-gi, in *A Treatise on Japan-Korean Unity* (J: *Naisen Ittairon*), wrote that conscription was the dream of all Koreans.[31] And Ueda Ryūdan, a Korean educated at Emory College, wrote *Sumera Chōsen*, which proudly heralded the draft and stated that "Koreans will never forget the conscription system for all eternity."[32] He was correct that Koreans would not forget, but not in the way he had hoped. Other works took a more familial and simplistic approach. *Conscript Brothers* (J: *Chōhei anisan*) contained letters and poems from grade school children that praised Korean soldiers, often their brothers, as heroes and role models. Children wrote, "I want to be a pilot," "The draft is a joy," and "This is for my brother who was drafted."[33] The goal of this compilation was to create a perceived public pressure on young men to serve in the military as well as to prepare the younger generation of Koreans to accept state demands on them.

Japanese propaganda assailed Confucian disdain for military service by cleverly turning to Korean tradition to promote the draft. Yi Pyŏng-do, a well-known Korean historian, likened the Korean youth of the 1940s to the warrior youth (K: *hwarang*) of the Silla dynasty. He said, "The fundamental meaning of *hwarang* is to live righteously, die righteously, and idolize music."[34] This effort to resurrect traditional Korean culture, which built on the efforts of the late Chosŏn dynasty, implied that the Korean draft was a restoration of a system that had existed in ancient times.[35] As part of the larger effort to integrate Koreans into the imperial ideology, the Mutual Assistance Society (J: *Kyōwakai*) encouraged Koreans to fight for the Japanese nation, because if they died, they would be enshrined at Yasukuni Shrine and would become gods that would be revered night and day.[36]

Some novels portrayed Koreans as active participants and heroes in the war. The 1944 novel *Captain Takeyama* (J: *Takeyama Taii*) was written about Ch'oe Myŏng-ha, a decorated pilot killed during Japan's invasion of Burma in early 1942. Like Yi In-sŏk, Ch'oe was glorified within Korean society as a hero and posthumously awarded the distinguished service medal (J: *shukunko*). The GGK anecdote surrounding Ch'oe encouraged youths to join the military and fight for Japan in imitation of Choe's bravery. *Volunteer Soldier Iwamoto* (J: *Iwamoto shiganhei*), discussed in the previous chapter, also fits in this genre, since it was published in 1943.

The Japanese colonial regime used film, a novel technology in Korea, to draw large crowds and deliver a promilitary message. Seven feature films on Koreans in the military were produced during the war.[37] *Love and Vows* (J: *Ai to chikai*, 1945), directed by Imai Tadashi, told the story of an orphaned boy who accepted the fatherly love of a Japanese family (and nation) and decided to reciprocate by volunteering to become a kamikaze pilot.[38] And *Mister Soldier* (J: *Heitaisan*, 1944), directed by Pang Han-jun and produced by the press section of the Korean Army, was made to "introduce the courage and diligence of the soldiers in the military through a portrayal of their strict training and homelike army life" as well as to strengthen the relationship between the family and the military. The training camp was presented to the viewer as a new family for young men, with the commanding officer as a father and the officer corps as older brothers. *Mister Soldier* showed a Korean family visiting a military camp. While there, they witnessed soldiers engaging in sporting activities and generally enjoying military life. The film presented training camps as places of camaraderie and happiness; recruits were seen eating cookies and drinking soda.[39] Movies such as these were shown throughout Korea and were used to win the support of potential recruits and their families by reducing the cultural barriers to soldiering. Much of the effort that was put into promoting the draft system went to waste because most movies were in Japanese. Colonial propaganda lacked flexibility because it approached Koreans not as ethnic Koreans but as Japanese. Korean-language propaganda was a small part of imperialization (J: *kōminka*) policies. Another hindrance to the GGK's propaganda efforts was that most Koreans lived in rural areas, where it was difficult to disseminate propaganda.

State propaganda called on Korean youth to fulfill their newfound responsibilities to the nation. State organs explained the essence of the draft (namely, its history and purpose) but, beyond the pan-Asian ideals of East versus West, did not explain why Koreans should support the draft. For many Koreans it was incomprehensible that they should risk their lives for the sake of Japan.[40] Japan failed to explain what Koreans had to gain by fighting for Japan or what would happen to Korea if Japan won the war. Prior to 1944 propaganda did not address whether Koreans would be granted full citizenship or would remain second-rate subjects. Propaganda was a one-way funnel in which the Koreans were told what to think and how to act.

THE EDUCATION CAMPAIGN

In 1943, Governor-General Koiso Kuniaki pushed to implement more completely the educational reforms of 1938 that were supposed to raise the quality of the Korean education system. These reforms removed all bureaucratic distinctions between Japanese and Korean schools, qualifying all graduates of these schools for service in the Japanese army. But, as of 1943, the 1938 reforms had not been uniformly executed throughout the peninsula: Some rural schools continued to offer a four-year curriculum, and the quality of education for Koreans remained substandard by Japanese standards. Prior to 1943, Korean students did not receive martial training in their schools; Koiso's reforms rectified this shortcoming by including twelve hours per week of military training in the curriculum for Korean students.

Another problem Koiso faced was that, as of 1942, the education system in Korea was not compulsory, so tens of thousands of conscription-age men had no formal schooling or too little schooling, and thus did not qualify for the draft. Only three-quarters of school-age Korean boys had attended elementary school, and only 52.4 percent graduated.[41] And, despite prior reforms to extend elementary schooling to six years, of the 77,062 elementary school graduates in 1942, 20,249 graduated with a four-year curriculum. Clearly, not all schools had the resources to comply with the reforms of 1938. Improving the education system in Korea and, by extension, the preparedness of potential recruits—namely, improving their Japanese language skills—was a Herculean task that had to be addressed during the thirty months leading up to the draft.

Japanese language proficiency among conscripts was essential to the implementation of the draft because Koreans were integrated into Japanese units. Approximately 20 percent of Korean men between the ages of seventeen and twenty spoke Japanese fluently.[42] Internally, the army expressed concern that Koreans with inadequate Japanese language skills would be unable to follow orders during training, and, more important, be useless on the battlefield—essentially rendering them deaf and mute in battle. At the foundation of these problems lay the low school-attendance levels among Korean youth.

A second education-related issue was special training camps for young men. The Korean education system failed to provide men with the proper ideological and martial training to be efficient soldiers. Such shortcomings necessitated a quick remedy. The Japanese army opined that Korean youth who had not finished elementary school were ignorant of the importance of military service and "needed more respect for the idea of time and sharing things." Furthermore, military officials bemoaned that Koreans "possessed a dullness of morals" and that the Koreans' dietary habits would disrupt battalion harmony.[43] Training camps were considered the solution to these and the language problems.

On October 1, 1942, the GGK announced compulsory, unpaid training for Korean men between the ages of seventeen and twenty-one who had not finished five years of school. Basically, all men who had not finished elementary school had to undergo one year of Japanese-language and basic military training.[44] Of those targeted for the draft, roughly half, nearly 125,000 men, needed special training before enlistment.[45] Exemptions from training camps were available to men who had finished or were attending volunteer soldier training centers, were serving as military civilians (contract workers with the military), or were in prison. The military expected preenlistment training camps (J: *seinen gunrensho*) to address the above issues as well as to impress upon Korean men the significance of the war, promote a spirit of national service, and teach Koreans army nomenclature. The military expected that this would also render the Korean recruits politically harmless. Army administrators hoped that the training would make Korean men into useful soldiers, laborers, and civilian employees of the military.

On December 1, 1942, training began at 715 public and 26 private training centers.[46] By 1943 the number of training camps had ballooned to 2,699, with an enrollment of 75,376 men. There were an additional 300 centers in Japan. Thereafter, the number of trainees fluctuated. In 1944 the number of trainees declined to 41,381, but in 1945 rose to 68,288.[47] By war's end, 210,000 Korean youths had been trained at these centers. To control costs, most training centers were located at national schools and administered by national school principals, and training was overseen by Japanese veterans.

The curriculum of the training camps was similar to that used at the volunteer soldier training centers. The one-year six-hundred-hour program consisted of three-hour training sessions four times a week. The training included heavy doses of indoctrination in which recruits learned songs that extolled the fatalistic glory of dying for the emperor. Some began to believe that it was their duty to die.[48] Instruction was in Japanese, and the curriculum centered on math, Japanese morals, ethics, history, and language, as well as military regimentation (marching and saluting)—not the use of guns. Oral histories indicate that some Koreans trained with wooden guns, but others did not even have those. Recruits also learned the basic daily routine of cleaning, calisthenics, and other military rituals. Training often included labor excursions to work in rice fields and on public works. Training camps for Koreans living in Japan provided 240 hours of free training, conducted in Japanese, in the evenings to accommodate the work schedules of the young men.[49]

ADMINISTRATIVE ISSUES

On the administrative front, the GGK was unprepared to implement the draft forthwith. Laws had to be altered or revised, and family records had to be updated. The former was necessary to establish a legal foundation for action to facilitate the smooth and even implementation of conscription laws. Japan's legalistic traditions demanded that, if only superficially, the appropriate laws be revised to rationalize the mobilization of Koreans. The colonial regime's prewar laxity in its enforcement of laws stymied the immediate wartime conscription of Koreans, and its inability to determine the whereabouts of Koreans placed a large portion of the Korean population beyond the nexus of power.[50]

The legal foundation for the Korean draft depended on revisions to the wording of several clauses of the Military Service Law, the Family Registry

Law (J: Keisekihō), and the Imperial Constitution, rather than on the prom-
ulgation of new laws. The Family Registry Law was amended by inserting
sixteen Chinese characters into Article 27 of the law code.[51] Specifically,
military service originally applied only to individuals subject to the Family
Registry Law within Japan proper (J: *naichi*). The cabinet added provisions
to the Family Registry Law that extended it to all peoples who lived under
Japan's rule—namely, Koreans and Taiwanese.[52] These laws were perma-
nently altered. Had Japan won the war, Koreans would have remained
subject to conscription in the postwar period.

The most important and difficult administrative task was the updating
of Korean family registries (J: *koseki*; K: *hojŏk*). It was impossible for the
army to institute the draft in Korea with any semblance of legality in 1942,
partly because too many registries contained incorrect information on
potential recruits' addresses, ages, and even genders. Thus, updating the
registry system was a necessary precursor to the draft. Family registries
were, and remain, official documents that contain demographic information on individual families. The records provide each individual's name,
birth date, relationship to the household head, and gender.[53] Individuals
whose names were listed on registries located in Japan were Japanese citizens. For this reason, Koreans could not transfer their registries to Japan.

Family registries, if properly maintained, contained information that
identified and located individuals subject to the draft. They listed a potential conscript's age, gender, residence, and criminal record. The Military
Service Law required the head of house to report to city authorities when
a household member turned twenty years old. Local authorities passed
the names and addresses on to the military, who then mailed conscription
notices to the men. To implement the draft successfully, the GGK needed
accurate registries. Yet the colonial bureaucracy had been lax in its enforcement of registry maintenance laws, so too few Korean registries contained
the accurate entries necessary for the draft. As a result, the regime suffered
for this neglect, while countless draft dodgers reaped the sweet rewards of
relative freedom from service. Prior to the colonial era, Korea and Japan
had each had family registry systems dating back many centuries. The two
systems differed on rules related to family heads, adoption, and types of
data entered into the registries. More important, the Japanese had a strong
tradition of reporting registry changes; Koreans, especially the lower

classes, did not. Thus, from the beginning of the colonial era, the Korean registry system, by Japanese standards, was in severe disarray.

The GGK passed laws in 1914 and 1922 to rectify problems within the Korean family registry system and to bring it in line with the Japanese system. For example, in 1922 the GGK introduced a temporary registry system that required individuals who moved away from their permanent residence for more than ninety days to report this change.[54] However, the populace and bureaucracy in Korea met these revisions with indifference, so there was little improvement in the upkeep of the registries.[55] The accuracy of the family registries worsened during the massive internal migrations of the 1920s and 1930s because few Koreans filed temporary registries. This negligence in the enforcement of the registry laws was central to the delay of the draft.

The infamous name-change policy, introduced in 1939 centered around family registries. This unpopular measure encouraged Koreans to adopt Japanese family names for bureaucratic encounters with the state at schools, at city halls, and in other legal matters. This policy became a major part of the assimilation process by unifying Korean family registry practices with those of Japan's. The name-change policy dealt largely with family registries and public affairs, and not so much with household matters.

In 1942 the Korean family registry system had three major problems that prevented the immediate implementation of the draft. First, the colonial regime estimated that half of all Koreans in Korea, Japan, and Manchuria were not on a family registry or had not filed the proper forms for temporary residency.[56] The colonial regime estimated in 1942 that, within Korea alone, almost 41 percent of Koreans needed to file temporary notices but had not.[57] This problem needed to be rectified before the draft could be implemented, because men not listed on a family registry were not eligible for the draft, while those who had not filed temporary registries would not receive draft notices. A second problem dealt with incorrect biological information. Many individuals' ages on the registry did not match their biological ages. One explanation for this was that the infant mortality rate in Korea was around 16 percent, so parents often did not notify local authorities of a child's birth until they thought the child would survive. When parents reported a child's birth, sometimes years later, the birth year was often incorrectly recorded. No small number of families failed to report the birth of a child at all.[58] Likewise, the death of a child occasionally went unreported, which left phantom individuals that the government might waste time attempting to draft. Some registries did not record gender, so confusion arose as to whether an individual should be sent a draft notice; some registries listed men as women and vice versa. As table 3.1 shows, nearly two-thirds of the registries had an error in the age, gender, or address column. If the age and gender were incorrect, it was impossible to know who was a twenty-year-old and therefore subject to military duty.

A third problem was that many families had ghost or multiple registries. Ghost registries were records that families abandoned because there was no head of household. In other instances, Koreans abandoned registries when the family moved to a new area and established a new residence without notifying authorities that the original had been superseded. This meant that one individual was listed on multiple registers and was mailed multiple draft notices. Given these three problems, the GGK recognized that it had to update the family registry system prior to the implementation of the draft system. The colonial regime diverted 6.5 million yen to straighten out the family registries and make other draft preparations.[59] But first the GGK had to determine the depth of the problem, so government authorities conducted an investigation of the registries in Kyŏnggi and Seoul. This survey found an average of two mistakes per registry. Table 3.1 lists the types of errors and the percentages of registries that had such errors.

TABLE 3.1   Family Registry Mistakes in Kyŏnggi Province and Seoul as of 1941

Types of Mistakes on Registry	Percentage with Errors
No record of an individual who left home	10.7 percent
People listed on multiple registries	11.0
Registry with family member not listed	19.5
Wrong age	62.6
Wrong information in the columns (gender, residence)	63.5
No head of house (not maintaining registry)	18.4

Source: Higuchi, *Senjika Chōsen*, 40.

On October 15, 1942, the colonial regime attempted to correct these registry errors by requiring Koreans to update their family records. Koreans living away from their hometowns had two weeks to file a temporary residence or be fined. Much of the detective work of rectifying family registry problems fell to patriotic unit heads, who then reported changes to local government offices. Colonial authorities implemented a system of mutual surveillance in which patriotic unit heads notified each other when an individual or family moved in or out of their jurisdiction. The government hoped to force families to file changes when a family member moved out, moved in, or was born. These heads also assumed authority over ration cards to ensure that families followed procedures. This, in many cases, forced families to comply with registry laws because a family's rations depended on the number of people listed on the family registry; it would have been difficult for a family to hide an extra person. This made the family registry a semicompulsory system, but full compliance was never reached. The GGK estimated that in late 1943, Koreans filed only 80 percent of changes to their registries.[60]

A final administrative problem for the regime was the Korean demand for suffrage. Prior to the war, the GGK claimed that Koreans were denied voting rights because they did not pay "blood" taxes (i.e., military service) as did Japanese citizens. This argument was no longer feasible after the extension of compulsory military service to Koreans. Demands for enfranchisement were discomforting to the regime because Koreans now bore all of the duties of citizenship, yet were denied equal rights. The GGK had no clear response to these renewed demands. Yet policymakers discussed conscription and suffrage in tandem, as if they were connected issues. For example, on May 9, 1942, when Emperor Hirohito was given a presentation regarding the Korean draft, he inquired whether enfranchisement should be considered in exchange for the draft.[61] Diet members also considered the issue during their debate on the draft. However, Governor-General Minami opposed extending voting rights in return for conscription because, he argued, Koreans might think that they had bargaining power and push to expand their ethnic desires. He considered the two issues to be unrelated.[62] Minami's stance exemplifies Japan's concern for maintaining mental domination over its colonial subjects. Men of Minami's ilk felt "that if [Korean] gratitude and enthusiasm [for the draft] were truly genuine, they would not raise the issue" of enfranchisement; calls for representation in the diet were taken as examples "that most Peninsulars do not yet truly have a thoroughgoing consciousness as Japanese."[63]

Nevertheless, the suffrage movement gained momentum in 1944 when

Koiso became prime minister. Koiso felt that enfranchisement was inevitable after the enforcement of Korean conscription and hoped to secure Korean loyalty by extending citizenship and other rights to Koreans. In April 1945 the Koiso cabinet granted Koreans representation in the diet beginning in 1946, but the war ended before this became a reality.

The colonial bureaucracy exhibited an ability to balance social reality with Japan's wartime needs. The regime could easily have followed the precedence of the French or British in Africa and shanghaied men or merely sent quotas to villages from the beginning. Instead, the GGK altered laws in accordance with the ideological notions of legality embedded in Japanese culture. The GGK ensured that the legal foundation for the draft was in place prior to the recruitment of Koreans. Of course, laws were altered for the sole benefit of Japan, which turned the issue into a problematic consequence of ideological hegemony.

The GGK's preparations for the draft reflect the prewar shortcomings of the colonial regime's social policies. The discourse on the backwardness and underdevelopment of Korean culture reinforced an ingrained distrust among the Japanese that had to be uprooted. These widespread prejudices contributed to a limited view in government circles of how Koreans might contribute to the expansion and defense of Japan's empire. Thus, when the military moved to implement the conscription system on the peninsula, it found that Korean society, specifically men, lacked the necessary language skills, patriotic fervor, and martial training to enter the military. The military could not overlook these problems, because of the serious defects in the family registry system. The effort to rectify the problems discussed above makes the GGK look less like an evil totalitarian regime and more like a short-sighted administration caught unprepared for a major change in policy.

IMPLEMENTING THE DRAFT

On August 1, 1943, the GGK and the Korean Army enacted the draft with much pomp and ceremony. The crown jewel event to celebrate the draft was an elaborate Shintō service at the Chōsen Shrine located on top of South Mountain (Namsan) in southern Seoul; in attendance were the governor-general, numerous Korean elites, and 90,000 flag-waving students. In a radio address, Yun Ch'i-ho welcomed the draft with a speech titled "What Can Equal Our Joy Today at the Formal Beginning of the Enforcement of the Conscription?"[64] Between this ceremony in August 1943 and the day the first Korean conscripts entered the army in December 1944, the army had much work to do. The rectification of the family registry was merely the first step; the army still needed to mail draft notices, conduct physical exams, classify potential recruits, and provide training for men who lacked the necessary qualifications. In each area, the colonial regime moved methodically according to the Japanese precedent used during the Meiji Restoration to contain the potential backlash of Korean public opinion.

In autumn 1943, the military mailed out 273,139 conscription notices to twenty-year-old men. Draft notices informed potential recruits of when and where to report for the conscription exams. Potential draftees had to return the notice to the local military district office in order to register for the exams. In some instances, the police and local officials personally delivered draft notices, because some youths could not read the notice, which was written in Japanese. Another reason for hand-delivering notices was to guarantee delivery of notices and to prevent recruits from running off once they received the summons. The delivery of conscription notices often devolved into a game of cat and mouse in which authorities established contact with men to guarantee the return of draft notices and to establish surveillance over flight risks. Men encountered pressure on all fronts to register for the draft and to undergo the exams. Police authorities, educators, and patriotic unit heads hounded the families of men who failed to respond to the draft summons. Policemen made daily visits to family members of draft dodgers, and in some instances dragged fathers to the police station for interrogation. In a few cases, fathers were fired from their jobs when their sons deserted.

Of the 273,139 draft notices sent out, 231,424 (84.7 percent) were returned. The 41,715 (15 percent) unreturned notices indicate that there were ongoing problems with the family registry as well as successful draft dodgers. Similar problems emerged among the Korean population in Japan. Nearly 40 percent of the conscription notices mailed to Koreans in Japan went unanswered, largely because the notification was either sent to an incorrect address or ignored by the recipient.[65] Once registered, potential draftees underwent physical and mental examinations to determine their draft classification.

The Korean Army conducted examinations from April 1 to August 20, 1944. Korea lacked sufficient numbers of doctors to man the exam stations, so the Kantō (C: Kwantung) Army in Manchukuo dispatched fifty doctors to assist with the physicals. Examiners inspected potential conscripts in three areas: physical condition, Japanese language ability, and mental fortitude and ideology. Conscripts were classified into one of seven classes: A, B-1, B-2, B-3, C, D, and F. Classes A and B-1 were classified as eligible for active duty. Class A recruits had to be at least 1.55 meters tall, have good eyesight, and be in good physical condition. Ideally, active-duty recruits had an elementary-school diploma and could speak Japanese without difficulty. Ideologically, the army looked for men who had no connection with or sympathy for the independence movement. Class B-1 recruits also had to be 1.55 meters tall, but had poorer eyesight and were in worse physical condition.

Those in Classes B-2 and B-3 were shorter and had poor eyesight. These men served in the Conscript Reserves and could be called into active service. Class C recruits served in the Second National Reserve Army. Class D were unfit for service. All of the above classes were available for labor conscription and service as civilian employees of the military. Class F recruits qualified for a temporary economic or physical exemption from service for one year. Approximately 22 percent of Koreans qualified for economic hardship exemptions.[66]

The draft in Korea was more limited in scope than in Japan because the government viewed Koreans as a source of labor, not as soldiers. Korean conscription targeted only twenty-year-olds (compared to nineteen- and twenty-year-olds in Japan), required stricter physical attributes, and allowed Koreans more exemptions from military service. For Japanese men, the army used the draft as a trump card to secure soldiers. The army conscripted or called up Japanese men on the reserves from industries, regardless of their technical skills, a policy that hurt industrial production. However, for Koreans, labor conscription was equivalent to military service and exempted many Koreans from the draft. Quite literally, Koreans evaded military conscription through labor conscription to the same positions in industries from which Japanese laborers were taken. Additionally, Korean civilian employees of the military were exempted from military duty. These policies, nonetheless, ensured that the Japanese nation benefitted from Korean labor and soldiering.

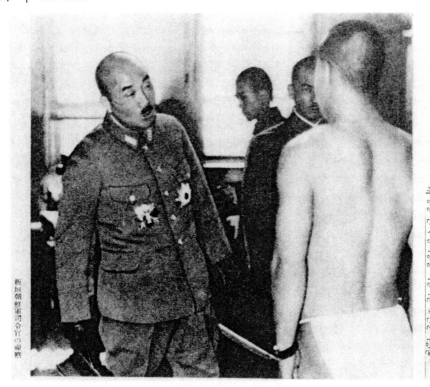

FIG 3.1 Physical examination of prospective military draftees.

Military exams also tested a recruit's Japanese language ability, which Japanese authorities considered essential to effective soldiering. Technically, Koreans who lacked adequate Japanese language skills were not to be drafted, but government documents and oral histories indicate the army ignored this policy. Army Vice-Minister Shibayama Kenshirō estimated that only 23 percent of Korean men entering the military spoke proficient Japanese in casual conversation.[67] Military officials used training camps to prepare Koreans for service in the army. Also, colonial authorities considered Japanese language proficiency emblematic of the assimilation process because it was the best way to weaken the Korean cultural identity.[68] Yet only 38.2 percent of young Korean men had graduated from elementary school—the cornerstone of Japan's assimilation policies.[69] The low Japanese-language proficiency and elementary-school-graduation levels are central to understanding Korean society's unpreparedness for the draft and, by extension, the haste (but not desperation) with which the GGK implemented the draft.

During the examination process, army examiners probed each candidate's ideology in an effort to identify "dangerous elements" (J: *kiken bunshi*). Army authorities worried that Korean nationalists or Communists might infiltrate the military and foment discontent from within or establish links with the Chinese and pass on military intelligence.[70] However, there is no evidence that any Korean was excluded from service because of ideological beliefs. In fact, colonial authorities considered military service—the embodiment of assimilation policies—a way to force Japanese ethnicity on Korean youth.

Of the 218,659 men in Korea expected to undergo the military exams in 1944, 206,057 (94 percent) showed up.[71] In some instances, the police and Chōsen League officials had to pressure recalcitrant youths to undergo the examination. Nearly 6,300 could not be located. Men who failed to submit to the conscription examination without just cause could be fined up to one hundred yen.

A number of problems arose during the exam process that originated with the family registries. Women, very young boys, and obviously older men showed up for the examination—all indicating incorrect birth information on the registry. It is also possible that families purposefully sent older men or women as replacements for qualified young men to capitalize on the confusion surrounding the registries. Despite government publicity, many Koreans did not understand the purpose, process, or nature of the draft. In some cases, families sent "replacement" siblings for a young man who was out of town or sick under the presumption that the army wanted any family member. Some mothers came to the exams saying their last good-byes to their sons, thinking that they would be shipped off to war that day. Problems also arose due to a shortage of translators. When one recruit took out and opened a small knife, he was quickly subdued by the examiner and the police, who assumed that he was going to attack the examiners. After much confusion and yelling, it turned out that the man simply wanted to make a blood pledge to serve Japan.[72]

Korean men sought to avoid classification as A and B-1 so they would not be eligible for active duty. Some showed up for their physical exams and acted deaf, sick, or mute in an effort to be exempted from the draft. Others intentionally failed the eye exam; a handful drank soy sauce to trigger an irregular heartbeat.[73] One potential draftee rubbed lead powder on his chest to give the appearance of a lung malady.[74] Examiners scrutinized, and some say abused, those who feigned a physical malady. Army officials challenged individuals who claimed to be disabled by isolating them for several days and closely observing them. In one instance, the police drove a nail into the shoulder of a Korean pretending to be mute, causing him to cry out in pain.[75] A few Koreans cut off a finger or toe to evade conscription. Those convicted of attempting to evade the draft by failing the physical exam risked being sentenced to three years in prison, but in most cases they were still enlisted and sent to the battlefront.

Of those examined, 33.5 percent (69,441) were classified as Class A candidates (making them available for active service), 30 percent (61,817) as Class B-1 (also available for active service), 16 percent (32,969) as Class B-2 (available for the First Conscript Reserve), 11.1 percent (22,666) as Class B-3 (available for Second Conscript Reserve), and 9.1 percent (17,545) were ineligible or temporarily exempted from the draft.[76] Thus 63.5 percent (131,258) were eligible for active duty, but of these only 24.7 percent (55,000) were placed on active duty in the army or navy, compared to nearly 90 percent of Japanese that same year. Those placed on active duty entered the barracks on December 1, 1944.

After the exams, Korean conscripts returned to their hometowns to await deployment. Many local authorities gave recruits a hero's welcome by holding congratulatory parties. Dozens of people, including policemen, attended these events to praise the soldier—some even spoke in honorific and deferential language. Koreans classified as A and B-1 were accorded a degree of respect by the bureaucracy, especially the police. Kang Tae-hŭi, of Kwangju, claimed that no one, not even the police, bothered him after he received his conscription notice, because "most [people] looked at me as a dead man walking."[77] Some conscripts went so far as to pick fights with police because they figured they were going to die in battle, so they decided to vent their anger on the police first.[78]

From August 1943 to December 1944, the Korean Army conducted the draft process in a rather orderly manner. It mailed out draft notices, examined recruits, and classified them in accordance with the Military Service

Law. This process exemplifies the slow, methodical approach to Japan's mobilization of Korea despite the regime's declining war conditions. The recruitment of men in 1945 was increasingly desperate and disorderly, but by no means chaotic.[79] The GGK and the army frequently ignored laws out of necessity by conscripting Koreans through extralegal means such as shanghaiing and recruiting underage men. The wartime survival of the nation took precedence over the niceties of adherence to state laws. As Japan's ability to conduct war deteriorated, government authorities worried less and less about legally rectifying their actions and relied more and more on police coercion and mutual surveillance to prevent negative Korean responses.

DRAFT EVASION

Most studies of the Korean conscription system focus on coercion and the victimization of Korean draftees. However, history is rarely so bifurcated. There is no denying that the colonial regime strong-armed men into the military, but the colonial regime did not rely solely on coercion, nor did it have complete control over Korean society; there was room for Koreans to control their own destinies. A large number of Korean men obeyed their conscription notices without any resistance. Many enlisted in the military after considerable foot-dragging; others successfully evaded the draft. Draft dodging was a common choice for a plethora of reasons, and grew more common in the last year of the war. An examination of this phenomenon as well as the Japanese response illustrates the colonial regime's incomplete grasp of Korean society.

Much like the volunteer systems, military service provided economic and social opportunities for unemployed men or peasants on the verge of starvation. Unfortunately, oral histories and government documents do not provide details about the extent to which Koreans enthusiastically complied with or quietly acquiesced to coercion. The social climate in postwar South Korea harbored prejudice against individuals who willingly cooperated with the Japanese colonial regime. Thus veterans of the Japanese military unvaryingly portray themselves as victims who attempted to evade service as long as possible.

Korean men evaded the draft for numerous reasons. The two most common were familial obligations and the failure of government assimilation policies. Young men had family obligations that, in their minds, outweighed loyalty to the state. Sons were needed on family farms as workers; also, a son was expected to carry on the family name, especially if he was an only son. Compounding this problem, from the point of view of the Japanese state, was that parents feared the loss of a son. Too few Koreans accepted the emperor-centered state ideology and instead felt that they were dying a "dog's death" for Japan.[80] This was not wholly pro-Korean nationalism, but Korean resistance showed that assimilation policies had not won the hearts and minds of most of the younger generation.[81] While parental concern for a child is universal, Korean parents lacked the patriotism of Japanese parents that prepared them to offer their sons' lives for the emperor. The failure of assimilation among Koreans is conveyed in the following postwar quote from Kang Pyŏng-ju, a bank manager from North P'yŏngan:

> That "One Body, One Spirit" slogan did not fool us, however! It sounded good on paper. Supposedly it meant that we, both Japanese and Koreans, were all children of the Divine Emperor and therefore should be treated equally. But actually, the Japanese desperately wanted to find ways to use Korean manpower, especially men from age eighteen to about forty, for their military use—by now many of their own men had been killed in the war. So we were not fooled. They wanted us to carry out their war effort.[82]

Kang aptly conveys the resentment that many Koreans felt toward Japanese coercion in general and toward the conscription system in particular. After three decades of discrimination and economic underdevelopment, most Koreans lacked a personal connection to either the GGK or Japanese ideology. Many exhibited their true opinions through evasion, desertion, and other forms of noncooperation that grew more pervasive as Japan's mobilization policies became more coercive and Japan's defeat more apparent. Koreans understood that the Japanese lacked faith and trust in the "peninsulars" and preferred not to arm them.

Evasion was the most common form of resistance to the draft. But not all methods of draft evasion were illegal. Thousands evaded military service by finding work in factories designated as critical to the war effort, because employment in these facilities exempted them from the draft; others joined patriotic labor corps. A handful of students enrolled in medical or science majors that allowed students to defer military duty. Some parents forced their sons to marry, which made them the sole providers of their own households, in an effort to qualify their sons for economic hardship exemptions. Conversely, other parents rushed marriages so that their sons would produce heirs prior to deployment. Girls willingly married these men to avoid state demands for labor or recruitment into the rumored (and true) system of military prostitution.

Of course, some methods of evasion were illegal. The most common of this type was draft dodging. Young men and their families were creative in their efforts to dodge the draft. Poor families relied on wit and bravado alone to evade military service. Without money, the poor could not afford to purchase extra food to supplement their rations while hiding a draft dodger, nor could they hide on an expansive estate like the sons of rich landlords. Running away was often the best option. One man evaded enlistment based on the advice of a shaman:

> I received a military draft notice, but I really didn't want to go into the army. I was married and we had a child, but that didn't make any difference to the Japanese. They wanted all the help they could get.
>
> Somebody said, why don't you go to a fortune teller to get advice? So I went. He told me to run away because my lot as a soldier would be a very bad one. I took his advice and went to my aunt several villages away. I stayed in hiding for six months and twenty days and then the war was over.
>
> My parents got into trouble because I ran away. The police went to my house every single day, demanding to know where I had gone. Sometimes the police went, sometimes the township officials, asking the same things over and over.[83]

This young man's story illustrates the pressure the state exerted on deserter's families. More importantly, it showcases the choices that Koreans had despite increased government pressure—and many chose to flee from the draft. In 1944 the colonial bureaucracy estimated that nearly 10,000 Koreans remained undrafted.[84] This constituted an untapped reservoir of men that slipped through the cracks of the regime's powerful mobilization machinery. While this was a small percentage of the total targeted population (over 205,000), it concerned the GGK. The colonial government investigated how these men were evading the draft and reported,

> Since the enactment of the conscription system, we have conducted an investigation into draftees whose whereabouts are not known … in order to grasp the total number of the undrafted. The survey results show that as of December 1, 1943, there were 9,767 undrafted men. Because there were so many, in March of this year we set up an investigatory body to find these Koreans. Throughout Korea we surveyed all areas looking for these missing persons. Together with this survey, we enacted a plan to apprehend all of the draftable men Korea and found 2,038 [of the 9,767].[85]

The GGK was effective in forcing nearly 205,000 men to take military examinations, but there remained enough room for thousands to slip through the cracks. Colonial authorities invested untold man-hours and resources in locating draft dodgers. Still, after all these efforts, the police located only one-fifth of the draft dodgers; the odds of evading the draft favored those willing to take the risk.

Given the importance of the family registries to the draft, they became a focal point of resistance—and an area in which the colonial regime was vulnerable to noncooperation. The temporary residence system provides insight into this topic. Koreans opposed the more stringent enforcement of the residency laws because they were concerned with increased government control over their lives, and many worried that the registry laws were a direct link to military service.[86] In opposition to registry laws and military service, Koreans used the system to their advantage. Parents bribed municipal officials to alter a son's birth date, purchased false death certificates from hospitals, changed their residence frequently without notifying the authorities, or filed false temporary registries, claiming that their son worked overseas.[87] The GGK records highlight this point,

> Among groups such as older women, the lower classes, and the unemployed, there are those who are taken with the wrong ideas that drafting equals death in war. They have caused their children of draftable age as well to flee to hiding places, or *attempted to evade [the draft] by changing their age in the family registry*, or because they became of draftable age, they have called off weddings [to conceal age].[88]

Calling off marriages helped to conceal the age of a potential recruit if, for example, the registry listed a twenty-year-old man as a fifteen-year-old boy.

Upper-class Koreans were unwilling to send their sons to war and had more resources at their disposal to evade conscription. Elites used their social and bureaucratic connections to help family members get exemptions from military service. Diet records state that "after the announcement of conscription, some of the educated and rich Koreans fled to China and Manchukuo";[89] the numbers are not known, but were in the hundreds, if not thousands. In one extreme case, Yi P'ung-ho, of Ch'ungch'ŏng, hired a local man to serve in the army on his behalf while Yi hid on the family farm. The young man successfully served for Yi and returned to the village after the war.[90] Of course, only the wealthy could afford this option.

There were also random occurrences of open violent resistance to the draft. One group of students in North Chŏlla made a list of pro-Japanese Koreans and planned to set fire to the neighborhoods where they lived; another group planned to make a bomb with gasoline, blow up a police station, and steal the weapons stored there. The police uncovered both plots before they were carried out. Such acts of resistance were foolhardy under the highly effective police state. Nevertheless, as the war drew to an unfavorable close for Japan, Koreans became increasingly bold in their resistance.

Resistance quickly caught the attention of a colonial government not famous for its tenderness toward Korean intransigence. The state suppressed opposition by using police surveillance and propaganda in tandem. Publically, the GGK continued to highlight pan-Asian ideals of East versus West, the brotherhood of Japan and Korea, peninsular loyalty to the emperor, and the progress of Korea under Japan. Interestingly, such propaganda was often dark and ominous, with slogans such as "It is a mistake to fear soldiering just because you might die. You will achieve glory on the road to heaven."[91] When propaganda did not win the support of intransigent Koreans, the GGK turned to coercion.

When a man did not comply with draft regulations, the state threatened family rations, which included rice, meat, fuel, sugar, and cloth; however, the colonial regime had no coherent policy for dealing with draft dodgers. Families faced the brunt of bureaucratic coercion when one of their own refused to submit to the summons. Yi Yong-gu dodged the draft by fleeing to his cousin's home in Manchuria. Once there, his cousin suggested that it would be better for the family if he, Yi, returned to Korea and enlisted.

By doing so, the cousin reasoned, he would spare his mother from police harassment.[92] Yi decided to enlist to spare his family from further government intimidation.

Harassment is also evident in the case of Kim T'ae-yong, a Korean conscript from South Hamgyŏng. Kim evaded enlistment for several months, but police and city officials visited his family every day, asking when he would enlist. Eventually the police took family members to the police office for interrogation. Kim finally enlisted to save his family from bureaucratic harassment. He was assigned to a unit in Manchuria ten days before Japan surrendered. The Soviet troops captured his unit and took him, along with approximately 7,700 other Korean soldiers and civilian employees of the military, to a Siberian labor camp where the men spent the next four years.[93]

Oral histories indicate that by 1945 state demands for soldiers increased as Japan's war fortunes declined. In response, government agents rounded up young men, in many cases without regard to legality. Chŏng Kŭm-jae of North Ch'ungch'ŏng, remembered, "During 1944 and 1945 I got four draft notices. Each time, I hid and they never enforced the notice. At least in my area, they just had to fill a quota. If some men didn't show up, they grabbed others."[94] This account highlights two themes: first, that Chŏng successfully ignored state demands, and second, that the GGK and Korean Army commandeered men. Im Hyŏn-su stated he and two others were seized by Koreans working for the Japanese. Im claimed that the GGK targeted tall, muscular men for on-the-spot recruitment, regardless of their age, but left small, scrawny men alone.[95] Japan never resorted to systematic kidnapping as the French did in West Africa, and there is no indication that the GGK resorted to wholesale abductions of large percentages of the men in a village for military service. Nevertheless, in the last months of the war, the colonial regime was less beholden to the legal strictures of mobilization because of the desperate war situation, but never fully abandoned the legalistic pretenses of mobilization. Even then, propaganda and indoctrination efforts continued as a palliative to the more visible coerciveness of state actions.

The exact number of Koreans who served in the Japanese army and navy is not known, so scholars are left to their best guesses. Part of the confusion is rooted in the calling up of Korean reservists and the commandeering of Korean civilians in the waning months of the war. The GGK seems to have abandoned bookkeeping in 1945, or the records for that year were destroyed following Japan's surrender. As a result, it is impossible to accurately determine the number of Koreans that served in the Japanese military. Furthermore, Japanese government statistics, compiled several years after the war, are contradictory. Some statistics combine military civilians with soldiers, while others list only those who were demobilized at the end of the war and do not account for deaths or soldiers released before the war ended.

According to Welfare Ministry (J: Kōseisho) documents released in 1953, a total of 209,279 Korean soldiers and military civilians were demobilized by the Japanese military: 186,980 in the army and 22,299 in the navy. Table 3.2 provides a provincial breakdown of Koreans demobilized from the army and navy as well as those killed while on active duty. The statistics in table 3.3 are widely acknowledged as representing the lowest number of Koreans that served in Japan's military. The number does not include reservists called into action, those released before the war ended, or soldiers unofficially demobilized on the spot when the war ended. *An Outline History of the Korean Army* (J: Chōsengun gaiyōshi), one of the most quoted sources for statistics on Korean military service, estimates there were 101,357 Koreans on active duty in the army, 9,366 in the army first reserve, and 20,000 in the navy, for a total of 130,723.[96] Table 3.3, taken from *An Outline History*, provides an annual breakdown of Koreans in the Japanese military, as well as the number on active duty and in the reserves. It includes volunteer and student volunteer soldiers from 1938 to 1943, but does not include the 2,000 naval volunteers from 1943 and 1944. Some scholars conclude that there were 186,980 soldiers in the army, and 22,299 sailors in the navy.[97] The highest estimate comes from Higuchi Yūichi, the foremost scholar on wartime Korea, who estimates that 213,719 Korean soldiers served in the Japanese military. In addition to regular conscription, Higuchi estimates that the Japanese army called up 58,000 Koreans from the reserves (29,000 each in 1944 and 1945) and mobilized another 22,000 as military laborers.[98]

The total military contribution of Koreans to Japan's war machine totaled between 286,000 and 367,000 soldiers, sailors, and military civilians. This said, Koreans had little impact on Japan's military capabilities. In the last two years of the war, Japan's army and navy swelled from 3.7 million in 1943 to 5.38 million in 1944 to 7.2 million at the time of Japan's surrendered in August 1945. Thus analysis of the mobilization of Koreans as

TABLE 3.2 Provincial Origins of Demobilized or Dead Korean Soldiers and Sailors

Home Province	Army Demobilized	Army Deaths	Navy Demobilized	Navy Deaths	Total
S. Kyŏngsan	6,291	603	2,634	42	9,570
N. Kyŏngsan	7,822	682	2,324	43	10,871
South Chŏlla	7,918	771	2,623	25	11,337
North Chŏlla	4,589	386	1,211	21	6,207
S. Ch'ungch'ŏng	5,998	352	1,363	20	7,733
N. Ch'ungch'ŏng	4,186	325	837	12	5,360
Kyŏnggi	10,374	612	1,568	18	12,572
Kangwŏn	6,221	292	1,459	36	8,008
Hwanghae	6,593	480	1,556	14	8,643
S. Pyŏngan	6,225	346	1,922	23	8,516
N. Pyŏngan	7,120	405	1,421	23	8,969
S. Hamgyŏng	8,982	291	1,415	21	10,709
N. Hamgyŏng	6,789	325	675	10	7,799
Total	89,108	5,870	21,008	308	116,294

Source: Kōseishō, "Chōsen zaiseki kyūrikukaigun," document 9-9; in Higuchi, *Senjika Chōsen*, 300–301.

TABLE 3.3 Number of Koreans in the Japanese Military

Year	Active Duty	First Reserve	Navy	Total
1938	300	100		400
1939	250	350		600
1940	900	2,100		3,000
1941	1,000	2,000		3,000
1942	2,250	2,250		4,500
1943	3,200	2,130		5,330
1943 (students)	3,457	436		3,883
Subtotal (volunteers)	11,357	9,366		20,723
1944	45,000		10,000	55,000
1945	45,000		10,000	55,000
Subtotal (draftees)	90,000		20,000	110,000
Total	101,357	9,366	20,000	130,723

Source: *Chōsengun gaiyōshi*, table 1. Student soldier statistics vary according to the source.

soldiers is more significant to the history of Korea and studies on colonialism than to the history of World War II.

KOREAN CONSCRIPTS IN THE MILITARY

On December 1, 1944, the first coterie of 45,000 Korean conscripts entered the Imperial Japanese Army, and 10,000 entered the Imperial Japanese Navy. Another 45,000 soldiers and 10,000 sailors entered on May 1, 1945.[99] As with regular Japanese conscripts, formal training for Koreans began the day they entered the barracks. Boot camp in the Japanese army consisted of the first three months in an assigned unit, even if that was at the battlefront. Korean soldiers went to the far reaches of the Japanese empire. Koreans were stationed in Southeast Asia, Japan proper, China, the Pacific islands, Okinawa, and Manchuria. As table 3.4 shows, the majority of Korean soldiers in the army (63 percent) remained in Korea or went to Japan proper, where they served as support troops. Troops that remained in Korea replaced two divisions of the Korean Army that were sent to New Guinea (in January 1943) and the Philippines (in December 1944).[100] Only a small percent were deployed to Southeast Asia, because by 1944 Japan was on the defensive and most of Japan's transport ships had been lost.

The duties of most Koreans varied from the mundane to the dangerous, but much depended on the unit commanders. Table 3.5 shows that the largest number of Koreans served as ordinary foot soldiers and artillerymen. These positions generally required no special skills or training. In some battalions, Koreans were given wooden guns to train with, while Japanese conscripts got real ones. One battlefield drill that some Koreans unfortunately had to participate in was the use of Chinese captives for bayonet practice. Sin Sang-ch'o was ordered to kill a Chinese prisoner of war (POW) because his student records (which his commanding officer possessed) indicated that he harbored seditious thoughts. However, Sin could not bring himself to kill the POW and subsequently faced increased scrutiny from his commanding officer.[101] Japanese recruits also participated in these horrid experiences.

TABLE 3.4 Korean Soldiers Demobilized, by Location

Location	Number
Japan Proper	16,379
Korea	43,888
Kurile and Sakhalin	395
Manchukuo	8,808
China	15,941
Taiwan	1,420
Philippines	3,107
Other SE Asian Islands	2,877
Burma	1,822
Other Pacific Islands	341
Total	**94,978**

Source: Kōseishō, "Chōsen zaiseki kyūrikugun gun'in," document 9-8; in Higuchi, *Senjika Chōsen*, 298–99.

TABLE 3.5 Korean Soldiers' Assignments, 1944–1945

Classification	1944	1945
Infantrymen	29,388	29,780
Heavy Artillery	0	260
Medium Artillery	610	645
Field Artillery	1,890	2,030
Anti-Aircraft	4,190	4,000
Combat Artillery	295	280
Mountain Artillery	1,430	1,500
Air Troops	2,050	1,100
Engineers	1,477	1,480
Radio Operators	0	120
Railway Troops	195	200
Shipping (senpakuhei)	600	700
Air Technicians	250	250
Tank Crews	2,030	2,060
Technicians	120	120
Cavalry Transport	475	475
Total	**45,000**	**45,000**

Source: *Chōsengun gaiyōshi*, tables 9 and 10.

Oral histories state that many Koreans served in noncombatant roles, particularly as laborers, indicating a lingering distrust of Koreans despite claims of brotherhood. On the other hand, in some units Koreans held positions requiring special skills, such as technicians and engineers. A handful became pilots, translators, tank drivers, and musicians—some positions required special schooling in Japan. At the pinnacle of respectability and veneration were Korean airmen, especially those who died as part of the Special Attack Corps (Tokkōtai). The first Korean kamikaze pilot died at the Battle of Leyte Gulf in October 1944. Newspapers, journals, and radio programs recounted beatitudes in his honor for months, making him the new Yi In-sŏk.[102]

A unique feature of Japan's mobilization of its colonial manpower was that Koreans were integrated into regular Japanese units; there was no all-Korean battalion, unit, or company. The French and British colonial empires maintained segregated battalions for colonial subjects, excepting the European commanding officers. Even blacks and Asians in the American military remained segregated until 1948. The Japanese army highlighted integration as a sign of racial equality. Yet, internally, the army had an informal policy that set limits on the percentage of Koreans per battalion: on the front lines Koreans comprised a maximum of 20 percent; in reinforcement units, 40 percent; and on the home front, 80 percent.[103] Most troops on the home front served in unarmed labor corps. The army claimed that this practice helped accustom Koreans to military life. Another possible explanation, suggested by prewar documents, is that military authorities lacked faith in the Korean soldiers' loyalties and capabilities. Specifically, officials feared that Koreans would either leak militarily sensitive information to China and the Soviet Union, or defect and join the war against Japan.[104] Integrated units provided the Japanese with the best surveillance of Korean soldiers.

By most accounts, Korean soldiers performed better than expected; infantry reports lauded them for heroism, bravery, being mentally tough, and adherence to duty.[105] The personal experiences of Koreans (as well as Japanese soldiers) in the military varied widely and depended on the temperament of their battalion commanders. Some Koreans felt like equals in the military because they received equal pay, rations, and fair treatment, in other units this was clearly not the case. Kim Hyo-byŏng, of South Chŏlla, stated that he was treated well by his commanding officer, who assigned Kim to be the unit's trumpeter. The officer even took Kim along with him on family vacations.[106] Others remember that, as long as they obeyed the rules, Japanese soldiers treated them as equals.[107]

In units at the battlefront, survival was the top priority, so there were Japanese soldiers who did not distinguish between Korean and Japanese. Korean soldiers in Southeast Asia suffered from exhaustion, starvation, and physical maladies alongside their Japanese comrades. This resulted in an esprit de corps between Japanese and Korean soldiers that Japanese authorities hoped would hasten the assimilation of Koreans. In some cases Japanese soldiers asked their Korean comrades to rescue their bodies if they died in battle.[108] Sŏn T'aesu, a naval volunteer soldier, worked at as an airplane mechanic at an airfield for kamikaze pilots. He stated that, other than never receiving pay, his Japanese associates treated him well. In fact, the pilots, knowing that they were about to die, gave him chocolates, cigarettes, and other items they no longer needed.[109]

Most units held Korean soldiers to the same code of conduct as Japanese recruits, making no allowance for ethnicity. This was a two-edged sword: If Koreans strictly adhered to the rules, they did not face discrimination; but if a Korean was unable to conform to the rules, regardless of the reason, he might be maltreated. Many Korean soldiers with advanced Japanese language skills encountered equality in the military because they hid their Korean ethnicity. They could do this because they had Japanese names, served in Japanese units, spoke fluent Japanese, and did not openly announce their ethnicity.

There were few advantages for Korean soldiers to reveal their ethnicity, so they lived by a "don't ask, don't tell" policy. This worked to Japan's advantage, because all soldiers were expected to conform to the strict martial culture. It also prevented conspiracies among Korean soldiers who might otherwise seek to escape en masse. Koreans could never be sure how many other Koreans were in their units because many of those with advanced Japanese language skills "passed" as Japanese. This differs from European colonial experiences in Africa, in which white soldiers were always given better rations and housing even though both black soldiers and white soldiers fought and died together. Even Filipino troops who fought alongside the Americans at Bataan received smaller rations than the Caucasians.

Of course, Koreans with poor language skills could not hide their ethnicity and were at the mercy of their battalion leaders. Life in the military was volatile and brutal for all recruits, regardless of ethnicity. In the last desperate days of the war, several battalion commanders in Southeast Asia and Manchuria used their troops as human suicide bombs to slow the Allied advance. Korean and Japanese men were fitted with makeshift suicide bombs made of TNT and were sent in waves against advancing American or Soviet troops. On Sumatra, nearly 250 Korean soldiers and military civilians were put into suicide squads and ordered to sacrifice themselves.[110]

Physical and emotional abuse were common fare for Japanese and Korean soldiers. But some officers targeted Koreans for extra abuse. In one unit stationed on Truk, a commanding officer mistreated Koreans who lacked Japanese language proficiency by assigning them the dirtiest and most dangerous labor duties. Pak Yun-sŏ and Kang Kong-sam, both educated Koreans, confronted the unit's officers about the ill treatment. The two men reasoned that Koreans were supporting Japan and therefore deserved to be respected and to be treated equally. The unit leader slapped Kang and said, "You are Chōsenjin [Korean], and that is why we call you 'Chōsenjin.' Why are you rebelling?" In response, Kang punched the unit leader in the face, which led to a group brawl between Koreans and Japanese. The naval police were called in and they arrested the leaders of the melee and interrogated them. The police ordered that the Koreans be treated more fairly. However, the commanding officer did not change his behavior, so Kang again attacked the commander, which led to another brawl. The naval police again arrested the ring leaders, but this time ordered that Kang and Pak be beaten for agitating the fight. The naval police reminded the Koreans that if they felt mistreated, they should a file a grievance through official channels instead of fighting.[111]

The majority of Korean soldiers suffered discrimination despite the GGK's and the army's claims of brotherhood. Discrimination often took the form of special restrictions on movement or access to information, and in some cases Koreans were kept under surveillance. Many battalions forbade Korean conscripts from having contact with nonmilitary personnel, while other units did not allow Koreans to leave the military camp on their days off. In other instances, army officials excluded high-ranking Koreans from meetings where sensitive information was discussed. Cho Su-hwan, of South Chŏlla, learned of Japan's surrender from a Japanese soldier under his command who attended a battalion meeting that Cho had been forbidden to attend.[112]

Soldiering was especially hard for Koreans who were not culturally or physically accustomed to a harsh, regimented lifestyle. Trainers and higher-ranking soldiers were notorious for their cruel treatment of all new recruits.[113] All soldiers, Japanese and Korean, suffered physical and emotional abuse that ranged from trivial to life-threatening, but most Koreans suffered extra tribulations because of their ethnicity. Yi Sang-hyŏp experienced mistreatment on a train while en route to his deployment in Manchuria; all Koreans in his unit were put in the cargo cars. When he complained to his superior that he was getting sores from sitting on hard crates, he was moved to a passenger car where Japanese recruits had comfortable chairs.[114] Other former soldiers remembered that the military left wounded Koreans for dead but rescued wounded Japanese.

Korean historians criticize the Japanese armed forces for discriminating against Koreans during the promotion process. At the end of the war, all but a handful of Koreans were privates, and very few were in the officer corps, especially when the percentages are compared to Japanese troops. However, this is partially, but not wholly, explained by the short time Koreans were in the military. Quite simply, Koreans had not been in the service long enough to advance in rank. Koreans in the service for several years, namely volunteer soldiers and military academy graduates, received promotions, although not necessarily at the same rate as their Japanese counterparts. In the Imperial Japanese Army, there were three Korean generals, two colonels, and 225 officers.[115] There are no verifiable numbers for in-the-field promotions. Unlike in other colonial situations, where colonial subjects were always subservient to troops from the metropole, Koreans had direct command over Japanese troops.

Hong Sa-ik was the highest-ranking Korean in the Japanese military at the end of the war. He graduated from the Japanese military academy in 1923 and quickly rose through the army ranks. In April 1934 Major Hong received a special command in Manchuria working at the Kantō Army headquarters in Xinjing (currently Changch'un). In 1944, at the rank of lieutenant general, he was transferred to the Philippines to oversee Allied POWs. He was stationed there when the war ended. Hong may have been transferred to avoid an anti-Japanese conspiracy between him and the 8,800 Korean troops in Manchuria. After the war, the United States held Hong accountable for the abuse of Allied POWs and executed him as a war criminal. Koreans familiar with Hong's case feel that the Japanese were scapegoated at the end of the war for prisoner abuse.[116]

Two Korean princes, sons of the deceased Korean King Kojong, were also high-ranking officers in the Japanese military. Prince Yi Kŏn, the head of the Korean royal family, was a colonel and received numerous decorations, such as the Grand Order of the Auspicious Stars, the Order of the Rising Sun, and the Red Cross Order of Merit. His half-brother, Prince Yi U, achieved the rank of lieutenant colonel and was the head of the Osaka Corps while concurrently serving as the head of an officers' school and infantry unit.[117] He died during the atomic bomb attack on Hiroshima at the age of thirty-four. Neither prince had a direct combat role.

KOREAN NONCOMPLIANCE

The causes of Korean resistance were similar to those of draft dodgers, namely, a resentment of coercive recruitment methods and a lack of loyalty to the Japanese nation. There were also problems that arose during the Koreans' time in the armed forces that contributed to resistance, chiefly, ethnic discrimination, a desire for self-preservation, and complaints about the miserable conditions of service and poor rations. Many of these can be attributed to an individual sense of injustice rather than to Korean nationalism.

Resistance within the military was generally nonconfrontational, with desertion being the most common form. Most Korean troops were stationed in northern Korea, Manchuria, and northern China, where they could flee to the homes of relatives or join guerilla forces to fight against Japan. Desertion was a dangerous undertaking because military law stipulated that those caught should be severely punished. Koreans stationed in the Pacific and in Japan proper rarely deserted because they had no place to run. Unfortunately, there are no verifiable statistics on Korean desertion.

Desertion was undertaken largely by small groups or by individuals. Koreans who were AWOL had a limited number of options available to them. The Japanese police searched the homes of family and friends first, so deserters usually did not return home. Besides, the food rationing system made it difficult and burdensome for families to feed an extra adult not listed on the registers. A common destination of deserters was territory controlled by the Chinese Nationalists or Chinese Communists. By late 1944, 175 Korean soldiers from the Japanese army had joined the Kwangbok Army, a Korean unit under the Chinese Nationalists, and roughly thirty Koreans joined the Fourth Red Army of the Chinese Communist Party.[118] However, the Kwangbok Army lacked the financial and material backing of the Chinese regime and was never allowed to attack Japanese units.

The largest and best-coordinated act of resistance within the military was an attempted en masse desertion by a group of Korean soldiers attached to the P'yŏngyang Division. This event, called the P'yŏngyang Incident, or the January 20 Incident, was organized by student volunteer soldiers. Kim Wan-yong, from Chūō Law School, and Pak Sŏng-hwa, an engineering student at Waseda University, began planning a large group desertion in October 1944 to help dozens of Koreans desert the army on January 20, 1945, and join the Korean independence movement in China.[119] Kim and Pak planned the desertion because Koreans in the military suffered discrimination during the promotion process; they learned that only 11 percent of Koreans who applied for officer training were accepted, but the rate for Japanese was 86 percent. Kim organized a secret society to recruit Koreans who wanted to go AWOL. The group's platform was that they would gather their strength and defect, fight for Korean independence, and directly and indirectly contribute to Japan's failure. They planned to defect to China once they had enough supplies. Kim and Pak reportedly recruited seventy Korean soldiers through word of mouth.

However, the group was betrayed by a fellow Korean, Im Yŏng-ho, whom they tried to recruit because his contacts with the police would have provided them with vital information to assist their defection. However, Im warned the police of the plan. Fortunately for the group, Im was not privy to the membership list, but the damage was done. The plan unraveled further when the police arrested Kim after he got into an altercation with a Japanese recruit. A police investigation led to the arrest of twenty-four of the group's members, who were sentenced to prison terms ranging from six to thirteen years. This incident was unsettling for the Japanese army because it showed that Koreans soldiers participated in subversive activities.

A comparable failed mass desertion took place in the 24th Taegu unit of the Japanese army. Student volunteer soldiers entered the Taegu unit in January 1944; however, they resented their recruitment and were concerned over the declining fortunes of the Japanese. In Spring 1944 Kwŏn Hyŏk-jo and Mun Han-u began to plot a group desertion of Koreans to take place in June. The first phase of their plan was to spread anti-Japanese propaganda among the Korean population to weaken public support for Japan; the second phase was to attack an armory, steal the weapons, and shoot hundreds of Japanese; the third phase was to poison the Japanese food supply to cause panic among the Japanese.[120]

The group, which had twenty members, set June 8, 1944, as the day for the attack. Their plans were thwarted when police learned of the plot, but Mun and Kwŏn decided to poison the food supply alone. Mun attempted to purchase poison but was unable to, so they called off the venture. Having failed at their first plan, the two students plotted a mass desertion as a statement against Japanese colonialism. On August 7, six of the six hundred Koreans in the Taegu unit escaped. A massive manhunt ensued, and all six were captured.[121]

Another choice available to Korean soldiers was surrender to Allied forces (see figure 3.2). The Japanese military indoctrinated all servicemen to believe that American troops killed prisoners of war. While this deterred some Koreans, thousands still surrendered. As POWs, Koreans sought the downfall of Japan. In March 1945 the 2,600 Korean POWs imprisoned in Hawaii donated almost three thousand dollars toward the purchase of US war bonds. An American army spokesman stated that the Koreans had requested to fight directly against the Japanese, but the Geneva Convention forbade this type of use of prisoners.[122]

The Japanese army and bureaucracy realized that the poor treatment of Koreans, as well as the language barrier, contributed to evasion and desertion. Army Vice-Minister Shibayama Kenshirō opined that the lack of Japanese language proficiency among Koreans led to miscommunication and frustration, resulting in the mistreatment and desertion of colonial troops. In January 1945 Shibayama stated in an internal army memo that in at least one situation "dozens of people became a group and tried to do something dangerous" owing to mistreatment. He recommended that battalion commanders handle Koreans in a more humane way and that Korean veterans

FIG 3.2 Korean laborers captured as prisoners of war in July 1944. These laborers had been constructing an airfield when they were captured on Numfoor during the Battle of Biak, which was part of the New Guinea campaign.

be used as mentors for incoming Korean recruits.[123] The GGK also recognized the problem and printed a handbook for officer training; it advocated that officers treat Koreans as equals of Japanese soldiers.[124] Some units, but not all, adopted the humane treatment for Koreans recommended by General Shibayama. For example, Yi Yong-gu attempted to desert his unit but was caught. When his unit commander asked why he went AWOL, Yi cited discrimination against Koreans. Generally, desertion was a capital offense, but in this instance Yi was returned to duty without punishment as a gesture of goodwill to boost the morale of Koreans.[125] Shibayama's suggestions and other efforts to improve the treatment of Koreans were either ignored or were too little and too late to have an effect on the treatment of Korean conscripts.

When the war ended on August 15, 1945, Koreans were spread through-out the Japanese empire. These Koreans had sweated, bled, and died for the Japanese nation and emperor, not for Korea. The spirits of Koreans who died in the service of Japan are enshrined at Yasukuni Shrine in Japan. The number of Koreans who died in the service of Japan's military is a hotly debated issue. Official Japanese documents claim that 22,182 Koreans died serving in the Japanese military: 5,870 in the army, 308 in the navy, and 16,004 serving as military contractors.[126] The number of deaths among Korean contractors were higher than that of active duty soldiers because they got caught in the crossfire of the American invasions of Pacific Islands (notably Tarawa and Okinawa).[127] Some statistics do not distinguish between soldiers and civilian employees of the military. As table 3.6 shows, those deployed to Southeast Asian regions, particularly the Philippines, suffered the highest number of casualties. Most scholars estimate that the number of deaths was higher. As shown in table 3.7, Higuchi Yūichi estimates that 50,884 of the 363,465 Koreans (14 percent) who served as soldiers and military civilians died or went missing in action.[128]

TABLE 3.6 Location of Korean Soldier Deaths

Location	Army Deaths
Japan Proper	55
Korea	108
Kurile and Sakhalin	23
Manchukuo	57
China	654
Taiwan	266
Philippines	2,156
Other SE Asian Islands	1,863
Burma	498
Pacific Islands	190
Total	5,870

Source: Kōseishō, Engokyoku, "Chōsen zaiseki kyūrikugun," document 9-8; in Higuchi, *Senjika Chōsen*. There were 308 naval deaths. See document 9-9 in same book.

TABLE 3.7 Survey of Korean Deaths according to Recruitment Method

Recruitment Method	Number	Deaths
Army Volunteers	17,664	2,473
Navy Volunteers	3,000	420
Student Volunteers	4,385	614
1st Coterie of Army Draftees	90,000	12,600
1st Coterie of Navy Draftees	20,000	2,800
2nd Coterie of Army Draftees	74,230	10,392
Army Civilian Contractors	74,838	10,477
Navy Civilian Contractors	79,348	11,108
Total	363,465	50,884

Source: Higuchi, *Senjika Chōsen*, 128. Deaths include those missing in action.

Japan lost control over Korean soldiers when Japan unconditionally surrendered to the Allies. The Soviets, Americans, and Chinese became responsible for the well-being of the Koreans. The repatriation of Koreans depended on their location when Japan surrendered. Some fought in the Chinese Civil War (1945–1949); others joined Indonesia's fight for independence. Many had to wait months before returning to their hometowns. Furthermore, the Soviet Union took 7,700 Koreans and 600,000 Japanese into Siberia and forced them to work for several years in dehumanizing and slavelike conditions to build the Soviet Union's infrastructure. Thus the tragedy of wartime mobilization was aggravated by international postwar politics.

CONCLUSION

The Tokyo and the colonial governments' decision to implement the Korean conscription system was not as automatic and simplistic as most studies imply. While it is true that the draft was implemented out of wartime necessity, government and military authorities had serious concerns over the Koreans' loyalty, ability, education, and potential to rebel. Koreans were ill prepared to enter the military, largely because of the colonial regime's prewar policies. Colonial administrators attempted to remedy these shortcomings as quickly as possible. The GGK and the army also carefully established a legal foundation for the Korean conscription system. As part of this effort,

Korean enlistment into the military was delayed thirty months to revise laws, intensify indoctrination efforts, update family registries, and prepare men for military service in training camps.

The recruitment of Koreans for military service followed a three-stage approach to secure compliance: propaganda and enticement to gain the cooperation of the targeted recruit; minor bureaucratic pressure on unwilling recruits and their families; and, finally, threats and police coercion, if necessary. Japan never abandoned its propaganda or indoctrination efforts to secure the compliance of the Korean people. Up to the end of the war, the GGK maintained the fiction that the draft was bestowed out of brotherly kindness and used Korean elites as talking heads to spread propaganda.

The Korean conscription system differed from the standard system used for Japanese citizens. These differences offer insight into Japanese concerns over Korean loyalty and combat worthiness. The scope of the draft was much narrower for Koreans than for Japanese. In both 1944 and 1945 the army enlisted only 45,000 Korean men out of roughly 220,000 possible recruits. Later, commandeering and call-ups increased the number of Koreans in the military. Had Japan desired to recruit 100,000 each year, it well could have. As a general rule, Japan remained within the legal framework it established for itself until desperation set in during the last months of the war. The 1944 cohort of Koreans was drafted according to existing laws, while the 1945 draft relied more on coercion and extralegal recruitment practices. Japan's growing desperation for manpower in 1945 obviated many of the niceties and legalities related to recruitment.

The Tokyo and colonial governments lacked faith in the Korean populace and did not want to empower large numbers of Koreans with military skills. Instead, the government preferred to mobilize Koreans as laborers. Koreans were not merely pawns or puppets in the mobilization process. An indeterminable number of draftees cooperated with the draft process and honorably served in the Japanese army or navy, and some were promoted to ranks above the Japanese in their units. Of course, there were men who chose not to cooperate and who exploited the colonial state's vulnerability to their advantage. Koreans evaded the draft, deserted the military, fled to distant lands, altered family registries, and disappeared from public life without serious recourse from the state. Herein we find a host of vulnerabilities within the colonial regime and see that many of its weaknesses were of the regime's own making. The GGK had not pushed for the use of the Japanese language until the late-1930s, had not strictly enforced the family registry laws, and had not provided an adequate education to the Korean people. These shortcomings shackled Korea's wartime potential and must be closely examined to provide a deeper understanding of the limited power of the GGK.

4 | MOBILIZATION OF COLONIAL LABOR

The Korean people's most significant contribution to Japan's war effort was their labor in Korea, Japan proper, Southeast Asia, and the Pacific. Korean wartime labor is best understood as an intensification of existing labor trends that began after the colonization of Korea. After 1931, when Japan became deeply embroiled in Manchuria, Japanese industries expanded rapidly throughout northern Korea, resulting in tens of thousands of workers moving into those industrial centers. After the outbreak of war with China in 1937, northern Korea underwent intensive industrialization and urbanization. Japanese industries on the Japanese islands also needed Korean labor to maintain production levels because the Japanese workforce confronted labor shortages as early as 1939; the labor situation worsened after Japan's attack on Pearl Harbor in December 1941 because hundreds of thousands of Japanese men joined the military. Additionally, between 1937 and 1945, the Government-General of Korea (GGK) mobilized an estimated 4.1 to 7.0 million Koreans as laborers in Korea, and more than one million in Japan and the South Pacific.

The nationalist historical paradigm emphasizes the victimization of the comfort women and the Korean laborers in the coal mines located on Hokkaidō. Japanese and Korean scholars compare the recruitment and use of Korean labor in Japan to that of the Atlantic slave trade.[1] While the plight of these individuals is undeniable, their story is not a complete account of Korea's wartime mobilization; any balanced account must include an overview of labor in Korea. The Korean wartime experience cannot simply be reduced to exploitation and victimization—rather, as with those who entered the military, Koreans were active agents throughout the mobilization process. As an analytical tool, calling Japan's use of Korean manpower a form of slavery fails on at least three counts: First, it does not account for the choices that Koreans had, whether it be to sign a contract or to change their employment (before or after the expiration of a contract); second, many Koreans received pay according to their contract; and third, the experiences of Koreans who worked in Korea are not adequately addressed. Scholars who compare Korean wartime experiences to slavery generally limit their analysis to Korean coal miners in Japan, where conditions were worst. There is no question that slavelike conditions existed in some industries; indeed, many unfortunate Koreans (and Japanese) were subjected to severe exploitation and physical and mental abuse, and had no choice but to work without pay, all while living in squalid conditions—but their story is part, not the whole, of Korea's wartime experience.

LEGAL FOUNDATIONS FOR LABOR MOBILIZATION

In the months following the outbreak of war with China in July 1937, Prime Minister Konoe Fumimaro's cabinet strengthened government control over the Japanese economy. In April 1938 the cabinet instituted the National General Mobilization Law (NGML) in Japan and extended it to Korea the following month. This law established government control over all aspects of Japan's economy, including labor, and formed the legal basis for the mobilization of Korea. However, the GGK implemented the NGML in Korea in a bastardized and piecemeal fashion because of the differences between Japan's and Korea's economies.[2]

The NGML established government power over the workforce. However, the central government enforced the law differently in Korea than in Japan in four ways. First, there was less worker training in Korea, despite the colonial government's rhetoric otherwise; second, in Japan the law targeted the urban population, but in Korea it targeted rural folk, so that by the end of the war, roughly 80 percent of the industrial workforce in Korea originated from the countryside; third, labor conscription in Korea was utilized much more broadly than in Japan; and fourth, Japanese women were subject to the NGML but Korean women were not. Korean women generally lacked the educational and technical training to be of use to industries affected by the NGML.[3] Thus, Korean women filled vacancies in agriculture and nonessential factories, such as textiles and food processing, from which men were requisitioned.

The most significant difference in how the NGML was enacted in Japan and in Korea was that labor recruitment in Korea took three forms: company-directed recruitment (K: *mojip;* J: *boshū*), government-directed recruitment (K: *kwan alsŏn;* J: *kan assen*), and labor conscription (K: *chingyong;* J: *chōyō*).[4] The first two methods were not used in Japan, thereby exhibiting the government's adaptation to Korea's particular economic and social conditions. Japan's actions were, until the last years of the war, careful and restrained because the Korean populace was not spiritually, patriotically, or educationally prepared to contribute to Japan's war effort. The GGK extended the more coercive conscription to Korea in 1942, three years after it was implemented in Japan. Furthermore, the GGK and Japanese industries incentivized labor mobilization, thereby reducing the need for conscription.

Company-directed recruitment (CDR), the first phase of labor recruitment in Korea under the NGML, delegated to individual companies the recruitment of Korean workers, but with government oversight. This was a continuation of existing business recruitment practices, but took on a more official character to meet business demands. The colonial administration allocated to private companies quotas that allowed them to recruit workers, directly or through recruiting agents, in government-designated areas. Direct hiring meant that companies located laborers in government-designated areas through newspaper advertisements, signboards, handbills, as well as through word of mouth and family connections with current employees; the prospective worker signed a contract with the companies without a middleman. Policemen and labor offices helped peasants find employment and assisted company recruiters looking for employees. However, local officials in Korea frequently demanded bribes for their assistance to recruiters.[5]

When direct hiring failed to secure sufficient numbers of workers, companies employed recruiting agents, many of whom were Korean. Companies often paid commissions to agents to gather laborers. For example, agents for the Hokkaido Coal and Steamer Company who recruited more than five workers in one trip received a cash bonus and travel vouchers from the company.[6] Recruiting agents were responsible for securing a signed contract between the laborer and the company. In certain cases, agents accompanied the workers from the village to the company.

The colonial bureaucracy was deeply involved in CDR even though it was technically a private affair. Since the GGK limited recruitment to government-designated areas, company agents rarely knew the local population and had to rely on provincial and village authorities, such as the police, patriotic unit heads, city clerks (who oversaw the family registries), and village headmen, to locate able-bodied men. Policemen frequently assisted in recruiting available laborers by pressuring young men and their families with impromptu visits to persuade men to sign contracts. Once signed, employment agencies and city clerks handled the necessary paperwork.[7] In fact, a number of recruiters bribed local officials (with money, women, and alcohol) to gather laborers for them. All too often, agents relied on deception and government assistance to secure the cooperation of Koreans. Recruiters might promise higher wages than would be paid, agree to shorter contracts than were realistic, lie about the nature of the work, assure workers that the work environment was safe (knowing that the work was dangerous), or promise educational opportunities outside of work that did not exist.[8] In doing so, recruiters focused on fulfilling quantitative recruitment goals, not on honest business practices. In the end, the worker was disgruntled and the business did not hire qualified workers.

The direct hiring of Koreans by companies makes it difficult to determine the total number of Koreans mobilized under CDR, because each business recruited and transported its own workers. Nevertheless, CDR proved insufficient to recruit the desired numbers of workers for industries and mines in Korea and Japan because private companies lacked the force of law to compel Koreans to sign a contract and leave their hometown. Furthermore, CDR became too expensive for private companies to recruit the needed numbers of laborers from the sparsely populated Korean countryside. To sustain the industrial workforce, the government took a more active role through government-directed recruitment (GDR) to assist companies in Korea and Japan in drawing labor from the rural regions.

Government-directed recruitment, as the title implies, entailed greater bureaucratic involvement in labor recruitment. Companies and cartels requested labor from the GGK, which in turn assigned a recruitment quota to employment agencies. Central to GDR was worker registration

(J: *tōroku*), which began in Korea in June 1939. Recent graduates and laborers with specific technical skills were required to register with the government.[9] Officials used this information to locate labor for strategic industries. The government initially required only skilled laborers between the ages of eighteen and forty, such as engineers, experienced industrial labor, and train conductors, to register. Later, registration was extended to unskilled laborers, unemployed men, and merchants; eventually it included day laborers between the ages of sixteen and forty-five.

The twin engines of GDR were employment agencies and the Korean Labor Assistance Association (J: Chōsen Rōmu Kyōkai). Employment offices played a vital role in the centralization of the government's supervision of labor. The colonial regime nationalized six labor recruiting offices (in Seoul, Taegu, Pusan, P'yŏngyang, Shinŭiju, and Hamhŭng) in January 1940 to assist in the recruitment of laborers. They collected registration information on recent graduates and the unemployed and shared this information with strategic industries. The government then recruited and shipped laborers to the designated workplaces. The number of people mobilized through these offices (for CDR, GDR, and conscription) rose from 12,000 workers in 1937 to 50,289 by 1942.[10] Most laborers recruited under GDR hailed from rural agricultural regions in the southern parts of the peninsula where the GGK thought there was a surplus of labor. A statement by a labor recruiter for the Joban Coal Mine in Mito, Japan, offers insight into the process,

> Korean labor is only in the south since the north is an industrial zone where there is no surplus labor. And so, in each province in southern Korea we go to the provincial office and tell them that Joban Coal Mine needs this number of laborers and say "send them." And since the provincial office knows which county has the most available men, we can go to that county. County authorities order each village to send a certain number of people. Workers are not asked to come to the office, but authorities retrieved them for us. The village head takes responsibility to hunt down that number by a certain date. There is no concern whether he was the oldest son or not.[11]

The above quote reinforces the point that the Japanese attempted to create and to abide by a system of laws, whether the Koreans knew it or not. Labor

recruiters had to go through government offices if they wanted the cooperation of the police and the village head man. Of course, the GGK wrote
and altered laws to force men into certain jobs; conversely, the GGK could
have done all this without the niceties of revising laws. Thus, it is important to understand how and why the colonial administration made efforts
to legitimize its actions. In many instances, illiterate farmers did not have
an opportunity to review the legal documents, all written in Japanese, as
they were being requisitioned. Nor did many laborers have time to inform
their families of their recruitment—creating the perception that they were
kidnapped.

Government-directed recruitment was more effective at gathering labor
than CDR because government recruiters had the force of law to levy labor.
Provincial and village authorities, under the direction of the GGK, assumed
greater responsibility for locating (through family registries) and recruiting the best-qualified men as laborers. Policemen and neighborhood heads
visited the selected man's residence and pressured him to sign a contract.
These colonial officials bolstered a recruitment network that served the
labor needs of industries in Japan and Korea. The GGK also used other legal
mechanisms to channel labor into strategic industries.

Table 4.1 shows that from 1939 to 1945, between 44,263 and 76,617 workers were recruited per year through GDR, totaling 402,053. This recruitment
caused regional labor shortages in Korea early in the war. In fact, the Agriculture and Forestry Bureau within the GGK opposed shifting rural farm
labor to urban factories because they worried that rice production might
decline.[12] The cabinet ignored this warning and continued heavy recruitment in the countryside, thereby requiring women to assume responsibility
for agricultural production.[13] Toward the end of the war, adult labor was in
such short supply that the colonial regime mobilized students as laborers.

The majority of laborers recruited through GDR worked in construction
on public works, in shipyards, and on defensive fortifications (83 percent).
A large number were also destined for mines in Japan and Korea (10.7
percent). People important to the military (J: gunyōin) served the military
in various capacities, including as laborers in army-owned industries.
Relatively few worked in factories (5.5 percent). The bureaucratic-led GDR
was more effective than the private-led CDR, yet this system fell short
of industry needs because it was only a method of recruitment; it lacked

the legal mechanisms to keep laborers at their positions. The government needed conscription to force laborers to remain in the positions for which they were recruited.

TABLE 4.1 Koreans Mobilized through Government-Directed Recruitment

Year	Gunyōin*	Mining	Transport	Construction	Factories	Total
1939		2,735	647	41,907		45,289
1940		2,714	901	57,912		61,527
1941	1,085	1,494	646	43,662		46,887
1942	1,723	4,943	278	42,086		49,030
1943	1,328	11,944	186	40,150	5,316	58,924
1944	4,020	14,989		54,394	3,214	76,617
1945	4,312	2,071	252	37,628		44,263
Total	**12,468**	**40,890**	**2,910**	**317,739**	**8,530**	**382,537**

Source: Unno Fukuju, "Chōsen shokuminchi ni okeru nōgyō seisaku no tenkai: Toku ni rōdōryoku seisaku to no kairen ni tsuite (The development of the agricultural policy in colonial Korea: Centering on its relation to the labor policy)," *Meiji Daigakuin bunkagaku kenkyūjo kiyō* 32 (December 1992): 271.

*Gunyōin people of importance to the military.

Japan's demands on Korean labor from 1937 to 1941 were relatively modest, largely because the conflict in China had not escalated into total war. Japanese officials remained confident that the Japanese military could win the war without placing heavy demands on its colonies. Labor conscription (K: *chingyong*; J: *chōyō*) began in Japan in 1939, but was not extended to Korea until after Japan entered into war with the United States. In 1942 the cabinet extended the Labor Conscription Law to Korea. As the war worsened, many bureaucrats felt that the Korean people, especially rural farmers, were not fully contributing to the war effort, so conscription became a way to tap into rural labor resources, real and perceived, and force Koreans to participate.[14] Conscription did not supersede CDR and GDR but rather supplemented them. Conscription gave the government full control over all aspects of labor, including the power to bind workers to their jobs. Conscripted laborers were national employees and could not quit or change jobs without government permission.

The procedure for labor conscription was similar to that of GDR. The government gave conscripted laborers one- to two-year contracts that could be voided only with government permission. As the war intensified, the government unilaterally extended these contracts to ensure that industries had sufficient numbers of workers. The law originally applied to men from the ages of twenty to thirty-five, but was later extended to include men from thirteen to fifty years old. There were two types of labor conscription: One requisitioned workers for a job, and the other forbid laborers from leaving a position (J: *genji chōyō*). With the former, the GGK assigned provinces a quota for a specific number of workers. Provincial leaders often handled labor conscription through county offices and police stations; with the latter, workers remained at their current positions but lost the ability to change jobs without government approval. Provincial governors sent a white conscription card (J: *shuttō meireisho*) to the worker who was drafted.[15] Labor conscription in Korea centered around conscripting a factory or mine and freezing all workers in that factory to their positions. In February 1943 the GGK conscripted seventy-three factories and fifty-six mines in Korea.[16] Women were not subject to conscription, but a small number with specialized skills were frozen to their positions.[17]

Conscription was not widely employed in Korea until 1944, and even then it was largely limited to freezing workers to their positions. Table 4.2 shows that by the end of the war, 260,145 Korean laborers had been frozen to their occupations in Korea, as were another 265,896 requisitioned laborers. By the end of the war the Japanese government had conscripted 526,041 Korean laborers, most of whom were requisitioned for work in Japan. Only 135 were conscripted for the South Pacific, and none for China, Manchuria, or Taiwan. Positions at those locations were filled through CDR and GDR.

Unofficially, conscription notices for Korean unskilled laborers were passed from one individual to another, which was not possible among Japanese workers. Filial sons, if old enough, volunteered to go in their father's place when the father received a conscription notice. Kim Sang-ŏp, of North Chŏlla, volunteered to go in his father's stead when his fifty-four-year-old father was selected (by village lottery) for labor conscription. Immigration authorities in Japan discovered that Sang-ŏp, at sixteen, was too young for conscription and wanted to send him back to Korea, but Kim successfully argued that since he was already in Japan he should be allowed to work.[18] This and many other anecdotes reveal that age limits were ignored. Kim's father was legally too old for conscription, and the son was too young. Government authorities ignored legal strictures simply to acquire manpower.

TABLE 4.2 Labor Conscription of Koreans by Year and Location

Year	Korea	Japan	Pacific Islands	Total
1941		4,895		4,895
1942	90	3,871	135	4,096
1943	648	2,341		2,989
1944	19,655	201,189		220,845
	(153,850)			(153,850)
1945	23,286	9,786		33,072
	(106,295)			(106,295)
Subtotal	43,679	222,082	135	265,897
	(260,145)			(260,145)
Total	**303,824**	**222,082**	**135**	**526,042**

Source: Pak Kyŏng-sik, "*Taiheiyō Sensō toki ni okeru*," 34. Parenthesis indicate workers frozen to their positions.

LABOR MOBILIZATION PLANS

An important legal mechanism in the movement of Korean labor to Japan was the NGML's Labor Mobilization Plan (LMP; J: Rōmu Dōin Keikaku), which outlined the central government's annual labor needs in response to requests by Japan's industries. Japanese citizens (the unemployed, women, and students) filled the majority of LMP needs, with Koreans representing 3 percent (1942) to 8 percent (1939) of the allocated laborers. Under the plan, the central government assigned to the GGK an annual labor quota that the colonial government then divided among provincial employment offices. Historians of the national historical paradigm refer to the movement of Korean labor to Japan under the LMP as "forced mobilization," which implies that coercion was the main factor in the movement of laborers to Japan. Many studies highlight the plight of the coal miners in Hokkaido and southern Sakhalin as typical of all Koreans' experiences. While coercion was a factor in the recruitment process, and miners suffered abuse, the methods of recruitment and the workplace environment of Koreans cannot be uniformly summarized as coercive and exploitative. As is shown below, the wartime labor market offered Korean workers a multitude of economic opportunities when they looked for employment.

As shown in table 4.3, LMP demands for Korean labor fluctuated over the course of the war. In 1939 the central government assigned to Korea a quota of 85,000 workers, mostly for mines and factories in Japan. The quota grew each year, peaking in 1944 at 290,000, and then declining in 1945 to 50,000, due to Allied bombing that destroyed factories and unrestricted submarine warfare that cut off the strategic raw materials needed for productivity.

Koreans taken to Japan under the LMP were generally assigned to business cooperatives (control associations), usually in the mining sector. Mining industries needed Korean labor because too many Japanese men had been conscripted into the military. From 1939 to 1945, 318,546 Korean

FIG 4.1 Korean laborers take time off from working on the Uryū hydroelectric dam. This photo was taken August 31, 1941; the dam was completed in August 1943.

TABLE 4.3   Korean Labor under the Labor Mobilization Plan, 1939–1945

Year	Destination	Quota	Recruited	Ratio
1939	Japan	85,000		
	Sakhalin			
	Pacific Islands			
	Total	85,000	53,120	62.5
1940	Japan	88,800		
	Sakhalin	8,500		
	Pacific Islands			
	Total	97,300	59,398	61.0
1941	Japan	81,000		
	Sakhalin	1,200		
	Pacific Islands	17,800		
	Total	100,000	67,098	67.1
1942	Japan	120,000		
	Sakhalin	6,500		
	Pacific Islands	3,500		
	Total	130,000	119,851	92.2
1943	Japan	120,000		
	Sakhalin	3,300		
	Pacific Islands	1,700		
	Total	125,000	128,354	102.7
		(155,000)		
1944		290,000	286,432	98.7
1945		50,000	10,622	21.2
Total		**907,300**	**724,875**	**79.8**

Source: Pak Kyŏng-sik, "Taiheiyō Sensō toki ni okeru," 35; and TGSS, Diet 85, 1944. Reprinted in Kondō Ken'ichi, *Taiheiyō senka no Chōsen*, 153–55. The 1943 total was later revised up to 155,000.

men went to work in Japan's coal mines, and another 75,749 in metal mines, 129,664 went to construction and engineering companies, and 122,872 to factories.[19] To recruit these numbers, the state used company-directed recruitment from September 1939, GDR from January 1942, and labor conscription from September 1944. Under CDR, from 1939 to 1941 around 63.6 percent of the quota was fulfilled. Through CDR and GDR, 92 percent of the quota was met in 1942 and eventually surpassed labor needs in 1943 (the only year the quota was met). A combination of CDR, GDR, and conscription were successfully used in 1944.

Tables 4.3 and 4.6 show the relative successes and failures of the LMPs, which called for 907,300 Koreans to be sent to Japanese industries. Of this, 724,743 (73 percent) were recruited, but only 604,429 actually made it to Japan.[20] Of the 120,014 men recruited who did not arrive at the workplace, a large percentage deserted or reneged on their contracts. Another contributing factor to the loss of workers was that recruiters signed on unqualified or unhealthy men; nearly 16,000 labor recruits were denied entry into Japan because they failed mental or physical exams that screened for contagious diseases and threats to public safety.

The Korean population in Japan grew from 1,030,394 in 1939 to 2.1 million in 1945. The LMP accounted for a significant part of this increase, but not all. For example, the 1944 LMP brought nearly 300,000 to Japan, but the population grew less than 200,000, indicating a significant flow of Koreans back to Korea. The exodus of Korean labor from Japan suggests that Japanese industries allowed individuals to leave upon the completion of their contract or that scores deserted their workplaces to return to the peninsula.

The central government established a system of employment passports to control the movement of Japanese and Korean labor. All workers, Korean and Japanese, were given two employment passports and needed both to secure employment. Japanese workers received passports from city officials and reported family registry changes to city hall. But in Japan, the government administered Korean workers' passports through the Mutual Assistance Society (J: Kyōwakai) because Koreans, as noncitizens, were restricted in their dealings with city offices. Korean laborers in Japan were required to join and to file their address with the Mutual Assistance Society; this was done so that the Korean's alien status would not be confused with that of regular citizens. The Mutual Assistance Society in Japan proper issued Korean labor passports and oversaw temporary registry changes.[21] Once hired, the worker gave one passport to their employer, who held the passport to prevent the employee from deserting. Many companies and workers ignored this system late in the war, allowing for the unofficial movement of Japanese and Korean workers.

The LMP strained labor reserves on the peninsula because hundreds of thousands of Korea's best workers were exported to Japan. Korea's quotas under the 1944 plan would have been higher had colonial authorities not opposed the demands of the central government. When the plan called for a drastic increase in Korean labor, the colonial administration grumbled that the emigration of Korea's best workers to Japan hindered war production in Korea. The governor-general office stated,

> Demand for laborers has annually grown. The central government now requests we send 290,000 workers in 1944. However, due to the limitations of the labor supply in Korea and extension of contract periods of Korean workers in Japan, sending laborers causes serious difficulties for us. Therefore, we must devise a stricter policy to reform how the labor quota is filled. We have decided from September this year to establish a labor reserve system, and, if possible, find more people through general conscription.[22]

In 1944 the colonial regime expanded age limits for targeted laborers to include older and younger demographic groups, especially students. Through such means the GGK met 98 percent of this quota.

METHODS OF RECRUITMENT

Many studies of Korean labor in Japan's war emphasize the coercive and deceitful tactics used by recruiters and government authorities. The colonial regime recruited labor with a carrot-and-stick approach. The colonial state offered Koreans enticements (the carrot) that included high wages, opportunities to learn marketable skills, and the chance to escape military service. The GGK and corporations offered incentives before relying on force. A common method of enticement was to offer a young man a stable salary. If Koreans did not respond positively to enticements, the colonial regime resorted to coercion (the stick). Bureaucratic pressure and police visitations were used in varying degrees—mildly at first, but with increasing intensity if the worker was intransigent. The most intense forms of harassment were reserved for those who refused to cooperate or who evaded recruitment.

Any serious study of Korean participation in the war effort must account for the economic opportunities offered to Koreans. Japanese authorities encouraged Korean cooperation through economic incentives. Financial compensation offered Koreans a tangible motive to sign contracts and to work for war industries. Many men thought that employment as industrial laborers or as civilian employees of the military was better than sustenance farming. Thus poverty-stricken farmers considered recruiters who promised signing bonuses, high salaries, a stable career, and safe working conditions to be their saviors. This was especially true early in the war, when agrarian conditions were harsh. From 1939 to 1942 Korea experienced crop failures and low harvests in three of the four years.[23] The harsh life of rural Korea compelled many Koreans to seek jobs in the industrial centers of Korea and Japan. Some Koreans, tired of eking out an existence, begged government authorities to find them work.[24]

The promise of educational opportunities also attracted laborers. Koreans sought out employment opportunities to learn marketable skills as clerks, medical assistants, translators, and mechanics—skills that would benefit them for life. Young girls willingly joined the Young Women's Volunteer Corps (J: Teshintai; K: Chŏngsindae) after educators and police assured them that they would be able to continue their education while working. Police, educators, and business recruiters used these incentives to lure young people, especially women, to sign contracts.[25] Kim Chae-rim and her cousin, both fourteen-year-old girls, joined the Young Women's Volunteer Corps when their teachers told them that they could make money and continue their education in Japan. Without parental permission, they went to city hall and stamped the required documents. Both worked at a Mitsubishi factory in Japan for seven months with little food and no pay (the company put their wages in a forced savings account). Both of them ran away from the factory before their contracts expired to escape poor working conditions and Allied bombing.[26]

Large numbers of Koreans volunteered for labor conscription for personal reasons that included avoidance of military service and to escape a bad home environment. Others volunteered in order leave home. Kim Sŏng-ju, of South Chŏlla, joined the Young Women's Volunteer Corps to escape her domineering stepmother. To join, Kim stole her father's seal (K: tochang) and stamped the permission slip. The recruiters paid her ten wŏn to sign up.[27] She went to work at a Mitsubishi factory in Nagoya. There, the factory fed her well and paid her wages into a forced savings account, which she collected when her contract expired.[28] While this case is anecdotal, it is representative of countless situations in which personal circumstances pushed Koreans to cooperate.

Government recruitment of civilians employed by the military (essentially contract labor) was an interplay of cooperation, coercion, and inducement between the colonial government and Koreans. Military contractors gained employment with the army and navy by willingly applying or by NGML recruitment (GDR and conscription; J: *chōyō*). Thus, military contractors were laborers, not soldiers or sailors. The methods used by colonial bureaucrats to recruit civilian employees for the military included patriotic propaganda, lucrative salaries, and coercion, when necessary. Recruiters promised salaries that were double, even triple, peacetime salaries if recruits went to combat zones.[29] Civilian employees of the military earned salaries between 50 and 120 wŏn a month—a hefty wage considering that the average policeman earned eighteen wŏn a month.[30] Recruiters told young men that it would be better to volunteer and capitalize on the high wages—otherwise they might be conscripted and given a lower wages. This modus operandi indicates that coercion underlay many individuals' decision to volunteer as civilian employees of the military and as laborers. Nevertheless, high-paying positions resulted in competition among Koreans for skilled military civilian positions. Some jobs required that applicants take a physical or education-based exam to evaluate language and technical skills. The military rejected many applicants for high-paying jobs because they had performed poorly on one of these exams or because there were more applicants than positions.[31]

Conversely, there was very little, if any, competition for low-salaried menial laborer positions in the war zone. Recruiters often did not receive enough applicants to fill such positions, and when the number of applications was insufficient, or when recruitment quotas were not met, the recruiters resorted to deception, coercion, and brute force. Oral histories provide insight into how government coercion functioned. O Haeng-sŏk, for example, was called in to the police office and asked to sign up as a military civilian. He demurred several times, but eventually the police beat him and forced him to sign an employment contract. The GGK assigned villages quotas and showed little concern as to how they were met. Recruiting agents, working for corporations and the government, frequently resorted to questionable recruiting methods to meet these recruitment allocations. Provincial and village authorities, such as patriotic unit heads, helped fill

FIG 4.2
Kang Sam-bong
in April 1943. Kim
was seventeen
years old when he
became a civilian
employee of the
military. He worked
on Hokkaidō as a
metalsmith.

these quotas for industrial labor and for civilian employees of the military
by locating and pressuring young men and women to serve the Japanese
nation.[32] Some men believed that they were powerless to refuse their social
superior's entreaty to volunteer.

Village leaders and recruiters resorted to filling quotas by tricking
uneducated men into signing contracts without fully disclosing all of the
details. As discussed above, recruiters promised young men higher wages
than would be paid, safer working conditions than existed, and shorter

contract periods than actually existed. Recruiting agents promised potential laborers false salaries in places equivalent to Voltaire's El Dorado. These
broken promises later contributed to the Korean historical remembrance
of injustice; they were also a common source of labor disputes and desertion. As one example of many, a recruiting agent told Chŏng Kir-hong, of
North Chŏlla, that he would not need to take any extra clothing with him
if he took a job on Tinian Island in the South Pacific. The recruiter promised Chŏng high wages and assured him that when Japan won the war, he
would be recognized by the government for his hard work. However, when
he arrived, the work conditions were dismal, and he was treated poorly and
received a lower salary than the agent had promised.

There was also considerable pressure placed on Korean laborers to
comply with recruitment efforts. Often, this coercion took the form of
compulsion and commandeering. Oral histories indicate that individuals
were kidnapped while on the way to work, while working in a rice field,
and while sleeping at home. In some cases, military authorities commandeered laborers en route to industries to work as civilian employees of the
military. Some young men who attended recruitment rallies and seminars
were forced to sign contracts on the spot and were transported overseas
the same day.[33] While these men were technically recruited according to
the letter of the law, the iron-fisted methods that were used left them with
a sense of injustice. Kidnapping of laborers was the result of desperation
by recruiting agents and government officials to secure an adequate labor
supply for war industries. Japanese recruiting agents admit to kidnapping
Koreans. Kamata Sawaichirō, a Japanese recruiting agent in wartime Korea,
explained how it worked,

It was useless to hope that an adequate number of Koreans would volunteer
to become members of the labor force in Japan. So what Japanese local labor
offices would do is to wait until families were asleep and then in the middle
of the night they would swoop down on houses where potential male laborers
lived. Another method was to send trucks to the fields and load them up with
people who had no idea what was happening to them. When a certain seized
work force was thus assembled, the Koreans would be sent off to the mines
in Hokkaido or Kyushu. In this outrageous fashion, the local labor offices in
Korea would fulfill their responsibilities for labor recruitment.[34]

Yoshida Seiji, a Japanese official stationed in Fukuoka, states that he conducted slave raids in Korea to meet his labor-recruitment quota in Japan.[35] In contrast to the mobilization laws, the kidnapping of laborers was an extralegal activity that probably had tacit the approval of government officials because Japan's survival was at stake. The number of laborers kidnapped is not clear, but oral histories indicate that the number was rather small. According to oral accounts, kidnapping happened most often late in the war, when Japan was increasingly desperate. However, there is no indication that either the GGK or the Tokyo government took steps to prevent or punish recruiters who lied to or commandeered laborers.

Ironically, kidnapping merely shifted labor shortages from one factory to another. If a young man was picked up off the street on his way to work, his original employer would have to find a replacement, which could take weeks. Commandeering was an ineffective method of resource management. Sadly, Korean recruiting agents participated in the abduction of their own countrymen and women. Korean policemen and corporate recruiters frequently sided with the colonial regime in a calculated assumption that Japan would win the war and their status would improve based on their wartime loyalty.

SEMIOFFICIAL LABOR ORGANIZATIONS

The Japanese state mobilized Korean manpower through a plethora of semiofficial organizations that were part of its corporatist approach to mobilization. These organizations, also found throughout Japan proper, provided the government with an important grassroots instrument through which it disseminated official policies and propaganda, enforced rules and regulations, worked on labor projects large and small, and encouraged compliance on a more individual level. In essence, these organizations integrated state and society. Countless official and semiofficial labor groups formed, reorganized, and dissolved during the war period, so it is necessary to generalize the methods used by these organizations.

The National Service Corps (J: Hōkokutai) was the most widespread labor-oriented organization at the provincial and village levels. Branches of this corps operated in schools, rural villages, and urban industrial workplaces to assist in the war effort by constructing dams, managing mines, and clearing forests. This organization mustered large numbers of Koreans for construction projects, including 1,900,000 of the 2,454,724 Koreans mobilized in 1944. The duration and location of work projects varied from several days to six months, and up to a year. The government frequently extended the term of service to finish large projects.

The Women's Volunteer Corps, created in April 1944, was a special work group for Japanese and Korean women. The corps' official purpose was to give women a chance to serve Japan prior to marriage. However, it was a means to compel women to perform labor duties. This organization functioned differently in Korea than in Japan. In Japan, the volunteer corps recruited unmarried women ages sixteen and older who had special skills; in Korea, too few women had technical skills, so the organization focused on recruiting unskilled laborers; in some cases it recruited girls as young as fourteen.[36] Additionally, advertisements, patriotic unit involvement, and police coercion factored into recruitment methods. The corps mobilized women for agricultural and factory labor—often sending young girls to Japan on one-year contracts. Schools functioned as an important recruiting ground for the Women's Volunteer Corps, accounting for upwards of 75 percent of the women recruited.[37]

The Women's Volunteer Corps recruited single young women, making the organization an easy target of recruiters involved in military prostitution. Many women recruited by the corps ended up in brothels. As a result, this corps is frequently discussed solely as a recruitment center for comfort women, but such a view omits the wartime contribution to industrial production made by tens of thousands of women in this corps. While this study does not examine comfort women as an official category of mobilization, the experiences of these women varied greatly and cannot simply be reduced to victimization and exploitation in total.

Another semigovernmental organization involved in the mobilization of married women was the Patriotic Wives Association (J: Aikoku Fujinkai). In June 1941 this organization had 461,000 members, of whom 322,538 were Korean. The colonial regime utilized this semiofficial group to disseminate and to enforce state policies as well as to spread propaganda. Its main purpose was to unite the nation's women in one purpose and to cultivate a patriotic spirit so that women would not oppose the mobilization of their husbands and sons.[38] Women in this organization also made home visits in conjunction with the police as needed. Although this group was not specifically a labor corps, it typifies the GGK's use of corporatism to disseminate state policies among Korean and Japanese women living in Korea. It was one of many auxiliary organizations that pressured Koreans to serve the state in any and all manners, and provides insight into the GGK's cultural nexus of power.

The multifarious ways in which the GGK utilized Korean human resources was impressive; unfortunately, reliable numbers are available only for official forms of mobilization. Table 4.4 summarizes official labor mobilization statistics. It does not include factory laborers recruited directly by companies or laborers mobilized through CDR or through semigovernmental organizations. Private companies hired hundreds of thousands of laborers each year without government assistance and, therefore, are not included in official statistics. Table 4.4 shows that labor mobilization grew annually during the war and peaked in 1944, at almost two and a half million, largely in preparation for an Allied invasion. There are no statistics for 1945, but the number of people mobilized was probably higher than 1944 due to Japan's growing wartime desperation. The number of Koreans mobilized through GDR and conscription in 1945 dropped because businesses lacked the resources to sustain production and because the war ended in August. Statistics are deceiving, because workers recruited through CDR and GDR were probably frozen to those positions later in the war, thus one person could be counted in multiple categories or multiple times in a single category. It is also highly likely that many individuals were mobilized several years in a row and were counted each year. These statistics should be viewed as incidents of mobilization, rather than representative of a number of people.

TABLE 4.4   Total Number of Korean Workers Mobilized

Year	GDR	Conscription	Patriotic Units
1938	19,516		74,194
1939	45,289		113,096
1940	61,527		170,644
1941	46,887	4,895	313,731
1942	49,030	4,096	333,976
1943	58,924	2,898	685,733
1944	76,617	374,695	2,454,724
1945	44,263	139,367	Unknown
Total	**402,053**	**526,042**	**4,146,098+**

Source: Pak Kyŏng-sik, "Taiheiyō Sensō toki ni okeru," 34 and 37.

The above statistics also do not include the millions of Koreans who participated in nonofficial forms of mobilization, nor do they include student mobilization. The GGK expended massive resources seeking support from all Koreans for participation in projects that ranged from donating gold hairpins to giving funds to buy airplanes to attending send-off parties to stitching thousand-stitch belts (J: *sen'ninbari*) for soldiers to writing letters to men at the front to contributing to general relief movements. The overall labor and monetary contribution of Koreans is not known, but the Japanese war touched the life of every Korean in one way or another.

PROPAGANDA FOR LABOR RECRUITMENT

These tools of state were designed to incorporate Korean laborers into the war effort and imbue them with a sense that they were contributing to the survival of their nation, namely Japan. Prior to the implementation of the draft in 1942, government propaganda emphasized that Koreans' patriotic duty was, by and large, to labor for the nation. After the announcement of the Korean military draft, martial and labor propaganda went hand in hand. As with propaganda for military mobilization, the GGK took a dual approach to win Korean cooperation and to counter decades of negative public portrayals of Koreans as being lazy, untrustworthy, and plagued with cultural shortcomings. This effort was important because it shows an ideological shift in how the GGK approached the Koreans, who were now shown as being ready to assume the responsibilities of national service. Publicity also highlighted the brotherhood between Japan and Korea.

Labor-related propaganda targeted men and women, students and parents, as well as old and young. Newspapers, journals, movies, handbills, and radio broadcasts encouraged workers to increase production and adhere to state policies. Typical sloganeering demanded "Jūgunka! Seisanka!" (Enlist! Produce!).[39] One article reminded laborers, "When you are conscripted for a factory or mine, you are called to work for your country [not for profit]."[40] As with military mobilization, much of this effort went to waste because few Koreans could afford newspapers or radios.

The GGK portrayed the Korean people as loyal subjects and tried to create a social atmosphere that encouraged Korean cooperation. A March 3, 1942, Japanese-language radio program in Tokyo stated, "Koreans who in the past were not industrious are now working very hard. Koreans are certainly no longer lazy."[41] Propaganda minimized or ignored the coercive nature of the law and highlighted the duty of the Korean people to serve the nation. The GGK beseeched Koreans to be patriotic to the benevolent emperor. A publication in Korean and Japanese stated,

> The meaning of labor conscription [K: *chingyong*] is that one works for the emperor. It is an order under national law that people need to do whatever work is asked of them. The difference between military conscription [K: *chingbyŏng*] and labor conscription is that military conscription means obeying the emperor's law to fight in the war and labor conscription means serving our country by working hard. Therefore, it is not much different. It just differs how heavy or light they work.

In other words, military service was considered the most important, but labor service came a close second. The article continued,

> There are many people who think of labor conscription as punishment, but labor conscription is an honorable duty and is considerably different from disciplinary punishment. Labor conscription is an opportunity in wartime and is a citizen's important duty. Therefore, one must obey and happily serve.[42]

For Koreans, labor service was as important as military service; in fact, labor conscription exempted Korean men from soldiering. One result of this loophole was that thousands of young Korean men willingly complied with, or even sought out, labor conscription to avoid military service. This opportunity did not exist for Japanese men, for whom the military draft took precedence over other duties.

To encourage Koreans to participate in the war effort, media organs recounted anecdotes of sacrifices Koreans made for Japan. An August 20, 1944, Tokyo radio broadcast in English related the story of a Korean who allegedly left his critically ill son the moment he received a conscription notice. He went to work in a munitions plant in Nagoya and allegedly said, "Although I was born in [Korea], I am a full-fledged Japanese and I must not fail in fulfilling my duty as a Japanese."[43] An article from a 1944 magazine told the story of a Korean named Matsuda Nobuyo, who was living in Japan and was recruited through CDR to work in a Mitsubishi coal mine in Nagasaki. Matsuda, the eldest son in his family, received a letter from his family that his son was ill, but remained at work. Matsuda reportedly stated that he would not return to Korea for his son because his obligations to his nation were greater.[44] In short, model Koreans ignored their biological families to serve their country. Such stories contributed to a social discourse that portrayed colonial subjects as devotedly serving a paternalistic emperor.

Government authorities and semiofficial organizations attempted to secure ideological hegemony over Korea by showing films, organizing theatrical plays, and disseminating paraphernalia. In the first nine months of 1939, the GGK showed anticommunist and antispy movies 869 times to 814,533 people, and staged 631 plays of the same ilk for 533,965 people.[45] In 1944 over 1,900 film showings related to the war effort were seen by 2,945,000 viewers.[46] Similarly, in 1939 the colonial regime disseminated 255,560 posters and 2,240,236 flyers and handbills throughout Korea to combat communist influences. That same year, the GGK organized over 58,000 discussion meetings and 2,496 anticommunist labor groups. These propagandist efforts were part of the GGK's efforts at social engineering that had the larger goals of assimilation and creating a cultural environment in which Koreans naturally devoted their lives to the imperial state.

The GGK targeted Korean elites as both conveyors and targets of propaganda. As targets, the Korean intellectual class was viewed as an idle source of labor to be mobilized. Many colonial authorities opined that Korean intellectuals made minimal contributions to the war and offered nothing but criticism. Korean elites were encouraged to travel to the front lines to see the war effort firsthand. This, officials felt, would give them a more positive outlook on the war and help them to find ways to contribute to the empire.[47] Japanese authorities used local and national elites as mouthpieces of state policies to call for compliance with labor laws and greater productivity, and to pressure young men to volunteer for labor projects.

KOREAN WARTIME LABOR MOBILIZATION

Korean manpower became increasingly important to the Japanese war machine as the war progressed, because Korea was spared from strategic bombing and was closer to the battlefield in China. The industrial workforce in Korea, as of 1940, consisted of 346,424 miners; 591,494 factory workers; 437,752 construction workers; 130,377 workers in food processing; and 180,000 transportation workers. This nonagrarian workforce totaled 1.7 million, but was dwarfed by Japan's manufacturing and construction workforce of 8.1 million. In June 1943 Korea had 654 metalworking factories with 41,504 employees; 1,354 machine tool factories with 47,821 employees; and 927 chemical factories with 63,778 employees.[48] Korea also had textile, lumber, food, and cement factories, but these industries were not designated as critical to the war effort and did not benefit from NGML mobilization.

A key contribution of Korean labor was in the mining industry. There were nearly 350,000 Korean miners in Korea alone. In October 1941 the coal mining industry in Japan proper had a labor force of 323,692, of which 40,936 (12.7 percent) were Korean, many of whom were in Hokkaidō. Three years later, the mining labor force grew to 408,159, with 134,477 Koreans (33 percent). Not only did the percentage of Koreans in mines increase, but Koreans generally worked the most dangerous positions—making up two-thirds of the miners working the face where the ore was extracted.[49]

As qualified and experienced Japanese men left their skilled positions, the GGK and Japanese corporations confronted a shortage of workers with educational or technical training. Unfortunately for Japan, the Korean labor pool lacked the training to fill these positions. This was an area in which Japan's manpower policies proved to be shortsighted and unproductive. Koreans generally lacked the education, training, and experience of the Japanese workers that they replaced, thereby hindering production. Replacing one skilled Japanese laborer with a Korean farmer (or Japanese student) hurt the qualitative and quantitative output of industries.

Recruitment for industrial labor also showed little concern about workers' training or qualifications, resulting in a qualitatively deficient workforce. As of 1943, only 20 percent of factory and mine workers had more than three years' experience at their jobs, and among industrial workers, half had less than one year's experience at their position and another 30 percent had only one to two years' experience.[50] Most Koreans left the mines and factories once their contract expired. This was especially harmful to the mining industry because it took two years for a new miner to become 80 percent as efficient as an experienced miner.[51] In an effort to keep productive workers, many companies unilaterally extended employee contracts (with government backing) to retain workers so they could sustain production.

At their place of mobilization, many Koreans experienced disappointment and outrage that the actual conditions of their employment were much worse than recruiters promised. All too often, Koreans received lower wages, worked longer hours, and had more demanding duties than promised by recruiters. Ethnic discrimination was common. Koreans received lower salaries than the Japanese for the same work because many companies considered Koreans less productive and less reliable than Japanese workers.[52] Another factor contributing to higher Japanese wages was that most companies factored an employee's age, gender, education, experience, and family size in determining wages. However, companies paid Korean employees based solely on their time with the company—which resulted in lower wages. Korean wages were often 60 to 80 percent of what their Japanese counterparts earned.[53] One mining company set the maximum Korean wage at 80 percent of a Japanese worker in a similar position.[54] In some companies, Koreans were paid the same as Japanese workers but were expected to work longer hours.

Some Korean workers felt that their employer treated them as an expendable source of labor that was to be exploited and then discarded if they were hurt or became unproductive.[55] In the Chikuhō coal fields on Kyushu, Korean workers were estimated to be 20 percent more likely to die on the job than their Japanese counterparts.[56] Other companies reduced salaries or refused to feed workers who were suspected of shirking their duties; other employers made no pretension of paying wages.[57] Koreans considered this sort of treatment contradictory to government proclamations of brotherhood and equality between the two peoples.

Many companies practiced forced savings, in which a laborer's wages were held in government-authorized bank accounts until the end of the contract period. This system ensured that both Korean and Japanese laborers contributed financially to the building of the empire, and prevented employee desertion.[58] For example, an employee making 74 yen per month would take home less than 13 yen after the company deducted for room and board, war bonds, compulsory savings, and remittance to family members.[59] Frequently, work conditions were so horrible that workers left the company before the end of the contract and lost the money in their savings account. When the war unexpectedly ended, these accounts were frozen by the Japanese government, and many laborers never received the money from their accounts.

The work conditions that many Koreans faced were bleak. Korean workers frequently worked twelve to sixteen hours a day, seven days a week. The government delegated much of its authority over labor management to individual companies. This absence of governmental oversight gave corporations a dominant position in labor affairs. Foremen and security guards often physically and mentally abused employees thought to be malingering. Korean workers at mines and factories were beaten for minor rule infractions (often caused by language problems), not meeting quotas, or for not showing respect.[60] Police records acknowledge that Korean workers suffered exploitation and mental and physical abuse, and lived in fear of company overseers and police organs.[61] The government, offering only rhetoric, did little to restrain corporate abuse of employees; there were no concrete measures to stop abuse. Japanese authorities and businesses emphasized production at all costs and tolerated the abuse of laborers. Workers had little recourse to mistreatment other than to desert or to strike.

The exploitation and abuse suffered by Korean miners and factory workers were an important, and undeniable, part of the Korean wartime experience. But exploitation did not relegate Koreans to the status of hopeless pawns in Japan's war. Some Koreans found ways to profit from the war, evade service if called upon, or desert if mobilized. These experiences are of equal importance to the Korean wartime experience. It should be noted that Japanese workers also experienced abuse and exploitation from their employers. This said, Japanese citizens were mobilized to protect their empire; Koreans, on the other hand, were mobilized to reinforce their secondary status within Japan's empire.

Military contractors (J: *gunzoku*) contributed significantly to Japan's war machine by providing essential labor, often on the battlefront, that freed Japanese men for military service, thereby increasing the fighting potential of the military. Japanese authorities preferred to mobilize Koreans as contractors instead of as soldiers because contractors required less training, needed lower Japanese-language proficiency, had fewer legal barriers to mobilization, and were not armed. The Japanese army and navy used contractors in nearly every territory occupied by the Japanese empire. Civil-

FIG 4.3 Photograph of a labor unit assigned to construct a dam. Time and location are not known.

ians employed by the army and navy performed an array of duties for the military: They constructed coastal artillery embankments, built bridges, worked as janitors, built airfields, tended horses, guarded prisoners of war (POWs), worked in shipyards, and metalsmithed. Some occupied highly skilled positions as mechanics, machinists, truck drivers, translators, and accountants. A handful held management positions in which they supervised unskilled workers.

The qualifications to become a military contractor depended on the type of service for which one applied or was recruited. High-paying technical positions required a middle school diploma or specific technical training, although most contractors worked as manual laborers. Conscripts classified by the military as unfit for active military duty and men who attended military training camps were targeted to serve as military contractors. By law, laborers had to be graduates of a national school and be at least twenty years old.[62] Frequently the military ignored age and educational requirements and recruited men as young as sixteen.

PRISONER OF WAR GUARDS

The experiences of Korean prisoner-of-war guards merit special attention because debate exists regarding the degree of agency surrounding their actions, namely the abuse of Allied POWs. The Japanese army employed 3,223 Koreans as POW guards.[63] Guards had two-year oral contracts, which were extended each year until the end of the war. In 1942 approximately 1,400 were sent to Indonesia, 800 to Thailand, and 800 to Malaysia to help guard nearly 50,000 Allied POWs. Taiwanese civilian employees of the military guarded POWs in the Philippines and in Borneo.[64] Korean guards received two months of special training that focused on indoctrination and Japanese culture; there was little training on how to handle POWs and none related to international laws governing the treatment of prisoners.[65]

Korean POW guards developed an infamous reputation for abusing POWs and causing many deaths.[66] Yet Korean guards were emotionally and physically trapped between two international forces. As employees of Japan, Korean guards followed orders from their Japanese commanding officers. These orders frequently required guards to push POWs to their physical limit to ensure prisoner submission and to extract labor. Korean scholars opine that Korean POW guards were victims of a Japanese military that forced them to hit, kick, starve, and overwork prisoners.[67] The result was that Koreans, in the name of Japan, mistreated, starved, and overworked Allied prisoners in order to build roads, airstrips, and bridges. On the other hand, some Korean guards sympathized with the POWs because they felt that Korea was a slave of Japan, just like the prisoners. Thus, Koreans had reason to treat POWs better than their Japanese counterparts did. Numerous Korean guards gave cigarettes to the POWs, struck up conversations with prisoners (even expressing dislike for Japan), and went easy on them during work details.[68] But if a Korean was caught showing sympathy to POWs, he could be accused of being a spy and punished.

As a result of their direct contact with POWs, Korean POW guards became the object of hatred of Allied prisoners even though the guards themselves did not have the authority to provide better medical care, better housing, or even better food. After the war, the Allies established war crimes trials to hold accountable those involved in the abuse of POWs. The Allies estimated that 12,399 POWs died in Southeast Asia. Allied war crimes tribunals convicted 148 Koreans (and 173 Taiwanese), most of whom were POW guards, as Class B and Class C war criminals. One hundred and twenty-five were imprisoned and twenty-three were executed (fourteen were POW guards), including Lieutenant-General Hong Sa-ik.[69] Koreans claim that Japanese authorities scapegoated the Korean POW guards for the worst abuses committed against POWs. Historiography from the national historical paradigm portrays Korean war criminals as martyrs of their circumstances and Japanese imperialism because they were not properly prepared or trained for their duties as soldiers or POW guards. In the minds of Korean and Japanese scholars, the Koreans executed as war criminals are more a testament of Japan's evasion of its wartime responsibilities than evidence of individual Korean culpability.[70]

KOREAN CIVILIANS EMPLOYED BY THE MILITARY

The deployment of Korean civilians employed by the military, shown in table 4.5, depended on Japan's fortunes of war. The majority of civilian employees of the military mobilized in 1941 and 1942, the years Japan gained control over the South Seas, went to that region; in 1944 and 1945 most civilian employees of the military went to Japan to prepare for the defense of Japan against the expected American invasion. Japanese government documents claim that 145,010 Koreans served as military employees during the war. These numbers provide a minimum estimate. Most scholars place the actual number of Korean civilian employees of the military slightly higher, at 154,424 men: 70,424 in the army, and 84,483 in the navy.[71]

TABLE 4.5   Deployment Location of Korean Military Contractors by Year

Year	Japan	Korea	Manchukuo	China	South Pacific	Total
1939			145			145
1940	65		656	15		736
1941	5,396	1,085	384	13	9,249	16,127
1942	4,171	1,723	293	50	16,159	22,396
1943	4,691	1,976	390	16	5,242	12,315
1944	24,071	13,545	1,617	294	5,885	45,412
1945	31,603	15,532	467	347		47,949
Total	69,997	33,861	3,952	735	36,535	145,080

Source: Higuchi, *Kōgun heishi ni sareta*, 15; and Pak Kyŏng-sik, "Taiheiyō Sensō toki ni okeru," 38. The statistics from the two sources have minor variations (Pak's numbers have some errors in computation).

Mobilization for labor projects outside the NGML, at the provincial level, totaled upwards of 4.1 million people from 1937 to 1944, more people than industrial and military mobilization combined.[72] The most common forms of nonindustrial mobilization were rural work projects (such as farm production and clearing forests) and the construction of defensive fortifications, dams, and other large-scale projects. The GGK requisitioned labor to work on these projects for one- to six-month periods. All able-bodied people, men and women of all ages, were expected to participate in rural work projects. Some villages were assessed a labor quota to work on government-sponsored projects; some communities filled these quotas by lottery. Industrial workers, women, students, and soldiers frequently spent holidays and vacation days working on labor projects. Rural labor projects, including rice harvesting, were commonly accomplished by small work groups that were loosely based on traditional neighborhood groups. In 1941 workgroups accounted for 61 percent of the rice harvest and 38 percent of the wheat.[73]

KOREAN WOMEN

Government expectations of Japanese and Korean women were comparable in many ways, with several notable differences. The government demanded labor of single Japanese women, but Korean women were only indirectly affected by mobilization. Women were called to work on coastal observation posts, to assist with public safety during drills, and to take part in military drills. Propaganda targeting Japanese women emphasized that they be good wives and wise mothers, while propaganda for Korean women focused on productivity.[74] In other words, the GGK did not emphasize or protect the sanctity of Korean motherhood because the regime was not concerned with maintaining familial bonds within the Korean household. As the war situation grew desperate, the GGK requisitioned women as young as thirteen and as old as fifty for work projects.

The GGK placed relatively few official demands on Korean women but expected them to assume the agricultural roles of men who had been mobilized as part of the war effort. The emphasis on productivity rather than families is seen in Governor-General Minami's attempt to increase the 1940 rice harvest. Minami called for the creation of temporary day care centers to give Korean women more time to focus on production. In response to this policy, by 1940 the state oversaw the creation of 11,799 nurseries that tended 321,684 children. The program rapidly expanded, and by 1944 over 34,700 temporary nurseries tended 915,003 children.[75] Nurseries got women out of the home and put their children in the government's care, where they could be indoctrinated.

Women were bombarded with demands to take up new roles to serve the nation as factory workers. In 1941 women made up 20.3 percent of the factory workforce, 7.3 percent of mining, 7.8 percent of transportation, and 24.5 percent of office workers.[76] By 1945 these numbers grew to 20 percent of construction labor, 15 percent of mining, and 28 percent of manufacturing.[77] By 1945 nearly 1.2 million Korean women were employed in industries ranging from communications, mining, and electricity to chemicals, ceramics, and construction. Work organizations encouraged women to sacrifice family time to provide labor to the state in order to share in the glory as people of the emperor (J: *mitami ware*). They were also called upon to cooperate with the government during difficult times and to take leadership roles in their family if the men were called to duty.[78]

ELEMENTARY AND MIDDLE SCHOOL STUDENTS

The colonial state increasingly mustered elementary and middle school students as laborers within and outside Korea. Student mobilization for provincial-level projects began in June 1938 with the Student Labor Patriotic Corps (J: Hakuto Kinrō Hōkokutai), which mobilized students under the slogan "Labor Service for the State."[79] Older students were used for heavy labor, while younger students were used for menial tasks. Boys built airfields, cleared trees for roads, gathered pine tar, dug air-raid shelters, and so forth; girls sewed military uniforms, made comfort bags for soldiers, cleaned shrines, and produced military paraphernalia.

The demands on student labor increased as the war progressed. Early in the war, schools mobilized students for provincial-level labor projects. Students could be mobilized for up to ten days to perform work duty. For example, in 1938, 6,000 students from thirty-two schools in Kyŏnggi worked six hours a day for ten days during their summer vacation.[80] In South Ch'ungch'ŏng, 235 schools mobilized 3,338 students for ten days to improve Shinto shrines, help agricultural production, and do other miscellaneous tasks. In 1941 the labor service for students increased to thirty days per year and eventually reached two months. In 1943 school hours were further reduced and the school year shortened to make students more available for labor service.[81] Eventually, Korean and Japanese students were requisitioned for labor service during school hours under the slogans "Learning by doing" and "Today's work rather than tomorrow's graduation."[82]

Although the number of students mobilized was extensive, it is impossible to quantify. There is no indication that student numbers are included in the general mobilization statistics. We know that during the war there were 3,245 youth organizations, with a combined membership of two million students who performed a variety of tasks.[83] A March 28, 1944, radio broadcast stated that "6,000 college and university youths, 100,000 middle school boys and girls, and 1,800,000 national school children are exerting all-out efforts" to improve Japan's military capabilities.[84] These numbers are impossibly high, considering there were 1.2 million Korean primary school students in 1939 and under 40,000 high school and college students within Korea.[85] Nevertheless, all students were required to divert their energies from the classroom to support the war effort.

KOREAN RESPONSES TO LABOR MOBILIZATION

Koreans responded to mobilization with active cooperation, quiet compliance, or resistance. As noted previously, these three options were not necessarily distinct categories, since active compliance could be a form of resistance. At the time of recruitment, Koreans had options available to them: they could cooperate and take advantage of economic opportunities or they could resist and face the repercussions. Nevertheless, government coercion did not turn Koreans into pawns moved about at the whim of the colonial regime.

Coercion was an important part of the recruitment process in meeting labor quotas, especially later in the war. Government authorities at all levels employed intimidation and deception to meet labor quotas for labor corps. Patriotic unit heads threatened to cut off rations, while police and women's organizations made frequent home visits to families to force compliance with labor policies. Often, families were told to send one able-bodied male for labor service—regardless of whether he was the father, husband, or only son. Thus, if the son ran off, the father or a brother might be expected to take his place. Young men considering evasion often complied, because if they did not go, their family members would be harassed.[86] Pressure to submit to labor mobilization came from government authorities, local elites, and even family members. Frequently, family members pressured a brother or son to comply so that the family would not face bureaucratic harassment. The following quote shows the intricate interplay of pressure exerted on young men to comply to state demands. Chŏng Chae-su, of North Chŏlla, remembered,

> My draft call came the first of October, 1944, when I was twenty-one. I wanted to run away, but my elder brother said, if that happens, the Japanese will give the rest of the family a hard time. So for the good of the family, he begged me to stay put and go when I was called up. The authorities said it would be for one year. I told my brother, even one year is too long. I will run away. But he persisted.[87]

This pressure proved unbearable for men such Chŏng, who acquiesced to his family's pleadings and went to work in a shipyard in Kobe, Japan. Thus, young men frequently volunteered as a result of indirect government coercion and direct urging from family members.

The police force in Korea was also an active, dreaded presence throughout the mobilization process. Policemen wielded great social power and effectively enforced mobilizations laws. However, too often the police are portrayed as a faceless machine that functioned with absolute precision. Instead, individual policemen were human and prone to gullibility and, in some cases, ineptitude. For example, the police targeted O Haeng-sŏk, of South Chŏlla, for labor mobilization. On three occasions the police called O, then eighteen years of age, into their office and filled out an application on his behalf—one time a policeman even signed the application for him. However, O eluded their pressure by claiming that he had a venereal disease. The police finally became suspicious of his story when they saw him running around town. The police had a doctor inspect O and found that he had lied about his condition. The police beat him for his dishonesty and shipped him off to Singapore to work as a POW guard.[88]

Untold numbers of Koreans evaded labor recruitment by hiding, spreading rumors, or using violence. The easiest place for Koreans to avoid labor mobilization was in their home province. Their intimate knowledge of the surrounding geography and populace gave Koreans a home-field advantage over recruiting officers. Young men took refuge in forests and caves near their villages, as well as with relatives in neighboring villages. Some fled abroad. Yet wily recruiters found ways to force compliance. For example, eight young men of Changsŏng, Kangwŏn, hid from the police and labor recruiters in the nearby mountains to avoid labor recruitment. The police, knowing that the respect of one's elders was paramount in Korean culture, dragged the men's elders into the middle of the village and held them hostage under the midday sun. Within an hour, all of the men surrendered themselves to gain the release of the older men.[89]

An unusual form of evasion (and cooperation) was the use of impersonators. In 1939 the police in Hokkaidō discovered 121 stand-ins for another person. On another occasion, of the 32,797 Koreans recruited through CDR, 61 were found to have used false names or to have impersonated others.[90] Impersonators forged documents, presented another person's family registry, or simply showed up for roll call during final boarding and answered to another person's name. There is not much information in the sources about the motives of the replacements. Several possible explanations are that wealthy Koreans hired replacement workers, sons took the place of their fathers, or the impersonators stepped in to secure a stable job.

Korean students also had options available to them to avoid labor service. Younger students could technically drop out of school and leave the work site, because education was not compulsory.[91] However, older students who quit school could be mobilized for labor or military service if they were of the right age. Dropping out of school was not a simple choice because dropouts faced bureaucratic discrimination and an uncertain occupational future. It is doubtful that Japanese authorities would have allowed dropouts to resume school after the war. The choices that students—and all Koreans, for that matter—made during the war cannot be judged based on the hindsight that Japan lost the war. The GGK was the legal government of Korea that presented Koreans with economic and employment options. Laborers who took advantage of the wartime economy to better their livelihoods acted in a rational and reasonable manner. It was not automatically guaranteed that Japan was going to lose the war, nor was Korea's liberation guaranteed if Japan lost the war. If Japan had won the war, a dropout would have had little or no education with which to get a job.

Avoidance of labor conscription was handled by the police and by employment agencies. Police resorted to every possible trick and stratagem to enforce laws, uncover noncompliance, and find deserters. Those who did not cooperate faced arrest, imprisonment, constant surveillance, and manipulation of their financial security; legally, they could be punished with one year of imprisonment or fined one thousand wŏn. The government made use of its resources to locate those who evaded labor duty. Japanese authorities offered a five-yen reward to whomever provided information on deserters, and police who arrested escapees were given bonuses. One ploy that police used to locate deserters was to offer candy to young children in exchange for information about family members or neighbors who were suspected of avoiding mobilization. Students at school were quizzed about their home life.[92] Nevertheless, the government lacked the manpower to force complete compliance and, in most cases, relied on Korean cooperation to sustain the war effort in Korea.

Koreans responded to government recruitment efforts with simple forms of resistance. For example, they used rumors and gossip to spread information about the poor treatment of Korean laborers in Japanese mines, the forcible collection of women as military prostitutes, and so forth. Rumors spread throughout the southern regions of Korea, where labor recruitment was heaviest, and made recruitment of Korean laborers more difficult as the war progressed. Rumors exhibited a collective social psychology of resistance and exposed the failure of assimilation policies as well as the government's inability to impose its will on the Korean people. Between December 1943 and May 1945, the police monitored 1,344 rumors in Korea that included criticism of the colonial regime, gossiping about the war, and perusal of Allied propaganda.[93]

In 1942 the police investigated and arrested 718 people for spreading rumors or for expressing forbidden thoughts. Of this number, 409 were imprisoned and 197 fined. A prominent theme in many rumors was Japan's defeat, which likely contributed to foot-dragging as Koreans waited for the war to end. One man in Hwanghae was arrested for asking, "Even though Japan has fought Chiang Kai-shek for five years, they have not been able to win yet. So how could they win by starting a war with America and England, the largest nations in the world?" He was sentenced to prison for one year.[94]

A common method of resistance among laborers under contract was to desert while in transit. Workers destined for Japan or the northern regions of Korea had to transfer trains (or from train to boat) several times before reaching their workplace. Those seeking to escape would plead to go to the bathroom or to get a drink of water and never return. Brave souls even jumped from moving trains to effect their getaway. En route desertion was so common that agents often found it necessary to travel with those they recruited to reduce the likelihood of desertion.[95] Urban legend claims that some trains were sealed to prevent desertion.

A final form of evasion, largely limited to the last months of the war, was the use of violence. Such acts were generally the result of ethnic nationalism or of frustration with coercive and arbitrary recruitment. In most cases, violent actions were suicidal, literally and figuratively. In July 1945, Ch'oe Hae-ch'ŏn, of Kyŏngju, killed a policeman who attempted to enforce a conscription notice and then committed suicide before the police could arrest him. Part of his suicide note read, "I do not die at your hands. Do not bother me. I will die by my own hand. But there is something I have to say: Why are you trying to drag Koreans into your war? I am Korean. The reason I killed that policeman was because he tried to drag me into Japan's war."[96] Ch'oe's suicide, while personally destructive, prevented Japan from benefitting from his labor.

THE WORK ENVIRONMENT

Most studies on Korean industrial laborers highlight the exploitative work environment, with an emphasis on low pay and discrimination. While there is truth here, suffering is not the full story of wartime Korea. The emphasis on exploitation at the workplace omits the complex nature of Koreans' wartime experiences. Not every Korean suffered unmitigated exploitation or was forced to stay at their place of employment. Koreans mobilized under the NGML faced, and made, a plethora of choices at the workplace that included remaining at their place of employment (whether they liked it or not), deserting jobs, utilizing strikes and labor slowdowns, and resorting to acts of violence.

The experiences of Korean civilian employees of the military also varied widely, from pleasant and profitable to severely exploitative. Some employees were paid three times (or more) the average salary of Koreans in Korea, while others were paid a pittance; some contractors were paid on time every month and sent part of their wages to their families. Large numbers of workers' salaries were deposited into forced savings accounts that the workers could not, and still cannot, access; a number received no salary at all.[97] Whether a laborer was paid or not depended on the location and condition of the unit and was generally similar to the experiences of their Japanese comrades. Many contractors reminisced that the army and navy paid them the same as the Japanese and that in some units the Japanese treated them as equals. Chŏng Kir-hong, a laborer on Palau who willingly applied to become a civilian employee of the military, said that the Japanese gave him gifts of food, alcohol, and tobacco. In fact, he enjoyed his job so much that he wished he had gone earlier.[98]

Late in the war, the Korean contractors suffered from Japan's declining fortunes. As a general rule, the Japanese in the military suffered alongside Korean soldiers and laborers. The Koreans and the Japanese ate the same food (or suffered malnutrition) and received the same pay (or not). Chŏng Kir-hong, mentioned above, was transferred from Palau to New Guinea, where he was not paid for his labor and felt that he was treated like a beast of burden. Conversely, Son Yŏng-gwŏn was recruited by his high school principal in 1942 and sent to work as an airfield mechanic in Nagoya. Son stated that he was paid the exact amount that he was owed and was never mistreated by the Japanese. In fact, when he completed his mobilization term, he received severance pay.[99]

The national historical paradigm focuses on Japanese exploitation and Korean resistance and does not discuss wartime laborers who chose to stay at their place of employment. Untold numbers of laborers received stable wages (even if they were low) and had no incentive to quit, especially if they had familial obligations. While discrimination was common at most work-places, not all work environments were insufferable. In many instances, workers in Korea remained at their jobs because they worked in businesses that had a majority of Korean workers and, as a result, they believed that their existing position was the best available option.

Noncompliance and subversive practices increased in the waning months of the war. Police records related to acts of resistance show that economic and other personal reasons were the most common factors. Other causes included frustration, war weariness, and possible knowledge of Japan's situation in the war. Korean independence remained a distant, faint goal that offered limited motivation for such acts. Nevertheless, from 1944 until the end of the war, police records indicate that Korean national-ism and communism increasingly concerned the police, who feared that

Koreans would align with the Soviets. The colonial regime was careful to avoid pushing the Koreans into the arms of nationalists or communists. As a result, the police maintained diligent surveillance over suspected Korean nationalists and barraged the general populace with propaganda to ameliorate the more oppressive aspects of its governance.

Korean workers responded to and challenged colonial policies with individual acts of resistance such as desertions, labor disturbances, and, infrequently, violence. Open resistance was futile because vigilant police work prevented coordinated resistance activities in workplaces and kept Korean resistance fragmented and incoherent. Desertion had been present in the prewar years, and the practice grew more common during the war.[100] In the war economy, desertion had a more profound effect on production, corporate morale, and government hegemony. Japanese authorities recognized six reasons for workplace desertion among Koreans in Japan: use of recruitment as a means to travel to Japan; fear of workplace accidents and incidents; changing jobs at the instigation and invitation of others; dislike of long, hard hours; a yearning for city life; and dissatisfaction with the difference between the contract and the actual work conditions.[101] Actual conditions at work included discrimination against Koreans by Japanese coworkers and by the company. It is worth noting that four of the six causes above reflect a dissatisfaction with work conditions.

Concerns about wages and the extension of contracts factored into worker grievances, and the language barrier contributed to many disputes.[102] The personal needs of Koreans (food and pay) were the most pressing needs and factored greatly in desertion. Koreans left one employer for another when they were offered, or they heard of, higher wages at another company. It is noteworthy that businesses often ignored restrictions on labor (such as the passport system) and hired employees with little regard for legal barriers or proper procedures. This contributed to the Koreans' ability to desert without legal ramifications. The Saitama Police Bureau in Japan reported in 1945 that Koreans in Japan chased after the highest wages in spite of lacking the proper documentation.[103]

Another common cause of desertion was a desire to return to one's hometown, especially in cases where the government had unilaterally extended contracts for several years. This was particularly true among Koreans in Japan. Contracts of Koreans in Japan were for six months to two years, but in 1941 the Welfare Ministry and the Mutual Assistance Society extended their contracts by one year in an effort to provide Japanese businesses with sufficient numbers of laborers.[104] In the last year of the war, the labor situation in Japan neared chaos, and workers did not show up to work because they had to handle family emergencies such as looking for housing or because the factory had been destroyed by strategic bombing. From October 1939 to October 1942, the annual desertion rate among Korean laborers in Japan was 35.6 percent. In Hokkaido, where Koreans worked in isolated mines, desertion rates from 1939 to 1942 were around 13.2 percent. In contrast, prior to Allied bombing, Japanese worker absenteeism in Tokyo was 20 percent, but reached 49 percent in mid-1945 after Allied bombing.[105]

Desertion by Koreans in Korea was also common. Since their hometowns were more accessible, many simply left their jobs to return to their hometown. Within Korea, Hwanghae had the highest desertion rate, at 6 percent in 1942, but it increased to 31 percent in 1944.[106] Many fled to Manchukuo, a Japanese puppet state, where labor conscription was not enforced, or found work in another factory. The high desertion and absenteeism rates by Koreans and Japanese slowed productivity, increased accident rates, and diverted needed resources from production to labor recruitment. The high rates of desertion and absenteeism among Japanese workers show the inability of the wartime regime to properly secure hegemony over Japanese and Korean workers.

TABLE 4.6   Korean Workers Imported under Labor Mobilization Plans

Labor Mobilization Plan quota for Korea	907,300
Number allotted for mobilization	711,505
Actually taken to Japan	604,429
Decrease (sick, runaways, etc.)	328,540
Returned after contract	52,108
Repatriated malcontents/rejected	15,801
Whereabouts not known	209,750
Discovered and repatriated	4,121
Repatriated	14,626
Others	46,306
Remained at original occupation	288,488

Source: Tsuboe Senji, *Zainihon Chōsenjin no gaikyō*, 21.

Table 4.6 summarizes the recruitment numbers of Koreans for labor service in Japan under the LMP and provides an end-of-war summary of the destination of the laborers. Less than half of the Koreans taken to Japan remained at the position to which they were assigned, and roughly one-third (209,750) disappeared from government records. The government was able to locate only 4,121 of that number. The low number of deserters located by the government (about 2 percent) indicates that authorities made little attempt to track them down and focused instead filling vacancies. The High Police provide alternative statistics, and they state that, among the 760,342 Koreans mobilized under the 1939 to 1943 LMPs, 257,907 ran away and 13,389 (5.2 percent) were found.[107] Also, local and corporate officials were able to locate only one in thirteen escapees.[108] The government's failure to locate deserters showcases the Koreans' ability to disappear and ignore laws (particularly in Japan), despite the existence of potent bureaucratic mechanisms of control. Through these "weapons of the weak," the Koreans voiced dissatisfaction with their circumstances and exposed the central and colonial governments' vulnerability to desertion and raises questions about the GGK's power over Korean society.

Labor disputes (strikes and work slowdowns) constitute another form of workplace noncooperation. Labor disturbances included malingering, failing to put in an honest day's work, damaging equipment, and performing shoddy work. These were an important form of group resistance intended to improve work conditions or economic betterment, but management often turned to police protection to suppress resistance. Disturbances peaked in 1939, with 10,128 workers participating, but the number declined steadily thereafter. The GGK's records note that of the ninety-six labor incidents in 1940, wage-related issues caused seventy-five of them.[109] Businesses in Japan proper reported 384 instances of labor disputes by Koreans in Japan from April 1940 to December 1941. The police estimated that language problems caused 41 percent of these incidences.[110] The GGK claimed that the decline was due to a fair wage system and improved work conditions. A more likely reason was the probusiness mentality of the government, which quickly suppressed labor strife.

Control over Korean labor was an area of special interest for the police, who expressed concern over communist infiltration of factories and mines. The police intervened in strikes and labor disputes to protect production levels and to guard against socialist encroachment. In at least one instance, communists attempted to infiltrate semiofficial organizations and turn Korean workers against the Japanese. Two men, Pang Yong-p'il and Yu Ryu-rok, organized a group and planned to recruit 2,000 miners and railway workers for their group. However, the colonial police force arrested the two masterminds of this plot before serious harm occurred to production.[111]

More disturbing to the police was that, late in the war, Korean nationalism surfaced as a cause of resistance. A police publication carried the following interesting account of malingering:

> In the past there were no problems with ideological-oriented insurrections, but recently they have occurred. There were examples of recent ideological, or bad, elements that intervene and intentionally obstruct production in order to usher in the defeat of the empire. I will give one or two examples.
>
> First, an immigrant Korean, who is now in custody and being investigated for violating the Peace Preservation Law, intentionally agitated other workers. In August 1942, at Yūbari Mine in Hokkaido, ideological malcontent Ch'oe Wŏn-jŏng urged the other workers not to work and planned to promote national consciousness and proclaimed the idea of independence, saying, "If Japan loses the war, we can assist Korean independence by supporting the Allies. If Korea is to be independent, there will be no discriminatory treatment and concrete benefits will come to Koreans. In order to usher in Japan's defeat, we should neglect our work and not procure the coal from the mine."[112]

The police noted that the productivity of the miners slowed from clearing three meters and ninety centimeters per day to two meters and sixty centimeters. The police wryly noted their conundrum: If they arrested all agitators, production would grind to a halt; if they did not make arrests, the slowdown would continue and it would set a bad precedent for Koreans at other mines. The police arrested the ringleaders, but not all of the malingerers.

Despite the government's push for the brotherhood and unity of Korea and Japan, Koreans continued to experience discrimination from employers and local government officials, the consequence of which was the solidification of Korean ethnic identity. Korean students with advanced educations personally experienced the disconnect between colonial propaganda and reality. An August 1944 GGK document noted,

> As soon as the war started, students developed in their subconsciousness a deep defeatism along with a weakening of Japanese national consciousness. This came about because of the difficulty of entering college. There are those who have fallen into an anti-Japanese consciousness. As before, there are many people who, to a considerable degree, grossly overestimate the economic capability of the Anglo-American enemy and dream of an independent Korea. They want Japan to lose a drawn-out war of attrition. They consider it an unparalleled opportunity for Korean ethnic liberation. These thoughts go together with the narrow feelings that are particular to younger students and can lead to inappropriate actions. While this trend is seen only among a portion of the students, it is apparent they have banded together in secret societies and planned for unrest and polluted the sacred academic halls. There are people who are committing punishable acts.... Nearly all are ethnic incidents that look forward to an improvement of Korean spiritual [J: seishinteki] affiliation as well as intellectual, physical, and economic power. Through these activities, they show they are preparing for Korean independence. Furthermore, through changes in the recent war situation there is a tendency to assume the defeat of the empire and Korean independence.[113]

This quote hints at many causes and areas of resistance and indicates that Japanese authorities harbored deep concern over the rise of Korean nationalism. Unfortunately, the author does not provide specifics, but makes clear that students were working toward Korean independence a year before the end of the war.

Violence, another form of workplace resistance, usually erupted in response to frustration with poor work conditions. In one situation, a Japanese commander assaulted a Korean military civilian for not showing the proper respect. In retaliation, twenty-five Koreans assaulted the commander. The ringleader was punished with ten days in jail.[114] In another case, one Korean who served as a prison guard in Indonesia remembered that the military contractors were held after their contracts expired, which led to an exchange of gunshots between Koreans and Japanese.[115]

In one suicidal act of defiance on January 4, 1942, three Korean civilian employees of the military stationed near Jakarta, Indonesia, were told that they were being reassigned to Singapore. Outraged at the order, they stole guns and went on a shooting spree that killed or wounded a dozen Japanese, including a Japanese general. They committed suicide before they could be captured. The three had warned other Korean civilian employees in the military of their intentions and had told them to flee once they heard gunshots, but none of their comrades alerted the Japanese.[116]

In another violent act of resistance, in July 1944, twenty-nine men on Hokkaido organized themselves into the Taesang Mountain Bamboo Spear Movement and began a war of resistance against Japan by constructing a mountain fortress and making bamboo weapons. Over the course of twenty days, the Japanese police attempted three offensives to dislodge the group, but each failed. The rebellion ended when the police successfully cut off their food supply and captured the men as they foraged for food.[117]

CONCLUSION

The collective national memory of Korea places victimization and oppression center stage in the national story. However, the wartime history of Korea is a complex amalgamation of individual stories. Untold numbers of Koreans, both workers and recruiters, cooperated to their own economic benefit; large numbers cooperated with recruitment policies and benefitted themselves, but did so with the implicit understanding that, if they resisted, government authorities would follow through with coercive measures. Not every person mobilized suffered low wages, discrimination, or coercion. The national story must include the masses of people who quietly followed orders and labored in mines and factories or in the fields, as well as those who personally profited from cooperation.

Studies that emphasize resistance and victimization alone tend to ignore the extent of Korean cooperation and choice. There is no denying that the colonial regime successfully used coercion to mobilize hundreds of thousands of people. But those who seized opportunities for personal gain and those who benefitted from their wartime experiences should also be taken into account. Young men and women willingly signed contracts to escape poverty, to get away from provincial life, to pursue educational opportunities, or to seek a better-paying career. Of course, not all benefitted. An ancillary point is that it was largely the poorer Koreans who suffered the most coercive recruitment and ended up in the worst working conditions; this was also true for Japanese citizens. Thus, their story is as much about class as it is about ethnicity.[118]

It must be noted that Koreans did not passively submit to government demands. They resisted labor mobilization through everyday forms of resistance. Koreans evaded labor duty, deserted jobs, sabotaged equipment, and malingered at work. The colonial regime was unable to effectively prevent or respond to tactics such as evasion, desertion, or the spreading of rumors. What historical significance should be attributed to Korean resistance to labor needs? Did it affect Japan's war capability? A number of Korean and Japanese scholars extrapolate that Korean resistance threatened the fascist system.[119] Although this may overstate the power of Korean resistance, it is true that rumors, evasion, strikes, and desertion challenged the hegemony of the Japanese system, even if they lacked the coordination and breadth to factor in Japan's defeat.

CONCLUSION

Japan's imperial endeavor in Korea is a subject of extraordinary sensitivity and controversy, so one must approach it with respect for the pain of the Korean nation as well as for historical veracity. Japan's dominion over Korea brought both exploitation and modernization in a mixture that is hotly debated. Until recently, most academic accounts of Korea's colonial past have emphasized Japan's exploitation of Koreans, the victimization and suffering of the Korean people, and the activities of Korean nationalists in China and America. This field of research, collectively called the "national historical paradigm," is ingrained in the collective national memories of both North and South Korea and has taken on political meaning. However, the thirty-five years of Japanese colonial rule in Korea, especially the war years (which are considered the darkest hours), cannot be summarily categorized in purely negative outcomes (exploitation, victimization, and enslavement). Colonialism is too diverse and complicated to approach with mental blinders. Once we broaden our view beyond exploitation to include the legal and organizational aspects of mobilization, we discover much that is worth examining.

A close examination of Japan's mobilization policies in Korea helps illuminate the practical nature and modus operandi of the Japanese. Colonial authorities watered down the laws and policies used for Japanese citizens to suit social circumstances in Korea. The legal foundation carefully erected for Korea's mobilization indicates that the Japanese made an effort to legitimize their policies and to enlist Korean support. The Government-General of Korea (GGK) largely adhered to the laws until the last, desperate months of the war. These laws also show that the GGK delineated the boundaries between the responsibilities of Japanese citizens and those of Korean subjects. The ethnocentricity of Japanese citizens made them hesitant to trust Koreans or to empower them, even during a war. Underlying these concerns were worries that the Koreans might demand political equality without sharing full responsibility. Equally important, the abbreviated versions of mobilization laws show that Japan was concerned that significant numbers of Koreans were not properly prepared for military or industrial service to the state at the outbreak of the war.

The Japanese military had no legal provision for extensive Korean military service until the Korean Special Volunteer Soldier System in 1938. The Japanese army procrastinated inducting Koreans, because military service was a bastion of Japanese citizenship, and army officials, along with most Japanese, believed that Koreans were unworthy of and unprepared for military service. The volunteer system was designed to acculturate Korean society to military service over the course of three to five decades, before the implementation of the universal draft system. From 1938 to 1943, Koreans submitted over 800,000 applications for the volunteer soldier system, but the military accepted only 17,000 (one in forty) Koreans into the military. The low percentage of applicants inducted into the military is a testament to the limited military contribution expected of Koreans during the early years of the war. However, war with the United States led to a conscription system decades sooner than expected. Even then, the army instituted a more limited military conscription system for Koreans than existed for Japanese, and then delayed the enlistment of Koreans by thirty months. This is seen in the exemptions provided to Korean men if they were conscripted as laborers, worked as military civilians, or lacked an elementary education. The first two exemptions were not available to Japanese men. Also, only twenty-year-old Koreans were drafted, whereas the draft age for Japanese men decreased as the war progressed.

Labor laws were also altered to suit Korea's social and labor conditions. The National General Mobilization Law (NGML), the most important law in the mobilization of Korean labor, was altered to account for Korea's less-developed social and economic conditions: First, Korean women were not subject to the NGML, unlike numerous Japanese women; second, Korean men conscripted under the NGML were exempted from military service, a provision not available to Japanese men; and third, the law had three forms of recruitment—company-directed recruitment, government-directed recruitment, and conscription. The first two forms did not exist in Japan, and labor conscription was extended to Korea in 1942, three years after it was implemented in Japan. Even then, large numbers of Koreans were not conscripted until 1944.

The GGK, while powerful and capable of brutality, could not secure the complete, uniform compliance of Koreans. The colonial administration had an impressive amount of leverage within Korean society through policemen, city officials, and village heads, as well as through law enforcement agencies, schools, and the rationing system. Yet, despite this coercive capability, the colonial regime was vulnerable to noncompliance and resistance. In most instances, its inability to exert greater control over or make full use of the Korean people stemmed from myopic prewar social and educational policies. Too few Korean men could adequately speak Japanese, very few had martial training, and only a small number had been imbued with Japanese patriotism.

Japanese authorities approached mobilization with caution, so as not to drive Koreans into the arms of the Comintern and not to spark Korean ethnic nationalism. The March First Independence Movement of 1919 instilled an anxiety in the GGK that Koreans were not passive, powerless subalterns with limitless patience. The GGK had the power to arrest nationalists, to coerce the reluctant, and to subdue an uprising, but the regime thought it best not to antagonize the Korean people, especially during the war. Concerns over the extent to which Koreans would support the war effort, as well as a lingering Korean hostility toward Japan, contributed to the use of propaganda and the intensification of longstanding policies to assimilate Koreans. These imperialization (J: *kōminka*) policies, while unpleasant for the Koreans, offered Japan's war machine a reasonable alternative to the use of blatant force. However, social and political equality were not the intended outcome of assimilation; instead, assimilation was a rhetorical method to assuage wartime mobilization.

Untold numbers of Korean men refused to cooperate with the military and labor mobilization policies. Colonial authorities pressured young men and students to submit an application for the volunteer soldier systems. Yet government persuasion failed to achieve complete compliance, as half of all young men rebuffed government enticements. On the labor front, the colonial regime and the central government in Tokyo proved vulnerable to malingering, strikes, desertion, and other types of resistance. Evasion and desertion grew so prevalent that, by the end of the war, industrial and military recruiters increasingly resorted to extralegal measures to meet quotas.

Generally speaking, Japanese authorities sought to secure the cooperation of Koreans rather than rely on coercion and brute force. The mobilization process began with revisions of applicable laws to encourage Koreans
to accept their duty as Japanese subjects. Japanese government authorities
and businesses enticed cooperation with mobilization policies by providing opportunities for Koreans to escape poverty, move to the city, improve
their social status, and ingratiate themselves within the colonial nexus of
power. In conjunction with this, laborers were offered decent wages and
good working conditions; soldiers were promised glory. Only after these
enticements failed did the GGK apply small degrees of coercion—for
example, local officials visited individuals' families to remind them of
their responsibility. And if the targeted individual remained unmoved,
government officials proceeded to exert increasing amounts of coercion
and intimidation on the recruit and their family. Nonconformists became
targets of full-scale coercion and risked the economic and social well-being
of themselves and their families.

In regard to military service, many inductees sought out opportunities
to serve in the military as a way to gain glory, improve their social status,
and secure meaningful employment. A handful of Koreans sincerely supported Japan; others merely wanted to learn technical and military skills. It
is important to remember that the army enlisted only 3 percent of volunteer
solider applicants, indicating that applicants had to be proactive and show
an eagerness in order for the military to choose them over others. However, many men successfully evaded military service. Thousands refused
to cooperate with the volunteer or conscription systems and found ways
to disqualify themselves by dropping out of school, purposefully failing
physical or oral examinations, and so forth. Large numbers avoided military service by submitting to labor conscription, leaving Korea for China,
or altering family registries.

With regard to labor mobilization, Koreans were better able to control
their own fates. Large numbers of laborers cooperated with mobilization
policies because they were attracted by the wages or the opportunity to
learn a lifelong technical skill. Young men used economic opportunities created by the war to escape Korea's unpredictable agriculture-based
economy, which frequently suffered from drought, famine, and abject
poverty. Laborers who felt exploited, discriminated against, or misled by

recruiters often responded by deserting workplaces, malingering at work, or going on strike.

An intriguing yet little addressed part of this story is that Koreans were actively involved in the mobilization of other Koreans. Nearly one-third of the police force and a large number of patriotic unit heads were Korean. Policemen and patriotic unit heads, along with teachers, most often spear-headed government efforts to fill government quotas for labor projects, entreat applications for the volunteer soldier system, pressure young men to respond to conscription notices, and lead labor recruiters to the homes of individuals targeted for mobilization. These Koreans were critical to the Japanese government's recruitment of labor and soldiers; it is doubtful that Japan could have located and recruited Koreans as extensively without the assistance of Koreans underlings.

Japan's actions in Korea were, for the most part, within the norm of global colonial practice. The similarities to and differences from inter-national colonial mobilization practices provide a useful backdrop. The British and French had mobilized colonial subjects from India and Africa for service in both world wars, as well as decades earlier for local conflagra-tions. France mobilized its colonies in Indochina, West Africa, and North Africa; Great Britain mobilized its colonies in India, Malaysia, Caribbean, and Africa; and the United States mobilized the Philippine peoples. The interesting point here is that Japan was so hesitant to use its colonial sub-jects as soldiers.

Japan's colonial mobilization polices were distinct in several ways. Most notably, the Japanese military integrated Koreans into existing military units; the British and French created separate units for their colonial sol-diers. For example, in East Africa, Africans were attached to the King's African Rifles, which was not part of the regular British army. The United States Army segregated nonwhite citizens into their own units until after World War II. Furthermore, units of nonwhites received less training and were armed with inferior weapons, whereas Koreans and Taiwanese were theoretically equals with Japanese soldiers. Some Koreans received pro-motions that put them in direct command over Japanese comrades—an unheard of practice in Western colonialism. This is not to suggest that the Japanese were enlightened, rather, it is insightful to know that the Japanese used integration as an ideological tool to assimilate Korean men.

World War II was a total war; governments mobilized all available resources—including colonial subjects and minority populations. Colonial authorities had to consider how wartime mobilization might affect the colonial relationship. The wartime experiences of Korean and African soldiers, which included discrimination as well as technical training, stimulated racial consciousness. During World War I, Indian and African soldiers and laborers saw Europe firsthand and were shocked to see the social problems and military weakness of Europe. They learned to operate radios, drive heavy equipment, shoot guns, kill men in hand-to-hand combat, and do other things that would later facilitate their fight for independence. These skills and experiences were not soon forgotten in the postwar period and contributed to calls for equality. More importantly, colonial subjects witnessed the shortcomings of their European overlords. Britain's colonial rule in Africa and South Asia had been shaken by two world wars, and Africans and Asians no longer accepted their subservient status to whites. Nonwhite soldiers who traveled overseas met Europeans who were less educated and more ignorant than themselves. Such experiences left a deep sense of political consciousness within these men, thereby altering the dynamic of the metropole-colony relationship and speeding the decline of colonialism.

The colonial era, and particularly the Asia-Pacific War, remains a delicate issue in South Korea because national memory conflates the experiences of all Koreans into a single narrative that accentuates the exploitation of the Korean people. If all forms of state-sponsored mobilization are accounted for, more than seven million people, or rather, seven million instances of official mobilization took place from 1937 to 1945.[1] This number does not include the hundreds of thousands of laborers recruited outside the National General Mobilization Law (NGML), namely the role of women who worked in light industries and agriculture, and of students who spent school hours performing war-related work.

The true extent of the mobilization of Korea will never be known, because the Japanese government destroyed documents after Japan's surrender in August 1945. Other hindrances to a better understanding of the war period include the formation of two separate regimes, the devastating effects of the Korean War (1950–1953), and the subsequent Cold War chill between the two Koreas. It is impossible to calculate the number of Koreans who died during the Asia-Pacific War because many people from the southern provinces stayed in the north, and vice versa. As a result, many Koreans never returned to their hometowns, so it is not possible to know what happened to them during or after the war. Similarly, no serious reckoning of wartime mobilization took place prior to the outbreak of the Korean War, so no accurate casualty list has been compiled. To my knowledge, there has been no collaboration between the current governments in Korea to determine the number of wartime deaths.

In the absence of solid evidence, the number of Korean deaths during the war remains a contested issue. In 1953 the Welfare Ministry in Japan estimated that 22,182 Korean soldiers, sailors, and military civilians died during the war.[2] In fact, approximately 21,000 are enshrined at Yasukuni Shrine, which commemorates Japan's war dead. Some scholars place military deaths as high as 50,884.[3] To this should be added the deaths of laborers and civilians who died throughout the Japanese empire. For example, untold thousands died in the Allied bombings in Japan, and upward of 30,000 died from the atomic bombings of Hiroshima and Nagasaki. In all, the Japanese government has confirmed 131,955 Korean deaths related to wartime service.[4]

Most studies of laborers and soldiers include a discussion of the postwar plight of these men and women, namely in relation to repatriation and war crimes trials. The slow pace of repatriation of Korean nationals following World War II meant that thousands of Koreans were stranded for months, even years, in China, Southeast Asia, and other places, waiting to return to Korea.[5] In some instances, Koreans were unable to return to their homeland; over 40,000 Koreans who lived on southern Sakhalin, many working as miners, were forbidden by Stalin's regime from returning home. Only after the collapse of the Soviet Union have those on Sakhalin been allowed to return, but many lack the finances to do so.

While Koreans were victims of Japanese imperialism, they were also perpetrators of acts of aggression during Japan's war of expansion. This is a paradox of colonialism.[6] Koreans ignore the pain that their countrymen inflicted on others during the Asia-Pacific War. Korean soldiers and military civilians earned a notorious reputation in Southeast Asia, where they are remembered as aggressive, abusive, and violent—not as victims. After the war, 148 Koreans were sentenced as war criminals. Koreans need to become more global in their perspective and to establish links between their experiences and those of other former colonies. Instead, Koreans often pass the blame to Japanese overseers for the heinous acts committed by Koreans.[7]

Unfortunately, historical remembrance in South Korea has become rigidly politicized and excludes counternarratives that suggest widespread cooperation and acquiescence by average Koreans. The personal experiences of industrial laborers, volunteer soldiers, and conscript soldiers, when examined (unaltered) in large numbers, create an inconvenient truth for the national historical paradigm. Unedited oral histories show that many Korean laborers and soldiers were negatively affected, but, conversely, there was a good number who benefitted from the war. Within the Korean community on the peninsula and overseas, the fear of being branded as pro-Japanese hinders open discussion of people's wartime activities and sincere academic inquiry. For example, in 1999 the author had lunch with two elderly Korean men in Hawaii. One mentioned that he had worked with radios in Japan during World War II; when I mentioned my research on Korean laborers and soldiers during the war, he refused to discuss the subject any further—much to my chagrin.[8]

In the larger historical context, Japan's surrender in August 1945 came suddenly for the Korean people, who then fell victim to international politics: The United States and the Soviet Union divided the Korean Peninsula at the 38th parallel, which resulted in the emergence of independent regimes in the north and south in 1948. The division of Korea has contributed to the politicization of history, as regimes in North and South Korea have appropriated a particular notion of history and national identity to legitimize their raison d'être. Each government uses history, namely the resistance activities of its founding fathers, to bolster its ability to speak for the ethnic Korean nation. As a result, history in South Korea is designed to perpetuate the patriotic fervor of the South Korean population, not to build historical veracity. The passage of time has only recently fostered objective scholarship.

Korean historical remembrance of the colonial era is dominated by a sense of *han*, a lingering feeling of injustice. For many Koreans, there has been no closure to the wartime historical wrongs committed by Japan: laborers who worked in Japan are *still* unable to withdraw the money their employers automatically deposited into savings accounts; former soldiers are denied veteran benefits similar to those the Japanese government provides to Japanese veterans (because Koreans lost Japanese citizenship when the war ended); Korean atom bomb victims were denied benefits similar to those provided to Japanese victims of the atom bomb until 2005; and comfort women continue their litigation to win appropriate compensation for the abuse and pain they suffered while employed—some say "enslaved"—as military prostitutes. The ongoing suffering of these individuals remains a salient issue in contemporary diplomatic relations between the two Koreas and Japan; North and South Koreans demand that the Japanese government assume more accountability for the exploitation of Koreans during the war. However, the Japanese government has instead obfuscated the process by which victims can gain redress.

The Japanese government maintains that it no longer bears legal responsibility for compensating South Koreans for anything that happened during the colonial era, and that the 1965 normalization treaty absolved it of all legal claims from the South Korean government and its citizens.[9] As part of the treaty, Japan paid three hundred million dollars in grants and provided an additional five hundred million in loans as compensation to South Korea, the purpose of which remains a contested subject between South Korea and Japan. The South Korean government used most of the funds to build industries and infrastructure, providing minimal compensation to victims. Koreans feel that the treaty did not absolve Japan of all postwar claims made against their government, and that a reckoning still needs to happen. Partly for this reason, comfort women and laborers continue to seek redress through legal actions in Japan.

Former Korean soldiers, comfort women, laborers, and victims of the atom bombs have relied on litigation to correct the perceived injustices they experienced.[10] A sampling of the lawsuits shows the range of legal issues: Former Korean soldiers and military civilian prisoners of war who were taken to Siberia by the Soviet Union after the war are suing to gain pensions that are available to Japanese citizens of similar background. Bereaved families of the wartime dead have sued to have their relatives removed from Yasukuni Shrine. Laborers who had savings in Japanese banks or wages withheld by corporations could not access these funds following the war; these individuals have filed lawsuits to access to their hard-earned money. However, their litigation has not helped resolve any outstanding issues with the Japanese government.[11] The Ministry of Health and Welfare reimbursed one man for insurance payments he made during the war, a total of thirty-five yen (about thirty-five cents), there was no adjustment for inflation or interest.[12] And in December 2009 seven women who had been deceived into working in a factory in Japan for two years were similarly refunded premiums totaling ninety-nine yen—less than a dollar—each.[13]

It may be worth pointing out that the United States failed to fulfill its promises to 250,000 Filipino soldiers who joined the military to fight against Japan. A February 23, 2009, report by CNN stated that the United States had promised Filipino soldiers full veteran benefits. Many of these soldiers were captured by the Japanese and were part of the Bataan Death March. However, in 1946 President Harry S. Truman signed a bill that rescinded the original promise. After sixty years of petitioning and picketing, the Obama Administration finally agreed to provide fifteen thousand dollars to each Filipino veteran who was a citizen, and nine thousand to noncitizens.

More than compensation, Koreans demand that the Japanese government offer a heartfelt apology that specifically acknowledges the damage and pain inflicted on the Korean nation. Several Japanese prime ministers, including Naoto Kan in August and again in December 2010, expressed deep regret over the suffering inflicted on Koreans during Japan's rule. However, Koreans feel that these blanket statements, while a step forward from past statements, do not allay Korean anger. Ahn Young-hwan, spokesman for the Korean ruling Grand National Party, says that Naoto's statement "has no mention of illegitimacy of the forced annexation and Koreans forced to work as sex slaves or manual laborers by the Japanese army."[14] For Koreans, these apologies admit to no wrongdoing by Japan. Koreans seek a more detailed apology, as well as compensation for specific cases, such as the comfort women. Utsumi Aiko, a Japanese scholar with numerous works to her credit, supports the Korean cause. She states,

> Koreans were mobilized for the Japanese war effort as soldiers, sailors, civilian military employees, and military laborers. It would seem only natural that they be compensated in the same way as are Japanese. Yet the Japanese government only reiterates the Japanese nationality requirement [to receive benefits]. It is worth noting that ... Koreans did not relinquish their Japanese nationality by choice. Instead, they were unilaterally stripped of it through a

single notification from the Japanese government. If the Japanese government today regards these individuals as foreigners, then the morally appropriate action would be to compensate them with all due speed for the pains inflicted by colonizing them and for treating them as "Japanese" in the past. These former "Imperial soldiers" suffered from the Japanese government's pursuit of self-interest; today they struggle to receive compensation from the same government. For those from formerly colonized nations who served as soldiers, sailors, and civilian military employees, the Asia-Pacific Wars are not over.[15]

Japan's refusal to apologize in a straightforward manner and to compensate those who suffered have contributed to Koreans' sense of historical injustice. Until the Japanese rectify their historical remembrance, Koreans will likely continue to adhere to the nationalist historical paradigm that portrays Koreans as victims of Japanese totalitarianism. This paradigm, and the corresponding historical remembrance in the public sphere, keeps alive the suffering of individual Koreans; this suffering is then extrapolated to be Korean national suffering and national humiliation.[16] Korean historical studies will also continue to use politicized history as a moral weapon to shame the Japanese into an apology.

However, the Japanese, like most former colonial powers, have placed their imperial past behind them and have moved forward with a clear consciousness. Their colonial-era propaganda of equality and claims that their imperial rule brought modernity have become the established history in most colonial powers. The United States is no different; Americans remember themselves as a benevolent colonial power, but American history textbooks exclude references to the Philippine-American War as well as American abuses of the Filipino people. The Japanese, similarly, remember the contributions they made to Korea's economy and modernization, but minimize the negative effects they had on the lives of Koreans.

Because academics have historically focused on the exploitation and suffering of Koreans under the Japanese, it is all too often overlooked that Japanese citizens also experienced depravity and exploitation at the hands of their own government. Certainly, scholars must examine Korea within the larger international context of colonial mobilization, but it is also necessary to compare the experiences of Japanese citizens with their Korean counterparts. Korean and Japanese subjects alike worked and fought in depraved conditions; the diet of both peoples steadily declined during the war; and the populations of both experienced a great amount of demographic dislocation and widespread intrusion of the state into everyday life. The key difference is that Japanese citizens were fighting and suffering for their own nation—and stood to benefit through national pride and economic advantages; Koreans, on the other hand, were at the disposal of the Japanese state and stood to gain little from a Japanese victory.

Colonial regimes often treated colonial subjects as mere mercenaries and as an expendable resource. As individuals, they risked their lives for meager personal rewards. As subjects, their efforts helped to perpetuate the empire, which directly enhanced the suppression of their home country. What did the colonized person gain when the empire won a war or annexed a new territory? Little, if any, benefit went to their homeland or its indigenous population; conversely, the colonized peoples often stood to gain more at a national level if their colonial masters lost. This was the case for colonial Korea during the Asia-Pacific War. This is the great irony of colonial mobilization confronted by all colonial peoples.

NOTES

NOTES TO INTRODUCTION

1   Ōmura Kenzō, *Tatakō hantō shiganhei* [Fighting peninsular volunteer soldiers] (Seoul: Tōbusho, 1943), 132–46.

2   Higuchi Yūichi, *Kōgun heishi ni sareta Chōsenjin: 15nen Sensōka no sōdōin taisei no kenkyū* [Koreans who were forced to be imperial soldiers: Study on the general mobilization system during the Fifteen-Year War] (Tokyo: Shakai Hyōronsha, 1992), 120 and 131; and Hanil Munjae Yŏn'guwŏn, *Ppaeakkin choguk kkŭllyŏgan saramdŭl: Ch'ilpaengman Chōsonin kangje tongwŏn ŭi yŏksa* [Stolen country, taken away people: A history of seven million Koreans' forced mobilization] (Seoul: Asia Munhwasa, 1995), 82–84. Korean manpower constituted a small part of the overall Japanese military and workforce. In 1940 Japan had a workforce of 32.5 million laborers, with 8.1 employed in manufacturing and construction. The army had 376,000 on active duty (two million in the reserves) in 1940, and five million on active duty in 1945; the navy had 291,000 men in 1941, and 1.66 million in 1945.

3   Military service was considered a sacred right and obligation of all qualified Japanese men, even if not always eagerly welcomed by those inducted into the military.

4   For an excellent discussion of this, see James C. Scott, *Weapons of the Weak: Everyday Forms of Peasant Resistance* (New Haven, CT: Yale University Press, 1985), xvi.

5   Theodore Jun Yoo, *The Politics of Gender in Colonial Korea: Education, Labor, and Health, 1910–1945* (Berkeley: University of California Press, 2008), 8.

6   Joung Yole Rew (Chŏng-nyŏl Yu), *Japanese Colonial Government of Korea: Empire Building in East Asia* (P'aju, South Korea: KSI, Han'guk Haksul Chŏngbo, 2008), 240; and Kang Tŏk-sang, "Background to History-Related Conflicts between Korea and Japan," in *The Historical Perceptions of Korea and Japan*, ed. Hyun Dae-song (Paju, South Korea: Nanam Publishing House, 2008), 341.

7   Gi-Wook Shin and Michael Robinson, eds., *Colonial Modernity in Korea* (Cambridge, MA: Harvard University Press, 1999), 5.

8   See Pak Kyŏng-sik, *Chōsenjin kyōsei renkō no kiroku* [A record of the forced displacement of Koreans] (Tokyo: Miraisha, 1965); and *Nihon teikoku shugi no Chōsen shihai (ka)* [Japanese imperialistic domination of Korea], vol. 2 (Tokyo: Aoki Shoten, 1975), 163.

9   Aimé Césaire, speaking of European imperialism, captured the essence of the *kangje yŏnhaeng* paradigm when he stated, "Between colonizer and colonized there is room only for forced labor, intimidation, pressure, the police, taxation, theft, rape, compulsory

corps, contempt, mistrust, arrogance, self-complacency, swinishness, brainless elites, degraded masses." See Aimé Césaire, *Discourse on Colonialism* (New York: Monthly Review Press, 1972).

10 Miyata Setsuko, *Chōsen minshū to "kōminka" seisaku* [The Korean people and the "imperialization" policy] (Tokyo: Miraisha, 1985); Hayashi Eidai, ed., *Chōsenjin kōgun heishi: Nyūginiasen no tokushiganhei* [Korean imperial soldiers: Special volunteer soldiers of the New Guinea front] (Tokyo: Tsuge Shobō, 1995); and Utsumi Aiko, *Kimu wa naze sabakareta no ka: Chōsenjin BC-kyū senpan no kiseki* [Why was Kim tried? The trajectory of Korean BC-class war criminals] (Tokyo: Asahi Shinbun Shuppan, 2008).

11 Three examples include Chŏng T'ae-hŏn and Ki Kwang-sŏ, "Ilche ŭi panillyukchŏk Chosŏnin kangje nomu tongwŏn kwa imgŭm t'alch'wi" [The Japanese imperialist's inhumane mobilization of Koreans and wage exploitation], *Yŏksa wa hyŏnsil* 50 (2003): 403–28; Chŏng Hye-gyŏng, *Chosŏnin kangje yŏnhaeng, kangje nodong* [Korean forced displacement, forced labor] (Seoul: Sŏnin, 2006); and Yamada Shōji, Tadashi Koshō, and Higuchi Yūichi, *Chōsenjin senji rōdō dōin* [Korean wartime labor mobilization] (Tokyo: Iwanami Shoten, 2005). Yamada, Tadashi, and Higuchi defend forced mobilization studies against recent revisionist criticism.

12 George Hicks, *The Comfort Women: Japan's Brutal Regime of Enforced Prostitution in the Second World War* (New York: W. W. Norton, 1995); Yoshimi Yoshiaki and Suzanne O'Brien, *Comfort Women: Sexual Slavery in the Japanese Military During World War II* (New York: Columbia University Press, 2000); and Michael Weiner, *Race and Migration in Imperial Japan* (New York: Routledge, 1994).

13 Janice C. H. Kim, *To Live to Work: Factory Women in Colonial Korea, 1910–1945* (Stanford: Stanford University Press, 2009), 6.

14 Shin and Robinson, *Colonial Modernity in Korea*, 2.

15 Carter J. Eckert, "Epilogue: Exorcising Hegel's Ghosts: Toward a Postnationalist Historiography of Korea," in Shin and Robinson, *Colonial Modernity*, 365–66.

16 C. Sarah Soh, *The Comfort Women: Sexual Violence and Postcolonial Memory in Korea and Japan* (Chicago: University of Chicago Press, 2008), xii. Italics in the original.

NOTES TO CHAPTER 1

1 Lynn, "Limits of the Colonial State," 2–3.

2 Chong-sik Lee, *Japan and Korea: The Political Dimension* (Stanford: Stanford University Press, 1985), 6. Frank P. Baldwin, Jr., examines numerous sources for casualties. One source lists 1,199 killed and wounded, while another claims that Japanese police killed 7,645 and wounded 45,462. See Baldwin's "The March First Movement: Korean Challenge and Japanese Response" (PhD diss., Columbia University, 1969), 233.

3 Prasenjit Duara, *Culture, Power, and the State: Rural North China, 1900–1942* (Stanford: Stanford University Press, 1988), 5.

4 Daniel Byman and Matthew Waxman, *The Dynamics of Coercion: American Foreign*

Policy and the Limits of Military Might (New York: Cambridge University Press, 2002), 3.

5 Ibid., 3–5.

6 Han-Kyo Kim, "The Japanese Colonial Administration in Korea: An Overview," in *Korea under Japanese Colonial Rule: Studies of the Policy and Techniques of Japanese Colonialism,* ed. Andrew Nahm (Kalamazoo: Western Michigan University Press, 1973), 45.

7 Yi Ki-baik, *A New History of Korea,* trans. Edward W. Wagner and Edward J. Schultz (Seoul: Ilchokak, 1984), 353.

8 While the Japanese were not murderous, they were far from enlightened. Between 1939 and 1944 the regime imprisoned around 5,600 political prisoners.

9 Gi-Wook Shin and Do-Hyun Han, "Colonial Corporatism: The Rural Revitalization Campaign, 1932–1940," in Shin and Robinson, *Colonial Modernity in Korea,* 75.

10 This should be compared to the British in India. In 1922 Britain had 1,200 members of the civil service, 700 British police officers, and 76,953 soldiers to rule 315 million Indian subjects. Korea had a population of 24 million in 1943. See Judith M. Brown, "War and the Colonial Relationship: Britain, India and the War of 1914–1918," in *India and World War I,* ed. DeWitt C. Ellinwood and S. D. Pradhan (Columbia, MO: South Asia Books, 1978), 24.

11 Chulwoo Lee, "Modernity, Legality, and Power in Korea under Japanese Rule," in Shin and Robinson, *Colonial Modernity in Korea,* 37.

12 The Peace Preservation Law was enacted after the passage of universal male suffrage in 1925. It was designed to counter the growing power of labor unions and leftist movements. In 1941 the Diet expanded the scope of the law.

13 For a discussion of this historical animosity see Kang Tŏk-sang, "Background to History-Related Conflicts," 325–48.

14 Chōsen Sōtokufu, Jōhōkyoku, *Atarashiki Chōsen* [New Korea] (Seoul: Chōsen Gyōsei Gakkai, 1944), 55; and Maeda Hajime, *Tokushu Rōmusha no Rōmu kanri* [Labor management of special labor] (Tokyo: Sankai Dokan, 1944), 16.

15 E. Taylor Atkins, *Primitive Selves: Koreana in the Japanese Colonial Gaze, 1910-1945* (Berkeley: University of California Press, 2010), 148–50.

16 Maeda Hajime, *Tokushu Rōmusha,* 119. Also see *Chōsen Rōmu* 17, no. 3 (June 1942): 24–25.

17 *Shokugin Chōsa Geppō,* June 1941, 4–5.

18 *Chōsen Mesaretari* [Summoning Korea] (Pusan: Fusan Nippōsha, 1943), 23 and 31.

19 Rikugunshō Fukkan, "Chōsen shusshinhei toriatsukai kyōiku no sankō shiryō sōfu ni kansuru ken" [Case regarding remittance participation materials of treatment education of soldiers from Korea], Army Secret Order 2848, August 14, 1943, frame 0409; and Shōbei Shiota, "A 'Ravaged' People: The Koreans in World War II," *Japan Interpreter* 8, no. 1 (Winter 1971): 46.

20 Chōsengun Hōdōbu Kanshū, *Chōsen chōhei junbi tokuhon* [Preparatory reader on Korean conscription] (Seoul: Chōsen Tosho Shuppan, 1942), 64–78.

21 Sven Saaler, "Pan-Asianism in Modern Japanese History: Overcoming the Nation, Creating a Region, Forging an Empire," in *Pan-Asianism in Modern Japanese History: Colonialism, Regionalism, and Borders,* ed. Sven Saaler and J. Victor Koschmann (New York: Routledge, 2007), 10.

22 Hŏ Su-yŏl, "Chosŏnin nodongnyŏk ŭi kangje tongwŏn ŭi silt'ae: Chosŏn nae esŏ ŭi kangje tongwŏn chŏngch'aek ŭi chŏn'gae rŭl chungsim ŭro" [Conditions of the forced mobilization of the Korean labor force: Centering on the development of the forced mobilization policies within Korea], in *Ilche ŭi Han'guk singmin t'ongch'i*, ed. Ch'a Ki-byŏk (Seoul: Chŏmŭmsa, 1985), 305. This movement began in Japan one year prior to being implemented in Korea.

23 Mura Tokoo, "Tatakō Chōsen no tenbō" [View of fighting Korea], in *Tatakō Chōsen* (Tokyo: Asahi Shinbun Kaisha, 1945), 13.

24 Mark Caprio, *Japanese Assimilation Policies in Colonial Korea, 1910–1945* (Seattle: University of Washington Press, 2009), 10.

25 Jun Uchida, "'Brokers of Empire': Japanese Settler Colonialism in Korea, 1910–1937" (PhD diss., Harvard University, 2005), 466.

26 Mitarai Tatsuo, *Minami Sōtoku no Chōsen tōchi* [Governor-General Minami's Korea rule] (Keijō: Keijō Nippōsha, 1942), 27; Chōsen Sōtokufu, *Chōsen ni okeru kokumin seishin sōdōin* [National spirit mobilization in Korea] (Seoul: Chōsen Insatsu Kabushiki, 1940), 27–29; and Gi-Wook Shin, *Peasant Protest and Social Change in Colonial Korea* (Seattle: University of Washington Press, 1996), 136. For a theoretical discussion of this process, see Foucault, *History of Sexuality*, 94.

27 Wonmo Dong, "Japanese Colonial Policy and Practice in Korea, 1905–1945: A Study in Assimilation" (PhD diss., Georgetown University, 1965), 329.

28 Andrew J. Grajdanzev, *Modern Korea* (New York: Institute of Pacific Relations, 1944), 261.

29 Caprio, *Japanese Assimilation Policies*, 22.

30 Uchida, "Brokers of Empire," 427; and Michael Kim, "The Aesthetics of Total Mobilization in the Visual Culture of Late Colonial Korea," *Totalitarian Movements and Political Religions* 8, nos. 3–4 (September–December 2007): 483.

31 Carter J. Eckert, "Total War, Industrialization, and Social Change in Late Colonial Korea," in *The Japanese Wartime Empire*, ed. Peter Duus, Ramon Myers, and Mark Peattie (Princeton, NJ: Princeton University Press, 1996), 28. For a brief discussion of these two princes, see Yi Ki-dong, "Ilbon chegukkun ŭi Han'gugin changgyodŭl" [Korean officers of the Japanese army], *Sin Tong-a*, no. 299 (August 1984): 481–82.

32 Namiki Masahito, "Singminji sigi Chosŏnin ŭi chŏngch'i ch'amyŏ" [Korean political participants during the colonial era], in *Haebang chŏnhusa ŭi chaeinsik* [A rediscovery of history before and since liberation], ed. Chi-hyang Pak, Kim Ch'ŏl, Kim Il-yŏng, and Yi Yŏng-hun (Seoul: Ch'aek Sesang, 2006), 666–69.

33 Kyeong-hee Choi, "Another Layer of the Pro-Japanese Literature: Ch'oe Chŏnghŭi's 'The Wild Chrysanthemum,'" *Poetica* 52 (1999): 81–83. Ch'oe's "The Wild Chrysanthemum" was written in November 1942.

34 Yi Sŭng-yŏp, "Chosŏnin naesŏn ilch'eronja ŭi chŏnhyang kwa tonghwa ŭi nolli: Nokki Yŏnmaeng ŭi Chosŏnin ideollogŭ Hyŏng Yŏng-sŏp ŭl chungsim ŭro" [The logic of pro-Japanese Korean conversion and assimilation: Centering on the Green Flag's Korean ideologue Hyŏng Yŏng-sŏp], in *Kŭndae rŭl tasi ingnŭnda: Han'guk kŭndae insik ŭi saeroun p'aerŏdaim ŭl wihayŏ*, ed. Yun Hae-dong et al. (Seoul: Yŏksa Pip'yŏngsa, 2006), 230–38.

35 Caprio, *Japanese Assimilation Policies*, 196.

36 Yun Hae-dong, *Singminji kŭndae ŭi p'aerŏdoksŭ* [The paradox of colonial modernity] (Seoul: Hyumŏnisŭt'ŭ, 2007), 233–42.

37 Yun Ch'i-ho, *Yun Ch'i-ho ilgi* [Yun Ch'i-ho's diary], vol. 11, *1938–1943*, July 26, 1938 (Seoul: National History Compilation History, 1989), 80. Also see Mark E. Caprio, "Loyal Patriot? Traitorous Collaborator? The Yun Ch'iho Dairies and the Question of National Loyalty," *Journal of Colonialism and Colonial History* 7 no. 3 (2006), paragraphs 32–41.

38 Yi Sang-ŭi, "1930 nyŏndae Ilche ŭi nodong chŏngch'aek kwa nodongnyŏk sut'al" [Imperial Japan's labor policy and the exploitation of workers in the 1930s], *Han'guksa yŏn'gu* 94 (September 1996): 174–76; Soon-won Park, *Colonial Industrialization and Labor in Korea: The Onoda Cement Factory* (Cambridge, MA: Harvard University, 1999), 38–39; and Kobayashi Ei, "Chōsen Sōtokufu no rōdō ryoku seisaku ni tsuite" [On the Korean Government-General's labor force policies], *Keizai to Keizaigaku* 34 (1974): 58–65.

39 Takashi Fujitani, "Right to Kill, Right to Make Live: Koreans as Japanese and Japanese as Americans During WWII," *Representations* 99 no. 1 (2007): 15.

40 Caprio, *Japanese Assimilation Policies*, 153.

41 I-te Chen, "Japanese Colonialism in Korea and Formosa: A Comparison of Its Effects Upon the Development of Nationalism" (PhD diss., University of Pennsylvania, 1979), 160.

42 Bruce Cumings, *The Origins of the Korean War: Liberation and the Emergence of Separate Regimes, 1945–1947*, vol. 1 (Princeton, NJ: Princeton University Press, 1981), 26.

43 There has been a recent effort on behalf of the South Korean administrations to promote a national narrative that includes the military. The *hwarangdo* of the Silla dynasty, Yi Sunsin, and the *ŭibyŏng* are highlighted as exemplars of this military tradition. See chapters 5 and 7 of Sheila M. Jager's *Narratives of Nation Building in Korea: A Genealogy of Patriotism* (New York: M. E. Sharpe, 2003). However, throughout much of the Yi dynasty, social elites and commoners both considered military service onerous and something to be avoided.

44 Minami Jirō Denki Kankōkai, *Minami Jirō* (Tokyo: Minami Jirō Denki Kankōkai, 1957), 460–61; and *Chōsen Sōtokufu Teikoku Gikai setsumei shiryō* [Explanatory materials for the Imperial Diet, hereafter abbreviated *TGSS*], Diet 86, 1944, in *Ilcheha chŏnsi ch'ejegi chongch'aek saryo ch'ongsŏ* [Historical document collection of the policies of the wartime regime under Japanese imperialism] (hereafter abbreviated *ICCCSC*), vol. 22, ed. Kang Man-gil (Koyang: Han'guk Haksul Chŏngbo, 2000), 231.

45 *Asahi Shinbun*, Korea edition, May 15, 1942.

46 Rew, *Japanese Colonial Government*, 158.

47 Carter J. Eckert et al., *Korea Old and New: A History* (Cambridge, MA: Harvard University Press, 1990), 263–64. Also see Chōsen Sōtokufu, Dōjimukan, and Okayuki Takeshi, *Rikugun tokubetsu shiganhei tokuhon* [Army special volunteer soldier reader] (Seoul: Teikoku Chihō Gyōsei Kakkai Chōsen Honbu, 1939), in *ICCCSC* 56, 70–72.

48 Utsumi, *Kimu wa naze sabakareta*, 43.

49 See chapter 2 in Caprio, *Japanese Assimilation Policies*.

50 Chōsengun Sanbōchō, Koiso Kuniaki, "Chōsenjin shiganhei seido ni kansuru iken" [Opinion regarding the Korean volunteer soldier system], no. 354 (June 1937): frames 1130, 1136–43. Available at www.jacar.go.jp, ref. code c01004599600. For examples of this in Africa, see Ali A. Mazrui and Michael Tidy, *Nationalism and New States in Africa from about 1935 to the Present* (London: Heinemann, 1984), 19–20.

51 Melvin E. Page, "Introduction: Black Men in a White Men's War," in *Africa and the First World War*, ed. Melvin E. Page (New York: St. Martin's Press, 1987), 1.

52 David Killingray, "Guardians of Empire," in *Guardians of Empire: The Armed Forces of the Colonial Powers, c. 1700–1964*, ed. David Killingray and David Omissi (New York: Manchester University Press, 1999), 6.

53 Ibid., 10.

54 Anthony Clayton, *France, Soldiers, and Africa* (London: Brassey's Defence Publishers, 1988), 6.

55 Jaap de Moor, "The Recruitment of Indonesian Soldiers for the Dutch Colonial Army, c. 1700–1950," in Killingray and Omissi, *Guardians of Empire*, 56.

56 Many of the 200,000 sepoy mercenaries hired by the British East India Company revolted against the British presence in India. Several thousand British civilians and soldiers were killed during the mutiny.

57 Tan Tai Yong, *The Garrison State: The Military, Government, and Society in Colonial Punjab, 1849–1947* (London: SAGE Publications, 2005), 25; and Byron Farwell, *The Gurkhas* (New York: W. W. Norton, 1984), 72.

58 Moor, "Recruitment of Indonesian Soldiers," in Killingray and Omissi, *Guardians of Empire*, 58–61.

59 Ibid., 53–55

60 Farwell, *Gurkhas*, 23.

61 Page, *Africa and the First World War*, 5.

62 Charles J. Balesi, *From Adversaries to Comrades-in-Arms: West Africans and the French Military, 1885–1918* (Waltham, MA: Crossroads Press, 1979), 36.

63 Clayton, *France, Soldiers, and Africa*, 6; and Moshe Gershovich, *French Military Rule in Morocco: Colonialism and Its Consequences* (Portland, OR: Frank Cass, 2000), 174.

64 Balesi, *From Adversaries to Comrades*, 40

65 Gershovich, *French Military Rule*, 183–86.

66 Nancy E. Lawler, *Soldiers of Misfortune: Ivoirien Tirailleurs of World War II* (Athens: Ohio University Press, 1992), 22, 42.

67 Bales, *From Adversaries to Comrades*, 37; and Gershovich, *French Military Rule*, 184.

68 Hew Strachan, *The First World War in Africa* (New York: Oxford University Press, 2004), 3; and Killingray and Omissi, *Guardians of Empire*, 7.

69 Gershovich, *French Military Rule*, 183–86.

70 Andrew Selth, "Race and Resistance in Burma, 1942–1945," *Modern Asian Studies* 20, no. 3 (1986): 488.

71 David Killingray, "Military and Labour Recruitment in the Gold Coast during the Second World War," *Journal of African History* 23 (1982): 90.

72 Myron Echenberg, "Race, Ethnicity, and Social Class in the French Colonial Army: The Black African *Tirailleurs, 1857–1958*," in *Ethnic Armies: Polyethnic Armed Forces from the Time of the Habsburgs to the Age of the Superpowers*, ed. N. F. Dreisziger (Waterloo, ON: Wilfrid Laurier University Press, 1990), 50–51. The Armee d'Afrique was an exclusive force reserved for whites living in colonies.

73 Denis Judd, *Empire: The British Imperial Experience, from 1765 to the Present* (London: HarperCollins, 1996), 245.

74 Vincent Confer, *France and Algeria: The Problem of Civil and Political Reform, 1870–1920* (Syracuse, NY: Syracuse University Press, 1966), 97.

75 James K. Matthews, "Reluctant Allies: Nigerian Responses to Military Recruitment, 1914–1918," in *Africa and the First World War*, ed. Melvin E. Page (London: Macmillan, 1987), 96–98; and Killingray, "Military and Labour," 89–90.

76 Killingray and Omissi, *Guardians of Empire*, 10; and John H. Morrow, Jr., *The Great War: An Imperial History* (New York: Routledge, 2004), 310.

77 M. Y. Effendi, *Punjab Cavalry: Evolution, Role, Organisation, and Tactical Doctrine: 11 Cavalry (Frontier Force), 1849–1971* (Karachi: Oxford University Press, 2007), 281; and Judd, *Empire*, 245.

78 Yong, *The Garrison State*, chapter 3; and Effendi, *Punjab Cavalry*, 137.

79 David Killingray, "Labour Exploitation for Military Campaigns in British Colonial Africa, 1870–1945," *Journal of Contemporary History* 24 (1989): 489 and 493.

80 Ibid., 484–85; and Strachan, *First World War*, 3.

81 Confer, *France and Algeria*, 96–97.

82 *New York Times*, June 29, 1925, March 30, 1925, and February 12, 1939.

83 Nadzan Haron, "Colonial Defence and British Approach to the Problems in Malaya, 1874–1918," *Modern Asian Studies* 24, no. 2 (1990): 279.

84 *New York Times*, September 19, 1935; July, 27, 1941; and November 19, 1941.

85 Ronald Takaki, *Democracy and Race: Asian Americans and World War II* (New York: Chelsea House Publishers, 1995), 29–30.

86 Martin Thomas, *The French Empire at War, 1940–1945* (New York: Manchester University Press, 1998), 12.

87 Farwell, *Gurkhas*, 192.

88 Herbert Ulrich, "Forced Laborers in the Third Reich: An Overview," *International Labor and Working Class History* (October 2000): 192–218, available at http://journals.cambridge.org/action/displayJournal?jid=ILW

89 Paul H. Kratoska, ed., *Asian Labor in the Wartime Japanese Empire: Unknown Histories* (Armonk, NY: M. E. Sharpe, 2005).

90 It is useful to note that Japan's assimilation policies in Taiwan and Korea had historical precedence in Hokkaido and the Ryukyu Islands (Okinawa). Specifically, the Meiji government used compulsory education and military service as instruments to incorporate alien peoples into the Japanese nation. See Caprio, *Japanese Assimilation Policies*, 54.

91 Hui-yu Caroline Ts'ai, *Taiwan in Japan's Empire Building: An Institutional Approach to Colonial Engineering* (New York: Routledge, 2009), 203.

92 Wan-yao Chou, "The Kōminka Movement: Taiwan under Wartime Japan, 1937–1945" (PhD diss., Yale University, 1991), 160–65.

93 Ibid., 166; and E. Patricia Tsurumi, "Colonial Education in Korea and Taiwan," in *The Japanese Colonial Empire, 1895-1945*, ed. Ramon H. Myers and Mark R. Peattie (Princeton, NJ: Princeton University Press, 1984), 291.

94 Chou, "Kōminka Movement," 1. Official statistics for Koreans and Taiwanese do not include troops called up or on-the-spot conscriptions, which happened with increasing frequency in the last months of the war.

95 Chou, "Kōminka Movement," 115, 134, and 151.

96 Ts'ai, *Taiwan in Japan's Empire*, 173–80; and Chou, *Kōminka Movement*, 178.

97 Chou, *Kōminka Movement*, 200.

98 Ts'ai, *Taiwan in Japan's Empire*, 176.

99 Ken C. Kawashima, *The Proletarian Gamble: Korean Workers in Interwar Japan* (Durham, NC: Duke University Press, 2009), 211n2; and Chou, *Kōminka Movement*, 211.

NOTES TO CHAPTER 2

1   This chapter refers to the Korean Special Volunteer Soldier System as the "volunteer system," the Korean Student Special Volunteer Soldier System as the "student volunteer system," and the Naval Special Volunteer Soldier System as the "naval volunteer system."

2   Chōsen Sōtokufu, *Chōsen jijō* [Korea's situation] (Seoul: Chōsen Sōtokufu, 1943), 208.

3   Chōsengun Sanbōchō, "Chōsenjin shiganhei seido ni kansuru ken" [Management of the Korean volunteer soldier system], no. 713, November 24, 1938, frame 0680. Available www.jacar.go.jp, ref. code c01004253900.

4   Chōsen Kempeitai Shireibu, *Chōsen no hito no tokkō bidanshū* [Collection of anecdotes of Koreans], vol. 1 (Seoul: Chōsen Kempeitai Shireibu, 1932), 5. Japan had a compulsory military conscription system that required all eligible twenty-year-old Japanese men to serve two years.

5   Kawashima, *Proletarian Gamble*, 167.

6   Found in *TGSS*, Diet 73, 1937. Reprint in *ICCCSC*, vol. 3, 70–71. See also Uchida, "Brokers of Empire," 461.

7   *Maeil sinbo*, May 12, 1942.

8   Chōsengun Sanbōchō and Koiso Kuniaki, "Chōsenjin shiganhei seido," frames 1131 and 1139.

9   Hanil Munjae Yŏnguwŏn, *Ppaeatgin choguk kkŭllyŏgan*, 78.

10 Kikuchi Kenjo, *Chōsenjin to heieki* [Koreans and military service] (Tokyo, 1943), 1.

11 Chōsengun Sanbōchō, Koiso Kuniaki, "Chōsenjin shiganhei seido," frames 1130 and 1154; and Chōsengun Sanbōchō, "Chōsenjin shiganhei seido," frame 0686.

12 Chōboka Rikugunshō, "Chōsenjin shiganhei mondai ni kansuru ken" [Issue of Korean volunteer soldier], (January 1938, frame 0800. Available at http://www.jacar.go.jp, ref. code c01004411500.

13 Caprio, *Japanese Assimilation Policies*, 54.

14 Katō Yōko, *Chōheisei to kindai Nihon, 1868-1945* [Conscription system and modern

Japan, 1868–1945] (Tokyo: Yoshikawa Kōbunkan, 1996), 246; and *Chōsengun gaiyōshi* [Outline history of the Korean Army] (ca. 1954; reprint, Tokyo: Fuji Shuppan, 1989).

15 Chang Hyŏk-ju, *Iwamoto shiganhei* [Volunteer soldier Iwamoto] (Seoul: Kōa Bunka Shuppan Kabushiki Kaisha, 1944 / Tokyo: Chōsen Gyōsei Gakukai, 1944), 4.

16 Chōsengun Sanbōchō, "Chōsenjin shiganhei seido," frame 0682, also found in *TGSS*, Diet 74, December 1939, 54.

17 Chōsen Sōtokufu, *Chōsen Sōtokufu seimu sōkan jimu hikitsugi mokurokusho* [Catalogue of Korean government-general civil governor's office transfer], June 1942. Reprinted in *ICCCSC* 29, 342.

18 Chōsengun Sanbōchō, "Chōsenjin shiganhei seido," frame 0699.

19 *Tokkō geppō*, January 1938, 111.

20 Shirakawa Yutaka, "Chyan Hyokuchyu 'Iwamoto shiganhei' ni tsuite" [On Chang Hyŏk-chu's *Iwamoto shiganhei*], in *Iwamoto shiganhei*, by Chang Hyŏk-chu (Seoul: Kōa Bunka Shuppan Kabushiki Kaisha, 1944; reprint, Tokyo: Yumani Shobō, 2001), 2–4 (page citations are to the reprint edition).

21 Kajiyama Toshiyuki, *Clan Records: Five Stories of Korea,* trans. Yoshiko Dykstra (Honolulu: University of Hawaii Press, 1995), 58.

22 Fujitani, *Race for Empire,* 57–59.

23 Chōsengun Shireibu, "Chōsenjin shiganhei seido ni kansuru iken" [Opinion on Korean volunteer soldier system], June 1937. Found in *SAJAN*, reel 105, no. 678, f14254. Translation from Fujitani, "Right to Kill," 19.

24 Chōsengun Sanbōchō and Koiso Kuniaki, "Chōsenjin shiganhei seido," frame 1131.

25 Minami Jirō Denki Kankōkai, *Minami Jirō,* 472–73.

26 *New York Times,* August 6, 1939.

27 Rikugunshō, Chōboka, "Chōsenjin shiganhei mondai," slide 0800.

28 Chōsen Kōhō Kyōkai, *Yakushin Chōsen wo kataru* [Discussing rapidly progressing Korea] (Seoul: Chōsen Gyōsei Gakkai, 1942), 24.

29 Japanese men could volunteer for one year of military service prior to their two years of mandatory conscription at the age of twenty. This one year of service did not count toward the two years.

30 Higuchi Yūichi, *Senjika Chōsen no minshū to chōhei* [Korean people and conscription during the war] (Tokyo: Sōwasha, 2001), 116. The Korean diet (particularly garlic) and laxity with time were subjects of concern for naval officials.

31 Naikaku Sōridaiji, "Chōsenjin oyobi Taiwan hontōjin ni kaigun tokubetsu shiganheisei shinsetsu junbi no ken" [Establishing provisions of preparation for establishment of the naval special volunteer system for the people of Korea and the Taiwan mainland], May 8, 1943. Available at www.japar.go.jp, ref. code A03010132200.

32 Takamiya Taira, *Hantō gakuto shusinfu* [A record of peninsular students sent to war] (Seoul: Keijō Nippō Shahakkō, 1944), 107–8 and 306; and *Maeil sinbo,* October 20, 1943.

33 Takamiya, *Hantō gakuto,* 38–40; and *Keijō nippō,* October 26, 1943.

34 Takamiya, *Hantō gakuto,* 91–97.

35 Japanese students were similarly criticized for now showing concern for national affairs

as well as for their lackadaisical lifestyle. See Ben-Ami Shillony, "Universities and Students in Wartime Japan," *Journal of Asian Studies* 45, no. 4 (August 1986): 781–82.

36 Kang Tŏk-sang, *Chōsenjin gakuto shujin: Mou hitotsuno wadatsumino koe* [Korean students go to war: Another voice of the sea] (Tokyo: Iwanami Shoten, 1997), 371 and 374.

37 Ibid.

38 Chōsengun Shireibu, "Chōsenjin shiganhei seido," frame 699. Found in *SAJAN*, reel 105, f14254.

39 Rikugunshō Fukkan, "Chōsen shussinhei," frame 0410.

40 Fujitani, *Race for Empire*, 12. Assimilation was promoted in newspapers (*Maeil sinbo*), movies (*Chiwŏnbyŏng* [Volunteer]), and journals. For examples, see *Chōsen*, no. 275 (April 1938): 2, 14, and 45. This issue of *Chōsen* included articles by governor-general Minami Jirō, Korean Army commander Koiso Kuniaki, and Yun Ch'i-ho. Each played up these themes.

41 Chosen Sōtokufu, Jōhōkyoku, *Atarashiki Chōsen*, 48. Translation in Utsumi Aiko, "Korean 'Imperial Soldiers': Remembering Colonialism and Crimes against Allied POWs," *Perilous Memories: The Asia-Pacific War(s)*, ed. T. Fujitani, Geoffrey M. White, and Lisa Yoneyama, trans. Mie Kennedy (Durham, NC: Duke University Press, 2001), 205.

42 *Chōsen gyōsei* 21, no. 7 (July 1942): 3. Literally "same ancestors, same origins."

43 *Asahi shinbun*, March 11, 1938.

44 Yi Sŭng-yŏp, "Chosŏnin naesŏn ilch'eronja," 231.

45 *Samch'ŏlli*, July 1, 1940, 42–43. The *hwarang* were elite male warriors in their mid-teens.

46 *Chōsen gyōsei* 21, no. 7 (July 1942): 10.

47 Takashi Fujitani "The Masculinist Bonds of Nation and Empire: The Discourse on Korean 'Japanese' Soldiers in the Asia Pacific War," *Senri Ethnological Studies* 16 (2000): 134.

48 Gakumushō, "Chōsenjin kōminka kihon hōsaku" [Basic measures of Korean imperialization], n.d. Available at www.jacar.go.jp, ref. code b02031285300.

49 Tanaka Takeo, interview by Kang Tŏk-sang et. al., September 9, 1959. Transcript in Miyata Setsuko, ed., *Mikōkai shiryō Chōsen Sōtokufu kankeisha rokuon kiroku* [Unpublicized materials: [Sound] recording transcripts of people involved with the Government-General of Korea] (Tokyo: Gakushūin, 2000), 99 and 114.

50 *Tokkō gaiji geppō*, July 1940. Reprinted in *Jūgonen Sensō gokuhi shiryōshū* [Collection of secret documents of the Fifteen-Year War], *Tokkō gaiji geppō* 6, ed. Miyata Setsuko (Tokyo: Fuji Shuppan, 1987), 435–37.

51 Rikugunshō, "Chōsenjin shiganhei mondai," slide 0080.

52 Pak Kyŏng-sik, *Nihon teikoku shugi*, 29.

53 Dong, "Japanese Colonial Policy," 383–84, 395.

54 Chōsengun Sanbōchō and Koiso Kuniaki, "Chōsenjin shiganhei seido," frame 1156.

55 Ueda Ryūdan, *Sumera Chōsen* [Imperial Korea] (Tokyo: Nihon Seinen Bunka Kyōkai, 1943), 149–50.

56 *Sōdōin* 1, no. 2 (July 7, 1939): 21–24.

57 Kang Tŏk-sang, *Chōsenjin gakuto shujin*, 376.

58 Pak Kyŏng-sik, *Nihon teikoku shugi*, 27. *Tamayoke* technically means "protection against bullets" and was used in reference to Japanese soldiers protecting the nation, but Pak implies that state policies were created so that Korean youth would die instead of the Japanese.

59 *Chōsen nenkan 1939*, 132. And Chōsen Sōtokufu, Keimukyoku, "Rikugun tokubetsu shiganhei shigansha boshū ni kanshi shoji bengi kyōyo kata irai no ken" [Request for matters of providing accommodation for army special volunteer applicant recruitment], October 30, 1941). Found in *SAJAN*, reel 215.

60 *Kyōwa jigyō*, July 1943, 10–11.

61 *Keijō nippō*, January 18, 1938, and December 13, 1938.

62 Fujitani, *Race for Empire*, 262.

63 *Keijō nippō*, June 16, 1938; *Bunkyō no Chōsen*, no. 152 (April 1938): 158; and Chōsen Sōtokufu and Rikugunhei Shigansha Kunrensho, *Shiganhei Seido no genjō to shōrai e no tenbō* [Current situation of volunteer soldiers and views of its future state], November 17, 1939. Reprinted in *Senji taiseika Chōsen Sōtokufu gaikaku dantai shiryōshū* [Collection materials of extragovernmental organizations of the Government-General of Korea under the war system], 14. Kangwŏn (363), South Chŏlla (516), and North Chŏlla (303) were the only provinces with more than 300 applicants in 1938.

64 Chosen Sōtokufu, Jōhōkyoku, *Atarashiki Chōsen*, 47.

65 Ibid. 53.

66 The colonial regime shut down Korean language newspapers in an effort to force Koreans to learn Japanese. As a result, few Korean language primary materials remain. One notable exception is the *Maeil sinbo*.

67 Kim Hak-tong, "Chang Hyŏk-chu ŭi minjokchŏk kwa ch'inilchŏk chakp'um ŭi pigyo koch'al: Haebang ijŏn Ilbonŏ chakp'um ŭl chungsim ŭro" [A comparative study of Chang Hyŏk-chu's nationalist works and his pro-Japanese works: With a focus on his Japanese language works before liberation], *Ilbŏn yŏn'gu* 34 (December 2007): 201–5. See also Fujitani, "Masculine Bonds," 140.

68 Lee Sun-jin, "The Feature Films in the Colonial Period: Discontinuity and Continuity," in *The Past Unearthed: Collection of Feature Films in the Japanese Colonial Period*, trans. Kim Su-hyŏn (Seoul: Korean Film Archives, n.d.), 62.

69 Ibid., 58.

70 Chōsen Sōtokufu, Jōhōka, *Zenshinsuru Chōsen* [Progressing Korea] (Seoul: Chōsen Sōtokufu, 1942); and Chosen Sōtokufu, Jōhōkyoku, *Atarashiki Chōsen*, 48.

71 Kim To-hyŏng, *T'aep'yŏngyang chŏnjaenggi kyŏkchŏnji wa Chosŏnin hŭisaengja e kwan-han yŏn'gu: Nyuginia chiyŏk ŭl chungsim ŭro* [Research on the Pacific War battlefront and Korean victims: The New Guinea area] (Seoul: Ilche Kangjŏmha Kangje Tongwŏn Pi'hae Chinsang Kyumyŏng Wiwŏnhoe, 2006), 15.

72 Ōmura, *Tatakō hantō shiganhei*, 3 and 204–9.

73 The Japanese military granted special permission to a handful of Koreans to attend Japanese military academies and enter the military. There were roughly 120 Koreans who graduated from cadet school in Japan prior to 1937. For an account of these officers, see Yi

Ki-dong, "Ilbon chegukkun," 452–98.

74 Utsumi Aiko and Murai Yoshinori, *Chosŏnin panhang* [Korean resistance], trans. Pak Nam-ch'ul (Seoul: Kukmun Publishing Co., 1981), 58.

75 Yun Ch'i-ho, *Yun Ch'i-ho ilgi*, vol. 11, 175 and 260.

76 Yi Ki-dong, *Pigŭk ŭi kunindŭl: Ilbon yuksa ch'ulsin ŭi yŏksa* [Soldiers' tragedy: A history of Japanese military school graduates] (Seoul: Ilchogan, 1982), 261.

77 Cumings, *Origins of the Korean War*, 38.

78 *Keijō nippō*, October 31, 1943; and Takamiya Taira, *Hantō gakuto*, 23.

79 *Maeil sinbo*, November 12, 1943 (my translation).

80 *Maeil sinbo*, November 5, 1943 (my translation).

81 See two oral accounts in Miyata Setsuko, *Mikōkai shiryō*, 153–58 and 196–200.

82 Todd A. Henry, "Cheguk ŭl kinyŏm hago, chŏnjaeng ŭl tongnyŏhagi: Singminje malgi (1940nyŏn) Chosŏn esŏ ŭi pangnamhoe [Celebrating empire, fighting war: The 1940 exposition in late colonial Korea], in *Asea yŏn'gu* 51, no. 4 (Winter 2008): 101. For circulation information, see Lynn, "Limits of the Colonial State," 111. The *Maeil sinbo* had a larger circulation throughout all of Korea, with 96,000.

83 Henry, "Cheguk ŭl kinyŏm hago," 102.

84 *Maeil sinbo*, November 5, 1943.

85 Carter J. Eckert, *Offspring of the Empire: The Koch'ang Kims and the Colonial Origins of Korean Capitalism* (Seattle: University of Washington Press, 1991), 246; and *Maeil sinbo*, August 5, 1943.

86 *Keijō nippō*, January 19, 1944. Translation found in Eckert, *Offspring of Empire*, 1991, 247.

87 *Maeil sinbo*, November 5, 1943. The Green Flag League was a Korea-based organization composed of 3,000 educated Koreans and Japanese. It advocated military service and assimilation. See Yi Sŭng-yŏp, "Chosen Naesŏn Ilch'eronja, 218.

88 Shirai Atsushi, *Daigaku to Ajia Taiheiyō Sensō: Sensōshi kenkyū to taiken no rekishika* [Universities and the Asia Pacific War: Historicizing research and experiences historical] (Tokyo: Nihon Keizai Hyōronsha, 1996), 161–62.

89 Choong Soon Kim, *A Korean Nationalist Entrepreneur: A Life History of Kim Sŏng-su, 1891–1955* (Albany: State University of New York Press, 1998), 119. Kim Sŏng-su exemplifies this point. Kim denied writing this article. Some scholars claim that he did not write the article but that his name was attached to it without approval.

90 *Maeil sinbo*, November 19, 1943.

91 *Maeil sinbo*, November 7, 1943.

92 *Keijō ihō*, no. 241 (December 1941): 26.

93 Michael Kim, "Aesthetics of Total Mobilization," 492.

94 Yun Ch'i-ho, *Yun Ch'i-ho ilgi*, vol. 11, 153.

95 Im Hye-bong, *Ch'in'il sŭngnyŏ paekp'arin: Kkŭnnaji anŭn yŏksa ŭi murŭm* [108 pro-Japanese monks: A historical question that never ends] Ch'ŏngnyŏn Haksul, 50 (P'aju, South Korea: Ch'ŏngnyŏnsa, 2005), 287–91.

96 During the late 1930s the colonial regime forced Christians to bow to the Japanese emperor. Churches that refused to bow were either closed or amalgamated into progovernment congregations.

97 Chōsengun Hōdōbu Kanshū, *Chōsen chōhei junbi*, 112–13.

98 *Chōsen mesaretari*, 7.

99 Takumushō, Yamao Dōni, "Rikugun shigansha no senko wo ōsakashi ni oite jisshi suru no ken" [Matter of enforcement of screening army volunteers in Osaka], Kankei 835, November 7, 1941. Found in *SAJAN*, reel 215. Malcontents were considered ideologically questionable individuals.

100 Kangje Tongwŏn Kusul Kirŏkchip, *Kapcha-ŭlch'uk saeng ŭn kunin e kayahanda* [If you were born in 1924 or 1925, you must join the military] (Seoul: Kangje Tongwŏn Kusul Kirŏkchip, 2006), 76–89.

101 Higuchi, *Kōgun heishi*, 27–30.

102 Takumushō, Kanrikyokuchō, "Chōsen Sōtokufu rikugunhei shigansha kunreisho seito boshū ni kansuru Ken" [Case regarding Korean government-general army soldier volunteer training camp pupil recruitment], Kankei 1907, September 1, 1942. Found in *SAJAN*, reel 215; and Higuchi, *Kōgun heishi*, 32–34.

103 Chōsen Sōtokufu, *Chōsen jijō* (1942), 202.

104 Kang Tŏk-sang, *Chōsenjin gakuto shujjin*, 5–6.

105 Chōsengun Hōdōbu Kanshū, *Chosen chōhei junbi*, 62.

106 Higuchi, *Senjika Chōsen*, 62–68. The military training camps were slightly different from the youth training camps (*seinen gunrensho*), which emphasized nonmilitary training. As noted in the next chapter, the number of youth training camps increased dramatically after the announcement of the draft.

107 Kim Haeng-jin, interview by P'yo Yŏng-su, November 11, 2001. Available at the Independence Hall of Korea.

108 *Keijō nippō*, February 23, 1941.

109 Im Kwang-ho, interview by Yi Byŏng-rae, November 17, 2001. Available at the Independence Hall of Korea.

110 Kim Haeng-jin, interview by P'yo Yŏng-su, November 11, 2001. Available at the Independence Hall of Korea.

111 Miyata Setsuko, *Chosŏn minjung kwa "hwangminhwa" chŏngch'aek* [The Korean people and the "imperialization" policy], trans. Yi Hyŏng-nang (Seoul: Ilchogak, 1997), 43.

112 *Chōsen nenkan*, 1944, 60.

113 Chŏng Ki-yŏng, interview by P'yo Yŏng-su, November 11, 2001. Available at the Independence Hall of Korea.

114 John Young Sohn, *Korean Gakuhei: My Life in the Japanese Army* (Stillwater, MN: River's Bend Press, 2007), 34–37.

115 *Keijō nippō*, November 10, 1943.

116 Kang Tŏk-sang, *Chōsenjin gakuto shujjin*, 369.

117 *Tokkō geppō*, December 1941.

118 Fujitani, "Masculine Bonds," 134. Soldiers made very little money, but at least the youths were no longer an expense for their families.

119 Michael Kim, "Aesthetics of Total Mobilization," 483.

120 Chōsen Sōtokufu, Jōhōkyoku, *Atarashiki Chōsen*, 47.

121 Kang Tŏk-sang, *Chōsenjin gakuto shujjin*, 82.

122 Wŏn Cho-jang, "Hachimakishiki hatchō," in *Chōsenjin kōgun heishi: Nyūginiasen no tokushiganhei* [Korean Imperial Soldiers: Special Volunteer Soldiers of the New Guinea front], ed. Hayashi Eidai (Tokyo: Tsuge Shobō, 1995), 153–59.

123 Young Hoon Kang, "Personal Reminiscences of My Japanese School Days," in *Korea's Response to Japan: The Colonial Period, 1910–1945*, ed. C. I. Eugene Kim and Dorthea E. Mortimore (Kalamazoo: Western Michigan University, 1977), 287.

124 Ha ŭn-jin, "Ilche P'asijŭm (1937–1945): Chosŏn minjung ŭi hyŏnsil insik kwa chŏhang" [Japanese colonial fascism (1937–1945): Korean people's reality understanding and resistance] (PhD diss., Koryŏ University, 1998), 198–99.

125 Kawashima, *Proletarian Gamble*, 172.

126 Utsumi Aiko, *Chōsenjin "kōgun" heishitachi no sensō* [The Korean "Imperial Army" soldiers's war] (Tokyo: Iwanami, 1991): 46–47.

127 Fujitani, *Race for Empire*, 249–50.

128 Dong, "Japanese Colonial Policy," 341–45. Dong summarizes three police surveys from 1936. The results, while suspect, suggest that most Koreans had moved on with their lives, economically and politically. For example, 84.2 percent of students and 86.8 percent of farmers and laborers did not care or had given up on independence. And 77.4 percent of students and 84.9 percent of farmers and laborers did not care or were satisfied with the Japanese regime. See *SAJAN*, reel 105, frames 13545 and 13572.

129 *Maeil sinbo*, January 17, 1944.

130 Ōno Rokuichirō, interview by Miyata Setsuko et. al., on November 4, 1959. Transcript in Miyata Setsuko, *Mikōkai shiryō*, 47.

131 *Keijō nippō*, January 19, 1938.

132 *Korea Times*, November 8, 2009. Translation by *Korea Times*.

133 *Chogwang* 9, no. 6 (June 1943): 40.

134 *Keijō nippō*, January 18, 1938.

135 *Chōsen* no. 282 (November 1938): 111.

136 Hŏ Su-yŏl, "Chosŏnin nodongnyŏk," 305; and Kim Min-yŏng, *Ilche ŭi Chosŏnin nodongnyŏk sut'al yŏn'gu* [Research of Japan's Korean manpower exploitation] (Seoul: Hanul, 1995).

137 Higuchi, *Kōgun heishi*, 99–101. Resistance among Koreans in Japan was strong. In 1943, 894 Koreans in ten prefectures in Japan submitted applications, but 162 did not show up for the military examinations. The Home Ministry investigated each case and found that in fifty-two cases the individuals or their families opposed military service and thirty-seven claimed to be ill but were suspected of resistance. Others had moved and could not be found.

138 Chŏn Ki-ho, *Nambang kihaeng* [Accounts of travels to the South Seas] (Seoul: Kangje Tongwŏn Kunsok Sugijip, 2008), 18.

139 Kangje Tongwŏn Kusul Kirŏkchip, *Kapcha*, 76–89.

140 Shillony, "Universities and Students," 780.

141 *Keijō nippō*, October 31 and November 3, 1943.

142 Kang Tŏk-sang, *Chōsenjin gakuto shujjin*, 9 and 11.

143 *Keijō nippō*, November 3, 1943. The newspaper did not give his Korean name.

144 Found in *TGSS*, Diet 84, August 1944; Higuchi, *Kōgun heishi*, 80–81; and Kang Tŏk-sang, *Chōsenjin gakuto shujjin*, 370.

145 *Tokkō gaiji geppō*, August 1939. Reprinted in *Jūgonen sensō gokuhi shiryōshū* [Collection of secret materials on the Fifteen-Year War]: *Tokkō gaiji Geppō* 6, ed. Miyata Setsuko (Tokyo: Fuji Shuppan, 1987), 75–76.

146 Found in *TGSS*, Diet 73, 1938, 293.

147 *Tokkō geppō*, December 1942, 109.

148 Ibid.

149 *Keijō nippō*, June 4, 1938.

150 *Chōsen mesaretari*, 6.

151 Hayashi, *Chōsenjin kōgun heishi*, 132–33.

152 Chang Chun-ha, *Tolbegae* [Stone pillow] (Seoul: Sasangsa, 1971), 7.

153 *Bunkyō no Chōsen* no. 224 (July 1944): 9; and Kang Tŏk-sang, *Chōsenjin gakuto shujjin*, 83.

154 Kang Tŏk-sang, *Chōsenjin gakuto shujjin*, 10 and 81.

155 *Keijō nippō*, November 3, 1943.

156 Ibid.

157 Rikugunshō Fukkan, "Chōsen shusshinhei," frame 0410.

158 Kang Tŏk-sang, *Chōsenjin gakuto shujjin*, 312; and Chōsen Sōgakkai, "Rikugun toku-betsu shiganhei hishigan gakusei kinrō jōkyō chōsa" [Survey of the labor situation of army special volunteer nonapplicant students], April 20, 1944. Found in *SAJAN*, reel 219.

159 This rumor relates to the Nomonhan Incident, in which Japanese and Soviet troops clashed along the border between Manchuria, Korea, and the Soviet Union in 1939. The Soviets decisively defeated the Japanese.

160 Kim To-hyŏng, *T'aep'yŏngyang chŏnjaenggi kyŏkchŏnji*, 15.

161 *Chōsen shisō undō gaikyō*, March 18, 1939, Document 5 in *Jūgonen sensō gokuhi shiryōshū*, 241.

162 Higuchi, *Senjika Chōsen*, 107. Higuchi estimates that 58,000 reserves were called up by the end of the war.

163 Chōsengun Shireikan, Rikugun Taishi, "Honendo saiyō suheki Chōsenjin shiganhei saiyō jin'in narabi nyūei mata ha meshiatsumeri butai ni kansuru ken" [Number of Korean volunteer soldiers recruited for this year and corps enlisted or drafted] January 24, 1939. Available at www.jacar.go.jp, ref. code c01004411700. Unfortunately, I have not located statistics on subsequent volunteer units or reassignment.

164 Naikaku, "Kaigun tokubetsu shigan heisei jisshi no jiki oyobi tokubetsu shiganhei saiyō teiinsu" [Establishing the subject of the numbers of staff at the time of adopting the Navy Special Volunteer System], July 22, 1943]. Available at www.jacar.go.jp, ref. code A03010086100; Asahi Shinbunsha, *Tatakō Chōsen*, 10; and Chōsen Sōtokufu, *Shiganhei yori chōhei e* [From volunteer soldiers to the draft] (Seoul: Chōsen Sōtokufu Jōhōka, 1944), 7–8.

165 *Tōyō no hikari* 5, no. 8 (September 1943): 67.

NOTES TO CHAPTER 3

1 Naikaku Sōridaishin, "Chōsen oyobi Taiwan"; and Tanaka Takeo et al., interview by Miyata Setsuko et al., September 9, 1959. Transcript in Miyata, *Mikōkai shiryō*, 128.

2 *New York Times*, August 6, 1939.

3 Minami Jirō Denki Kankōkai, *Minami Jirō*, 467; and Tanaka Takeo et al., interview by Miyata Setsuko et al., September 9, 1959. Transcript in Miyata, *Mikōkai shiryō*, 128.

4 Rikugunshō Heibika, "Daitōa Sensō ni kan wo wakajinteki no kentō," January 20, 1942; and Utsumi, *Chōsenjin "kōgun" heishitachi*, 46.

5 Katō, *Chōheisei to kindai Nihon*, 227–28.

6 *Osaka Mainichi and Tokyo Nichinichi*, May 10, 1942. Original in English.

7 *Hyōgoken shakai jigyō*, July 1942. Document 5 in Higuchi Yūichi, ed., *Kyōwakai kankei shiryōshū: Senjika ni okeru zainichi Chōsenjin tōsei to kōminka seisaku no jittai shiryō* [Collection of materials related to the Kyōwakai: Materials on the actual conditions of Koreans in Japan during the war and assimilation policies], vol. 3 (Tokyo: Rokuinsho, 1992).

8 Tanaka Takeo et al., interview by Miyata Setsuko, August 26, 1958. Transcript in Miyata, *Mikōkai shiryō*, 23 and 144.

9 Asahi Shinbunsha, *Tatakō Chōsen*, 19–20. My translation, italics mine.

10 Asahi Shinbunsha, *Tatakō Chōsen*, 10. As noted in the previous chapter, this was a self-fulfilling prophecy for the Japanese. Colonial officials artificially bolstered the number of applications so that they could make this very claim.

11 Chōsengun Hōdōbu Kanshū, *Chōsen chōhei junbi tokuhon*, 31–32.

12 *Chōsen Nenkan* 1943, 60–61; *Nippu jiji*, May 17, 1941; and Asahi Shinbunsha, *Tatakō Chōsen*, 10.

13 Shirakawa Yutaka, "Chan Hyokuchu," postscript.

14 Chōsen Sōtokufu, *Shiganhei yori chōhei e*, 3

15 *Japan Times & Advertiser*, May 11, 1942.

16 *Nippon Times*, February 4, 1944. Original in English.

17 Masao Yamazaki, "An Outline of the History of the Army System." Quoted from "Koreans in the Japanese Imperial Army," accessed March 14, 2004, at http://home.att.ne.jp/sun/RUR55/E/epage12.htm (now defunct).

18 Tanaka Takeo et al., interview by Miyata Setsuko, August 26, 1958. Transcript in Miyata, *Mikōkai shiryō*, 100–108 and *Kyōwa jigyō nenkan*, August 31, 1943, 10–11.

19 Caprio, *Japanese Assimilation Policies*, 150.

20 Fujitani, "Masculine Bonds of Nation," 146.

21 Higuchi, *Kōgun heishi*, 165. For a fictional account written by a Japanese who lived in Korea during the colonial era, see Kajiyama, *Clan Records*, 58.

22 Tanaka Takeo et al., interview by Miyata Setsuko, August 26, 1958. Transcript in Miyata, *Mikōkai shiryō*, 103, 144, 151, and 164.

23 For an analysis of Japanese propaganda for Japanese citizens, see Barak Kushner's *The Thought War: Japanese Imperial Propaganda* (Honolulu: University of Hawaii Press, 2006).

24 Fujitani, "Masculine Bonds of Nation," 157.

25 Chōsengun Hōdōbu Kanshū, *Chōsen chōhei junbi tokuhon*, 104.

26 *Tōyō no hikari*, vol. 4 (June 1943): 65.

27 *Maeil sinbo*, December 25, 1943; and Hanil Munjae Yŏn'guwŏn, *Ppaeakkin choguk kkŭllyŏgan*, 38–39.

28 Ch'oe Chŏng-hŭi, "The Wild Chrysanthemum" (1942), translated by Sarah Frederick (1999, unpublished); and Kyeong-hee Choi, "Another Layer, 66–70. Choi notes that this story had a strong feminist undercurrent that challenged the male-dominated social values in Korea.

29 *Maeil sinbo*, December 8, 1943.

30 *Maeil sinbo*, November 20, 1943.

31 Kang Ch'ang-gi, *Naisen ittai-ron* [Treatise on Japanese-Korean unity] (Tokyo: Kokumin Hyōronsha, 1939), 201–6.

32 Ueda Ryūdan, *Sumera Chōsen*, 243.

33 Zensen Gakudō Tsuzukatashū, ed., *Chōhei anisan* [Conscript brothers] (Seoul: Kōa Bunka Shuppan Kaisha, 1944).

34 *Maeil sinbo*, November 26, 1943. Yi graduated from Waseda University in Japan and taught at Chungang School. He was an important figure in the writing of Korea's history during the colonial era.

35 *Tōyō no hikari*, vol. 4 no. 6 (June 1942): 8.

36 *Kyōwa jigyō*, (February–March 1943): 97.

37 Fujitani, *Race for Empire*, 305.

38 Ibid., 318–23.

39 Quote from the introduction of the movie. See also *Kokumin bungaku*, no. 4 (June 1944): 54–60.

40 Kim Chun-yŏp, *Changjŏm: Na ŭi Kwangbokgun sijŏl* [A strong point: My Kwangbok Army experience] (Seoul: Nanam, 1987), 45–57.

41 *TGSS*, Diet 86, 1944, found in *ICCCSC* 22, 215; Kang Tŏk-sang, *Chōsenjin Gakuto Shujjin*, 375; Wonmo Dong "Japanese Colonial Policy," 388; and Ha ŭn-jin, "Ilche p'asijŭm," 49–53. Around one-third of girls attended school.

42 Chosen Sōtokufu, Jōhōkyoku, *Atarashiki Chōsen*; and Chōsen Sōtokufu, *Shiganhei yori chōhei e*, 5.

43 Rikugunshō Fukkan, "Chōsen shusshinhei," frame 0411.

44 *Chōsen* no. 331 (December 1942): 4–7; and Kang Tŏk-sang, *Chōsenjin gakuto shujjin*, 373. The low graduation rate of Koreans paled in comparison to the 99-percent graduation rate of Japanese men.

45 *Chōsen nenkan*, 1943, 64; and Sin Chu-baek, "Ilche malgi Chosŏnin kunsa kyoyuk, 1942–1945" [Korean military education in the late colonial period, 1942–1945], *Han'il minjok munje yŏn'gu* 9 (December 2005): 258. Men as old as thirty were required to undergo special training because they worked as military civilians.

46 Chōsen Sōtokufu, *Shiganhei yori chōhei e*, 5.

47 Chosen Sōtokufu, Jōhōkyoku, *Atarashiki Chōsen*, 51; and Sin Chu-baek 2005, 166.

48 Yi Se-il, *Hawai p'oro suyongso Hanin p'oro e kwanhan chosa* [A survey on Korean POWs

in Hawaiian POW camps] (Seoul: Ilche Kangjŏmha Kangje Tongwŏn P'ihae Chinsang Kyumyŏng Wiwŏnhoe, 2008), 57–58. Some training camps provided as few as 300 hours per year. See Higuchi, *Senjika Chōsen*, 65.

49 Higuchi, *Kōgun heishi*, 36, 46, and 58; and Pak Kyŏng-sik, *Tennōsei kokka to zainichi Chōsenjin* [The emperor system state and Koreans in Japan] (Tokyo: Taihei Insatsusha, 1986), 228–29; and *Naganoken kōsei jibō* 5, no. 10 (October 1943). Found in Higuchi, *Kyōwakai kankei shiryōshū*, 331.

50 Fujitani, "Right to Kill," 15.

51 Chōsen Sōtokufu, *Kanpō* [Official gazette] no. 4584 (May 13, 1942); *Chōsen gyōsei* no. 23 (April 1944): 10–14; and Kang Tŏk-sang, *Chōsenjin gakuto shujjin*, 3.

52 Utsumi Aiko, "Japan's Korean Soldiers in the Pacific War," in *Asian Labor in the Wartime Japanese Empire: Unknown Histories*, ed. Paul H. Kratoska (Armonk, NY: M. E. Sharpe, 2005), 82.

53 "Household registers," *Kodonsha Encyclopedia of Japan*, 240. The Family Registry System remains in effect in Japan and Korea.

54 Chōsen Sōtokufu, *Chōsen jijō* (1943), 232–33. A temporary registry system existed in Japan.

55 *Bunkyō no Chōsen* no. 202 (July 1942): 13. Government records bemoaned the sorry state of Korean registries up to the end of the war.

56 Chōsen Sōtokufu, *Shiganhei yori chōhei e*, 4.

57 "Kiryū ni Kansuru Tōkei," *Koseki* (April 1943); found in Fujitani, *Race for Empire*, 69.

58 Ka Kaoru, "Sōryoku senka no Chōsen josei" [Korean women under total war], *Rekishi hyōron*, no. 612 (April 2001): 10. The Korean pronunciation of Ka's family name is "Ha." Proper registry maintenance remained a problem in the postwar era. The author's brother- and sister-in-law, who were born in rural Korea in the mid-1970s, are listed on their registry as being born two months apart, when in actuality they were born two years apart.

59 *TGSS*, Diet 85, 1944. Reprint in Kondō Ken'ichi, ed. *Taiheiyō senka no Chōsen oyobi Taiwan* [Korea and Japan during the Pacific War], vol. 2 (1961): 23; and Yi Myŏng-jong, "Ilche malgi Chosŏnin chingbyŏng ŭl wihan kiryu chedo ŭi sihaeng mit hojŏk chosa [Resident registration system enforcement and family registry system investigation for the draft in late colonial Korea], *Sahoe wa yŏksa t'onggwŏn* 74 (June 2007): 83–95.

60 *Koseki* 2, no. 11 (February 1943); and Higuchi, *Senjika Chōsen*, 48.

61 Katō Yōko, *Chōheisei to kindai Nihon*, 248.

62 Chōsen Kōhō Kyōkai, *Yakushin Chōsen*, 24; Minami Jirō Denki Kankōkai, *Minami Jirō*, 472; and Chōsen Sōtokufu, Jōhōkyoku, "Chōsenjin ni taisuru chōheisei jikō junbi ni kansuru," n.d. Found in *ICCCSC* 55, 535.

63 Quotes from Shihōshō Keijikyoku, *Shisō geppō*, no. 95 (June 1942): 18. Translation by Takashi Fujitani. See Fujitani, *Race for Empire*, 281.

64 Yun Ch'i-ho, *Yun Ch'i-ho ilgi*, vol. 11, 458. This was a Shintō shrine located on Namsan in southern Seoul.

65 Chōsen Sōtokufu, *Chōsen jijō* (1944), 232; and Pak Kyŏng-sik, *Tennōsei kokka*, 225.

66 Fujitani, *Race for Empire*, 70; *Kyōwa jigyō* (February–March 1943): 8; and Chōsengun

Hōdōbu Kanshū, Sugiura Hiroshi, *Chōsen chōhei tokuhon* [Reader on Korean conscription] (Keijō: Tosho Shuppan, 1943), 140.

67 Rikugunshō Jikan, Shibayama Kenshirō, "Chōsen shusshinhei no toriatsukka shidō sasshin kōjō ni kansuru ken rikugun ippan e tsuchō" [General army instructions on improving treatment of soldiers from Korea], Army Secret Order 308, January 26, 1945, frame 0466. Available www.jacar.go.jp, ref. code c01007867000. The author of this memorandum indicated that the lack of Japanese language skills among Koreans contributed to desertion.

68 Chōsen Sōtokufu, "Chōsen dōhō ni taisuru chōheisei jisshi junbi kettei ni tomonau sochi jōkyō narabi kono hankyō" [Measures and responses to the decision on the draft system enforcement preparation for Korean compatriots], May 1942. Found in *ICCCSC* 55, 435–37.

69 *Bunkyō no Chōsen*, no. 202 (July 1942): 16; and *Shokugin chōsa geppō* (June–July 1941): 13.

70 *Tokkō geppō* (March 1938): 125.

71 *TGSS*, Diet 86, December 1944, 120; and Pak Kyŏng-sik, *Nihon teikoku shugi*, 28. The second round of exams were held from February to May 1945.

72 Higuchi, *Senjika Chōsen*, 37.

73 Kangje Tongwŏn Kusul Kirokchip, *Kapcha*, 76–89.

74 Sohn, *Korean Gakuhei*, 41.

75 Sŏk Ch'ŏng-su, exerpts of interview. In Kim Yong-gwŏn, *Kkŭllyŏgan saramdŭl, ppaeakkin saramdŭl: Kangje chingyongja wa chonggun wianbu ŭi chŭngŏn* (Seoul: Haewadal, 2000), 38–49.

76 *TGSS*, Diet 86, December 1944, 89; and Higuchi, *Senjika Chōsen*, 88.

77 Kang Tae-hŭi, interview by U Su-mi, November 24, 2001. Available at the Independence Hall of Korea.

78 Kim Chun-yŏp, *Changjŏm*, 57.

79 Yi Pyŏng-ju, interview by P'yo Yŏng-su, November 11, 2001. Available at the Independence Hall of Korea. The second round of exams was held from February to May 1945.

80 Sohn, *Korean Gakuhei*, 108.

81 See the various polls in Dong, "Japanese Colonial Policy."

82 Hildi Kang, *Under the Black Umbrella: Voices from Colonial Korea, 1910–1945* (Ithaca, NY: Cornell University Press, 2001), 59.

83 Ibid., 130–31.

84 *TGSS*, Diet 86, December 1944, 89 and 120; and Chōsen Sōtokufu, Saimu Kyokuchō, and Mizuta Naomasa, "Shōwa 19nendo Chōsen Sōtokufu yosan ni tsuite" [Regarding the 1944 Government-General budget], March 29, 1944. Reprinted in *Taiheiyō Senka shūmatsuki Chōsen no jisei*, vol. 2, ed. Kondō Ken'ichi (Tokyo: Chōsen Shiryō Hensankai, 1961), 143.

85 Chōsen Sōtokufu, Saimu Kyokuchō, and Mizuta Naomasa, "Shōwa 19nendo Chōsen Sōtokufu," 143.

86 Yi Myŏng-jong, "Ilche malgi Chosŏnin," 98–99.

87 Ibid.

88 Chōsen Sōtokufu, Saimu Kyokuchō, and Mizuta Naomasa, "Shōwa 19nendo Chōsen Sōtokufu," 143. My translation. Italics mine.

89 *TGSS*, Diet 79, December 1941, 103.

90 Lee ŭn-hwa, son of Yi P'ung-ho, interview by Brandon Palmer, August 15, 2004, Honolulu, Hawaii.

91 Ueda Ryūdan, *Sumera Chōsen*, 259.

92 Chang Kyŏng-ok, "Chingbyŏng t'alch'ulcha kkŭt ŏmnŭn miro" [Draft escapees with nowhere to go], *Chŏnggyŏng munhwa* 234 (August 1984): 317–19.

93 *Hokkaidō Shinbun*, February 25, 1995. About 600,000 Japanese soldiers and civilians were taken to Siberia as forced to work as laborers in 2,000 detention camps. It is estimated that 10 percent of the POWs died in captivity. See *Korea Herald*, December 27, 2010.

94 Hildi Kang, *Under the Black Umbrella*, 130.

95 Im Hyŏn-su, interview by P'yo Yŏng-su, November 24, 2001. Available at the Independence Hall of Korea.

96 *Chōsengun gaiyōshi*, 83. *Chōsengun gaiyōshi* is a valuable resource on the Korean Army and Korean military mobilization. The authors of this book are not known, but were apparently officers in the Korean Army. Further, it is unclear what sources were used to write the book. There are some factual problems with this work, but given the dearth of other reliable materials, this work has remained the most-used source for statistics on Koreans in the military.

97 Utsumi, "Japan's Korean Soldiers," 87.

98 Higuchi, *Senjika Chōsen*, 101–8.

99 Utsumi Aiko, "'Daitōa kyōeiken' to Chōsenjin gunjin/gunzoku" [The "East Asia Co-Prosperity Sphere and Korean soldiers and military civilians], *Samchŏlli* 31 (Winter 1982): 87.

100 Miyata Hiroto, *Tatakō Chōsen* (Tokyo: Shinkansha, 2007), 22

101 Sin Sang-ch'o, *T'alch'ul: ŏnŭ chayujuŭija ŭi sugi* [Escape: Memoir of a liberalist] (Seoul: Nokmungak, 1966), 86–92.

102 Kim, "Aesthetics of Total Mobilization," 497.

103 Rikugunshō Sanbō Honbu Hensei Dōinka, *Shinajihen: Daitōa Sensōkan rikugun dōin gaikyō* [The China incident: A general history of army mobilization during the Greater East Asia War] (reprint, Tokyo: Fuji Shuppan, 1988), 436; and Utsumi Aiko, *Chōsenjin "kōgun" heishitachi*, 50.

104 *Tokkō gaiji geppō*, July 1939, 99–100; and *Chōsen shisō undō gaikyō*, February 28, 1940, 240–41. Reprinted in Miyata Setsuko, *Jūgonen Sensō*, 28.

105 Fujitani, *Race for Empire*, 265–67.

106 Kim Hyo-byŏng, interview with U Su-mi on November 24, 2011. Available at the Independence Hall of Korea.

107 Ibid.; and Chŏn Ki-ho, *Chosŏn iranŭn uri nara ka issŏkkuna* [I did not know our country was called Chosen] (Seoul: Kangje Tongwŏn Kunsok Sugijip, 2008), 85; and Kim Ki-chae, interview by U Su-mi, November 24, 2001. Available at the Independence Hall of Korea.

108 Kim Chae-yŏn, "Jūsatsu meirei" [Execution order], in Hayashi Eidai, *Chōsenjin kōgun heishi*, 115; and Kim Haeng-jin, interview by P'yo Yŏng-su, November 11, 2001. Available at the Independence Hall of Korea.

109 Kangje Tongwŏn Kusul Kirokchip, *Kapcha*, 76–89.

110 Yi Pyŏng-ju, interview by P'yo Yŏng-su, November 11, 2001, and O Haeng-sŏk, interview by Chŏng Hye-gyŏng, November 11, 2001. Available at the Independence Hall of Korea. Also, Kim Tae-yong, interview by Brandon Palmer, August 1997. Each of the three men interviewed survived being a human bomb. Yi passed out on the battlefield, O was too sick to be sent out, and Kim's unit surrendered before he was sent against the Soviets in Manchuria.

111 Chŏn Ki-ho, *Chosŏn iranŭn uri nara ka*, 19–33. Koreans considered "Chosŏnjin" to be a derogatory term.

112 Cho Su-hwan, interview by U Su-mi, November 25, 2001. Available at the Independence Hall of Korea. See also 1·20 Hakpyŏng Sagi Kanhaeng, *1·20 hakbyŏng sagi* [Chronicle of the January 20 student soldiers], vol. 2 (Seoul: 1·20 Hakpyŏng Sagi Kanhaeng, 1987), 98–103.

113 Chi Yŏng-im, "Kusul ŭl t'onghae pon Ilcheha Chejudo nae kangje tongwŏn ŭi silt'ae wa t'ŭkjing" [A look at the conditions and characteristics of the forced mobilization of Cheju under Japanese rule through oral statements], *Sahoe wa yŏksa* 72 (2006): 85.

114 Yi Sang-hyŏp, interview by Chang Sin, November 19, 2001. Available at the Independence Hall of Korea.

115 Utsumi Aiko, "Korean 'Imperial Soldiers,'" 202.

116 Yi Ki-dong, *Pigŭk ŭi kunindŭl*, 200–202.

117 *Keijō nippō*, May 28, 1940.

118 Kang Tŏk-sang, *Chōsenjin gakuto shujjin*, 364–67. Of the 175 Korean soldiers in the Kwangbok Army, there were 12 student soldiers, 159 from the 1944 compulsory draft, and 4 others.

119 1·20 Hakpyŏng Sagi Kanhaeng, *1·20 hakbyŏng sagi*, 98–103. See also Fujitani, *Race for Empire*, 285–86.

120 Kim To-hyŏng, "Ilche malgi Taegu 24 budae hakbyŏng t'alch'ul ŭi ko" [A study on the Korean soldiers' escape from the 24th battalion of the Japanese military in Taegu], *Kunsi* 65 (December 2007): 209–15.

121 Ibid., 217–22.

122 *Honolulu Advertiser*, May 17, 1945, and *Honolulu Star-Bulletin*, December 15, 1945.

123 Rikugunshō Jikan, Shibayama Kenshirō, "Chōsen shusshinhei," frames 0465–66. Available at http://www.jacar.go.jp. For another example of commanding officers using better treatment of Koreans to prevent desertion, see Chang Chun-ha, *Tolbegae*, 22–23. Chang's commanding officer punished a Japanese soldier for mistreating Korean recruits.

124 Takashi Fujitani, "Senka no jinshu shugi" [Wartime racism], in *Kanjō, kioku, sensō, 1935–1955* [Emotion, remembrance, war], ed. Narita Ryūichi (Tokyo: Iwanami Shoten, 2002), 260–62.

125 Chang Kyŏng-ok, "Chingbyŏng t'alch'ulja," 318–19.

126 Engokyoku Kōseishō, "Chōsen zaiseki kyūrikugun gun'in gunsoku no shosoku butaisho zaichi chikibetsu tokeihyō" [Statistical chart of Koreans on the registry of the old army as soldiers and military civilians (with unit) by region] (1962). Reprint, Document 9-8 in Higuchi, *Senjika Chōsen*, 298–99.

127 *TGSS*, Diet 85 1944. Reprinted in Kondō Ken'ichi, *Chōsen kindai shiryō: Chōsen Sōtokufu kankei jūyō bunsho senshū* [Modern documents of Korea: Anthology of important documents related to the Government-General of Korea], 5 vols. (Tokyo, 1961–1964), 156.

128 Higuchi, *Senjika Chōsen*, 121 and 128.

NOTES TO CHAPTER 4

1 Hayashi Eidai, *Kyōsei renkō, kyōsei rōdō: Chikuho Chōsenjin kōfu no kiroku* [Forced dislocation, forced labor: A record of Chikuho's Korean miners] (Tokyo: Gendaishi Shuppan, 1981), 83; and Chong-sik Lee, *Japan and Korea*, 14.

2 Miya Kōichi, *Chōsen chōyō mondō: Kokumin chōyōrei kankei hōrei* [Questions and answers on Korean labor conscription: Statutes related to national labor conscription laws] (Seoul: Mainichi Shinbōsha Shuppanbu, 1944). Reprinted in *Senjika Chōsenjin rōmu dōin kiso shiryōshū* [Collection of basic materials on wartime Korean labor mobilization], vol. 3, ed. Higuchi Yūkichi (Tokyo: Ryokuin Shobō, 2000), 238–41.

3 Kim Min-yŏng, *Ilche ŭi Chosŏnin*, 60 fn 48 and 61.

4 For an excellent discussion of these recruitment methods, see William Donald Smith III, "Ethnicity, Class, and Gender in the Mines: Korean Workers in Japan's Chikuhō Coal Field" (PhD diss., University of Washington, 1999), 231–46.

5 Kawashima, *Proletarian Gamble*, 33; William Donald Smith III, "Ethnicity, Class, and Gender in the Mines: Korean Workers in Japan's Chikuhō Coal Field, 1917–1945" (PhD diss., University of Washington, 1999), 243, 243.

6 Maeda Hajime, *Tokushu rōmusha*, 18. Maeda was the head of the Hokkaido Coal Mine Labor Department.

7 Koshō Tadashi, "Nihon Seitetsui Kaisha no Chōsenjin kyōsei renkō to sengo shori" [Korean forced labor by Nippon Seitetsu Corporation and their demand for compensation], *Keizaigaku ronshū* 25, no. 1 (June 1993): 30.

8 Kang Man-gil, "Ch'imnyak chŏnjaenggi Ilbon e kangje tongwŏn toen Chosŏn nodongja ŭi chŏhang" [Resistance of Korean laborers who were mobilized against their will in Japan during the aggressive war period] *Han'guksa hakbo* 2 (March 1997): 250.

9 Chōsen Sōtokufu Rōmuka Kanshū, *Kokumin chōyō no kaisetsu: Shitsumon ni kotaete ichimon ittō shiki ni* [Inauguration of national labor conscription: fashioned as detailed responses to questions one by one] (Seoul: Kokumin Sōryoku Chōsen Renmei, 1944), 24–25.

10 Hŏ Su-yŏl, "Chosŏnin nodongnyŏk," 320.

11 Pak Kyŏng-sik, *Nihon teikoku shugi*, 32.

12 Endō Akira, "Senjika no Chōsenjin rōdōsha renkō seisaku no tenkai to rōshi kankei" [Wartime Korean labor displacement policy development and labor and management], *Rekishigaku kenkyū*, no. 567 (May 1987): 9.

13 Naimushō Kanrikyoku, "Chōsen oyobi Taiwan no genkyō" [Conditions of Korea and Taiwan], July 1944. Reprinted in Kondō Kenichi, *Taiheiyō Senka* , 38–39.

14 Miya Kōichi, *Chosen no rōmusha* [Korean laborers] (Seoul: Tōbu Shosekikan, 1945), 240–43, 248. Reprinted in *ICCCSC* 88.

15 Miya Kōichi, *Chōsen chōyō mondō: Kokumin chōyōrei kankei hōrei* [Questions and answers on Korean labor conscription: Statutes related to national labor conscription laws] (Seoul: Mainichi Shinbōsha Shuppanbu, 1944). Reprinted in *Senjika Chōsenjin rōmu dōin kiso shiryōshū* [Collection of basic materials on wartime Korean labor mobilization], ed. Higuchi Yūichi (Tokyo: Ryokuin Shobō, 2000), 254. White slips were mailed for labor conscription and red for military conscription.

16 Ibid., 250 and 264–65.

17 Ibid., 234–36.

18 Kim Sang-ŏp, interview by Chang Sin, November 19, 2001. Available at the Independence Hall of Korea. Kim was too young at the time he was mobilized, but the age for mobilization was later lowered to thirteen.

19 Sonia Ryang, "Inscribed (Men's) Bodies, Silent (Women's) Words: Rethinking Colonial Displacement of Koreans in Japan," *Bulletin of Concerned Asian Scholars* 30, no. 4 (1998): 14–15 and note 29. Also see United States Strategic Bombing Survey, *Coals and Metals in Japan's War Economy* (1947), 17. Kondō Ken'ichi places these statistics (from 1939 to 1944) at 272,361 coal miners; 46,830 metal miners; 84,468 construction workers; and 40,547 factory workers. Kondō Ken'ichi, *Chōsen kindai shiryō: Chōsen Sōtokufu kankei jūyō bunsho senshū* [Modern documents of Korea: Anthology of important documents related to the Government-General of Korea], vol. 2 (Tokyo, 1961–1964), 153–55.

20 Jerome B. Cohen, *Japan's Economy in War and Reconstruction* (Minneapolis: University of Minnesota Press, 1949), 325.

21 Naimushō Keihōbu, "Chōsenjin no idō bōshi ni kansuru ken" [Matter of Korean migration prevention]. Found in *SAJAN*, reel 215. These passports were used only for employment purposes, not for foreign travel.

22 *TGSS*, Diet 85, 1944, 95.

23 Grajdanzev, *Modern Korea*, 119.

24 Cho Kyu-sun, interview by P'yo Yŏng-su, November 24, 2001; and Chang Sŏk-ch'an, interivew by P'yo Yŏng-su, November 24, 2001. Available at the Independence Hall of Korea.

25 Yamada Shōji, "Chōsen joshi kinrō teishintai no dōin to tenkōgyō e no Chōsenjin danshi no senji dōin tono hikaku kentō" [A comparison of the wartime mobilization of the Korean women's *teishintai* and Korean men in mining] *Hanil minjŏl munjae yŏngu* 9 (December 2005): 121–32.

26 Kim Chae-rim, interview, November 24, 2001. Available at the Independence Hall of Korea.

27 In Korea and Japan a seal is still used instead of a signature to sign official documents.

28 Kim Sŏng-ju, interview by Yi Hye-jŏng, 2001. Available at the Independence Hall of Korea.

29 Chen Yingzhen, "Imperial Army Betrayed," in *Perilous Memories: The Asia-Pacific War(s)*, ed. Takashi Fujitani, Geoffrey M. White, and Lisa Yoneyama (Durham, NC: Duke University Press, 2001), 183; and Chŏng Kir-hong, interview by P'yo Yŏng-su, November 24, 2001. Available at the Independence Hall of Korea.

30 O Haeng-sŏk, interview by Chŏng Hye-gyŏng, November 11, 2001. Available at the

Independence Hall of Korea. Also Chŏng Hye-gyŏng, "Ilche malgi Chosŏn kunnomuja ŭi silt'ae mit kwihwan" [A study on the Korean military employees in the late colonial period], *Han'guk tongnip undongsa yŏn'gu* 20 (August 2003): 69–73.

31 Pak Sŭng-gi, interview by Yi Pyŏng-nae, November 17, 2001; and Chŏng Kir-hong, interview by P'yo Yŏng-su, November 24, 2001. Available at the Independence Hall of Korea.

32 Eugene I. Knez, "Sam Jong Dong: A South Korean Village," (PhD diss., Syracuse University, 1959), 47; and Chi Yŏng-im, "Kusul ŭl t'onghae pon ilcheha Chejudo," 94–95.

33 Yi Kye-hyŏng, interview, December 3, 2002. Available at the Independence Hall of Korea. See also Smith, "Ethnicity, Class, and Gender," 245–50; and Nihon Shuppan Bunka Kyōkai, "Chōsenjin rōmu kanri no yōkō" [Outline of Korean labor control] (Tokyo: 1942). Reprinted in *Senji kyōsei renkō, rōmu kanri seisaku* [Wartime forced dislocation, labor control policies], vol. 1, ed. Pak Kyŏng-sik (Tokyo: Ajia Mondai Kenkyūsho, 1982), 25.

34 Shiota, "'Ravaged' People," 50.

35 George Hicks, *The Comfort Women: Sex Slaves of the Japanese Imperial Forces* (London: Souvenir Press, 1995), 55.

36 Chŏng Chin-sŏng and Yŏ Sun-ju, "Ilche sigi yŏja kŭl ro chŏngsindai ŭi silsang" [Conditions of the colonial era womens' corps], in *Hanilgan ŭi mich'ŏngsan kwaje*, ed. Han'guk Chŏngsindae Yŏn'guhoe (Seoul: Asea Munhwasa, 1997), 171–72. Also see Kim Chong-ju and Kim Chae-rim interviews. Available at the Independence Hall of Korea.

37 Yamada Shōji, Tadashi Koshō, and Higuchi Yūichi, *Chōsenjin senji rōdō*, 153.

38 Aikoku Fujinkai Chōsen Honbu, *Aikoku fujinkai Chōsen honbu gaiyō* [Summary of the patriotic wives' association head office] (1941). Reprinted in *ICCCSC* 52, 23–27.

39 *Chōsen rōmu* 4, no. 1 (February 1, 1944): 15.

40 *Kokumin bungaku* 4 (September 1944): 61.

41 Radio broadcast on March 3, 1942. Found in US Office of Strategic Services, Research and Analysis Branch, *Programs of Japan in Korea* (Honolulu: Office of Strategic Services, 1945), 15.

42 Miya Kōichi, *Chosen chōyō mondō*, 229–31. The Japanese and Korean texts were printed side by side.

43 Radio broadcast on August 20, 1944. US Office of Strategic Services, Research and Analysis Branch, *Programs of Japan in Korea*, 10.

44 Chōsen Sōtokufu, Jōhōkyoku, *Atarashiki Chōsen*, 56–57.

45 Chōsen Sōtokufu, Keimukyoku, Hōanka, *Chōsen ni okeru bōkyō undō* [Anti-communist movement in Korea] (Seoul: Maeil Sinbo, 1939). Reprint in *ICCCSC* 52, 324–28. This works out to exactly 1,550 people per showing. Furthermore, Kangwŏn, for some unknown reason, accounted for more than one-fifth (107,255) of the movie attendance and nearly one-fourth (176) of the showings.

46 Asahi Sinbunsha, *Tatakō Chōsen*, section 2, 15.

47 *Chōsen*, no. 326 (July 1942): 49.

48 Pak Kyŏng-sik, *Nihon teikoku shugi*, 162.

49 "A War of Coal," *Oriental Economist*, April 1944, 167.

50 Chōsen Sōtokufu, Rōmukyōkai, *Chōsen rōdō gijutsu tokei chōsa kekka hōkoku* [Statistical report on skilled Korean labor] (Seoul: Chōsen Sōtokufu, n.d.).

51 *Shokugin chōsa geppō* (June/July 1941): 8–9; and Cohen, *Japan's Economy in War*, 301.

52 *Shokugin chōsa geppō* (June/July 1941): 9.

53 *Chōsen shakai jigyō* 19, no. 9 (July 1941): 28.

54 Koshō Tadashi, "Nihon Seitetsui Kaisha," 33.

55 Koga Hironobu, "Tera to ikotsu" [Temple and ashes], in *Kesareta Chōsenjin kyōsei renkō no kiroku: Kanpu renrakusen to hidoko no kōfutachi* [Erased record of Korean forced displacement: Shimonoseki-Pusan ferry and miners of the fire broiler], ed. Hayashi Eidai (Tokyo: Akashi Shoten, 1989), 419. Koga stated that the company he worked for buried alive a Korean who was seriously wounded while working in a mine.

56 "Ethnicity, Class, and Gender," 284.

57 Some Koreans were recruited and paid as contracted (see interviews of Chang Sŏk-ch'an, O Haeng-sŏk, Cho Kyu-sun, and Kim Sŏng-ju), and many felt that they were not discriminated against by the Japanese (see interviews of Yi Kŭm-sun, Pak Sŭng-gi, and Yi Kye-hyŏng). Interviews available at the Independence Hall of Korea.

58 Kangje Tongwŏn Kusul Kirokchip, *Kulp'arŏ kundae kassŏ* [I went into the army to dig tunnels] (Seoul: Kangje Tongwŏn Kunsok Sugijip, 2008), 59–65.

59 Smith, "Ethnicity, Class, and Gender," 296.

60 Chŏng Chae-su, "Drafted to the Kobe Shipyards," in Hildi Kang, *Under the Black Umbrella*, 126. See also Im Jae-hun, interview by Nam Sin-dong, November 24, 2001. Available at the Independence Hall of Korea. Also Kangje Tongwŏn Kusul Kirokchip, *Kulp'arŏ kundae kassŏ*, 69–76.

61 *Chōsen shisō undō gaikyō*, August 31, 1939. Reprinted in *Jūgonen Sensō*, 185–88.

62 *Keijō nippō*, March 11, 1944.

63 TGSS, Diet 85, 1944. Reprint in *Taiheiyō senka shūmatsuki Chōsen no jisei* [Last days of the Pacific War: Governance of Korea], vol. 2, ed. Kondō Kenichi (Tokyo: Chōsen Shiryō Hensankai, 1961), 155.

64 Utsumi, *Kimu wa naze sabakareta*, 86.

65 Radio intercept, May 22, 1942, US Office of Strategic Services, *Programs of Japan in Korea*, 25.

66 Gavan Daws, *Prisoners of the Japanese: POWs of World War II in the Pacific* (New York: Quill, 1994), 104–5. POWs gave Korean guards nicknames such as "the Undertaker," "the Mad Mongrel," "Lizard," and "Slime."

67 Kim Do-hyung, "Haebang chŏnhu chaba chiyŏk Hangugin ŭi tonghyang kwa kwihwan hwaltong [Korean repatriation activities from Java and Indonesia prior to and after liberation]," *Hanguk kŭnhyŏndaesa yŏn'gu* 24 (Spring 2003): 158–59. See also Utsumi Aiko, "Lee Hak Rae, the Korean Connection, and 'Japanese' War Crimes on the Burma-Thai Railway," trans. Herbert Bix. JapanFocus.org, August 26, 2007.

68 Daws, *Prisoners of the Japanese*, 104 and 348.

69 Utsumi, *Kimu wa naze sabakareta*, 5. Utsumi Aiko, a Japanese scholar, provides the most extensive academic coverage of these individuals. See also Utsumi Aiko and Yi Ho-gyŏng, *Chosŏnin BC kŭp chŏnbŏm* [Korean B/C class war criminals] (Seoul: Tong Asia, 2007); and *Chōsenjin BC-kyū senpan no kiroku* [A record of Korean BC-class war

crimes] (Tokyo: Keisō Shobo, 1982). There were 984 individuals executed as war criminals, including 21 Taiwanese. A total of 3,429 people received prison sentences following the war; this included 147 Taiwanese.

70 See Utsumi, *Kimu wa naze sabakareta,* and "Lee Hak Rae."

71 Hanil Munjae Yŏn'guwŏn, *Paeakkin choguk kkŭllyŏgan,* 82 and 84.

72 Neighborhood groups have existed in Korea for many centuries. Japan formally co-opted these groups as village compacts during the Rural Revitalization Campaign, which was launched in 1932 and lasted until 1940. This campaign sought to alleviate rural poverty, encourage self-sufficiency, and increase state penetration at the village level. For a full discussion of this, see Gi-Wook Shin and Do-Hyun Han, "Colonial Corporatism: The Rural Revitalization Campaign, 1932–1940," in Shin and Robinson, *Colonial Modernity in Korea,* 70–96.

73 Higuchi Yūichi, "Taiheiyō Sensōka no josei dōin: Aikokuhan wo Chūshin ni" [Women mobilization during the Pacific War: An emphasis on the Patriotic Association], *Chōsenshi kenkyūkai ronbunshū* 32 (October 1994): 126–27. See also Knez, "Sam Jong Dong," 47.

74 Ka Kaoru, "Sōryoku senkano Chōsen," 11.

75 Higuchi, "Taiheiyō Sensōka," 126; and Chŏng Chin-sŏng and Yŏ Sun-ju, "Ilchesigi yŏjagŭllo," 168.

76 Miya Kōichi, *Chōsen no rōmusha,* 44; and C. Sarah Soh, "Aspiring to Craft Modern Gendered Selves: 'Comfort Women' and the Chŏngsindae in Late Colonial Korea," *Critical Asian Studies* 36 no. 2 (2004): 185–86.

77 Janice C. H. Kim, *To Live to Work,* 145.

78 Michael Kim, "Aesthetics of Total Mobilization," 492–94.

79 *Bunkyō no Chōsen,* no. 224 (July 1944): 21–22.

80 Hŏ Su-yŏl, "Chosŏnin nodongnyŏk," 328.

81 Some schools in the United States went to half-day classes so that students could work in factories and on the farms.

82 Yoo, *Politics of Gender,* 204.

83 Radio intercept, April 5, 1944, US Office of Strategic Services, *Programs of Japan,* 17.

84 Ibid.

85 Grajdanzev, *Modern Korea,* 266.

86 Chi Yŏng-im, "Kusul ŭl t'onghae pon Ilcheha Chejudo," 79.

87 Chŏng Chae-su, "Drafted to the Kobe Shipyards," in Hildi Kang, *Under the Black Umbrella,* 123.

88 O Haeng-sŏk, interview by Chŏng Hye-gyŏng, November 11, 2001. Available at the Independence Hall of Korea.

89 Hanil Munjae Yŏn'guwŏn, *Ppaeakkin choguk kkŭllyŏgan,* 118.

90 *Tokkō geppō,* November–December 1939, 182; and Monbushō Kyōgakukyoku, "Jihenka ni okeru Chōsenjin shisō undō ni tsuite" (Regarding Korean ideological activities during the [Sino-Japanese] incident) (1941). Document 8 in *Zainichi Chōsenjin kankei shiryō shūsei* [Compilation of materials on Koreans in Japan], ed. Pak Kyŏng-sik (Tokyo: San'ichi Shobō, 1976), 1220–24.

91 *Chōsen shakai jigyō,* no. 19 (June 1941): 43.

92 Gi-Wook Shin, *Peasant Protest*, 138.

93 United States Strategic Bombing Survey, *The Effects of Strategic Bombing on Japanese Morale* (Washington, DC: 1947), 112.

94 Higuchi, *Senjika Chōsen*, 202.

95 Hozumi Takanobu, "Rōdōryoku fusoku" [Shortage of manpower], in Hayashi Eidai, *Kesareta Chōsenjin*, 453.

96 No Yŏng-chong, "Ilche malgi Chosŏnin ŭi Pukhaedo chiyŏk kangje yŏnhaeng kwa kŏbu t'uchaeng" [The Hokkaido forced repatriation and resistance of Koreans at the end of Japan's imperialism], *Hanguk kŭnhyŏndaesa yŏn'gu* 17 (Summer 2001): 170.

97 O Haeng-sŏk, interview by Chŏng Hye-gyŏng, November 11, 2001; Pak Sŭng-gi, interview by Yi Pyŏng-nae, November 17, 2001; and Chŏng Kir-hong, interview by P'yo Yŏng-su, November 24, 2001. Available at the Independence Hall of Korea. Chŏng stated that he was paid sixty-nine wŏn a month as a military civilian when most Koreans were getting nineteen wŏn. Sŏ Hwal-wŏn-su stated that he was paid five wŏn a month.

98 Chŏng Kir-hong, interview by P'yo Yŏng-su, November 24, 2001. Available at the Independence Hall of Korea.

99 Chŏn Ki-ho, *Nambang kihaeng*, 14–19.

100 For a discussion of prewar desertion by factory girls, see Kim, *To Live to Work*, 120–23.

101 Maeda, *Tokushu rōmusha*, 133–37.

102 Based on my impression of *Tokkō gaiji geppō* records from July 1939 to July 1940.

103 Cohen, *Japan's Economy in War*, 339.

104 Chōsen Sōtokufu Rōmuka Kanshū, *Kokumin chōyō*, 16.

105 Cohen, *Japan's Economy in War*, 342

106 No Yŏng-chong, "Ilche malgi Chosŏnin," 176–78.

107 *Tokkō geppō*, February 1944. There were no statistics on the number of Koreans found in 1940. Excluding 1940, the recovery rate of runaways was 5.6 percent.

108 Smith, "Ethnicity, Class, and Gender," 283.

109 *Chōsen shisō undō gaikyō*, February 1939, 150; TGSS, Diet 79, December 1941, 73; *Tokkō geppō*, March 1943, 80–81; and Kang Man-gil, "Ch'imnyak chŏnjaenggi," 245 and 255.

110 *Tokkō geppō*, November–December 1939, 182.

111 *Tokkō gaiji geppō*, August 1939, 4–5.

112 Naimushō, Keihōbu, "Chian jōkyō ni tsuite: Keisatsu buchō kaigi ni okeru hōankachō setsumei yōshi" [Explanatory summary of (a speech by the police) public peace section head at a police chief conference], January 14, 1944. Found in SAJAN, reel 218, f88663.

113 Chōsen Sōtokufu Saimu Kyokuchō, Mizuta Naomasa, "Showa 19nendo Chōsen Sōtokufu," 69–70.

114 Utsumi Aiko and Murai Yoshinori, *Chosŏnin panhang*, 134–35.

115 Kasayama Yoshikichi, "Korean Guard," *Japan at War: An Oral History*, ed. Haruko T. Cook and Theodore F. Cook (New York: The New Press, 1992), 119–20. Also see Daws, *Prisoners of the Japanese*, 351.

116 Utsumi Aiko and Murai Yoshinori, *Chosŏnin panhang*, 164–80.

117 No Yŏng-chong, "Ilche malgi Chosŏnin," 171.

118 Smith, "Ethnicity, Class, and Gender," 310–11.

119 Higuchi Yūichi, *Kyōwakai: Senjika Chōsenjin tōsei soshiki no kenkyū* [Kyōwakai: Study of an organization that controlled during war] (Tokyo: Shakai Hyōronsha, 1986), 183.

NOTES TO CONCLUSION

1 This number assumes that 4.1 million were mobilized for rural projects, another 1.8 million students for various work projects; 1,103,782 through labor mobilization; and 130,723 as soldiers. The 4.1 million for rural mobilization does not include statistics for 1945. Koreans mobilized as military civilians and under the Labor Mobilization Plan are not included because they were counted under company-directed recruitment (CDR), government-directed recruitment (GDR), and labor conscription. It is more accurate to state 7.2 million instances of mobilization because a single laborer mobilized under CDR and GDR could later be frozen to their position or conscripted as a soldier or military civilian, thereby accounting for two instances of mobilization.

2 Utsumi, *Chōsenjin "kōgun" heishitachi*, 44.

3 Higuchi, *Senjika Chōsen*, 128.

4 "Names of 3,955 Additional Victims of Japan's military Draft during WW2 confirmed," *Joong-ang Ilbo*, February 12, 1997.

5 Kim To-hyŏng, "Chungbu T'aep'yŏngyang P'allau Kundo Hanin ŭi Kangje Tongwŏn Kwihwan" [Korean activities and repatriation from Palau after the Pacific War], *Han'guk Tongnip Undong Sayŏn'gu*, vol. 26 (June 2006): 231–51; Kim To-hyŏng, "Haebang chŏnhu Chaba chiyŏk Han'gugin," 152–75.

6 Yun Hae-dong, *Singminji kŭndae*, 20 and 26.

7 Kim Hyo Soon and Kil Yun Hyung, "Remembering and Redressing the Forced Mobilization of Korean Laborers by Imperial Japan," *The Asia-Pacific Journal: JapanFocus*, February 15, 2010. Journal available online.

8 This individual returned to Japan after the war and became a successful businessman there. The demand for individuals to conform to the nationalist historical paradigm is especially strong among former comfort women. See Soh, *The Comfort Women*, epilogue.

9 Toyonaga Keisaburō, "Colonialism and Atom Bombs: About Survivors of Hiroshima Living in Korea," in Fujitani, White, and Yoneyama, *Perilous Memories*, 388.

10 Soon-won Park, "The Politics of Remembrance: The Case of Korean Forced Laborers in the Second World War," in *Rethinking Historical Injustice and Reconciliation in Northeast Asia: The Korean Experience*, ed. Gi-Wook Shin, Soon-won Park, and Daqing Yang (New York: Routledge, 2007), 58–66.

11 Toyonaga Keisaburō, "Colonialism and Atom Bombs," 389–91.

12 Ibid., 390–91.

13 Kim Hyo Soon and Kil Yun Hyung, "Remembering and Redressing." See also William Underwood's two articles, "Names, Bones and Unpaid Wages (1): Reparations for Korean Forced Labor in Japan" at JapanFocus.org, September 10, 2006. The 99 yen in 1945 was worth several months' salary, but in 2010 could not buy a can of Coca-Cola.

14 "Japan Apologies Again for Colonial Rule of Korea," CNN online, August 10, 2010.

15 Utsumi, "Korean 'Imperial Soldiers,'" 215.

16 Many younger-generation Koreans harbor considerable animosity toward the Japanese. I taught English in Korea to elementary school students in the 1990s and had one student who refused to eat kimchi (the quintessential Korean food) because he erroneously thought it was a Japanese food.

BIBLIOGRAPHY

PRIMARY SOURCES

Aikoku Fujinkai Chōsen Honbu. *Aikoku fujinkai Chōsen honbu gaiyō* [Summary of the patriotic wives' association head office]. 1941. Reprinted in *Ilcheha chŏnsi ch'ejegi chŏngch'aek saryo ch'ongsŏ* [Historical document collection of the policies of the wartime regime under Japanese imperialism, hereafter abbreviated as *ICCCSC*], vol. 52, edited by Kang Man-gil, 1–76. Koyang: Han'guk Haksul Chŏngbo, 2000.

Asahi Shinbunsha. *Tatakō Chōsen* [Fighting Korea]. Osaka: Asahi Shinbun Kaisha, 1945.

Chang Chun-ha. *Tolbegae* [Stone pillow]. Seoul: Sasangsa, 1971.

Chang Hyŏk-ju (alias Noguchi Minoru). *Iwamoto shiganhei* [Volunteer soldier Iwamoto]. Seoul: Kōa Bunka Shuppan Kabushiki Kaisha / Tokyo: Chōsen Gyōsei Gakukai, 1944.

Chŏn Ki-ho. *Nambang kihaeng* [Accounts of travel to the South Seas] Seoul: Kangje Tongwŏn Kunsok Sugijip, 2008.

Chōsen Kempeitai Shireibu. *Chōsen no hito no tokkō bidanshū* [Collection of anecdotes of Koreans]. Vol. 1. Seoul: Chōsen Kempeitai Shireibu, 1932.

Chōsen Kōhō Kyōkai. *Yakushin Chōsen wo kataru* [Discussing of rapidly progressing Korea]. Seoul: Chōsen Gyōsei Gakkai, 1942.

Chōsen mesaretari [Summoning Korea]. Pusan: Fusan Nippōsha, 1943.

Chōsen Sōgakkai. "Rikugun tokubetsu shiganhei hishigan gakusei kinrō jōkyō chōsa" [Survey of the labor situation of army special volunteer nonapplicant students]. April 20, 1944. Found in *Selected Archives of the Japanese Army-Navy, 1868–1945* (hereafter abbreviated as *SAJAN*), Library of Congress Microfilm, reel 219.

Chōsen Sōtokufu. "Chōsen dōhō ni taisuru chōheisei jisshi junbi kettei ni tomonau sochi jōkyō narabi ni kono hankyō" [Measures and responses to the decision on the draft system enforcement preparation for Korean compatriots]. May 1942. Reprinted in *ICCCSC* 55, 421–56.

———. *Chōsen jijō* [Korea's situation]. Seoul: Chōsen Sōtokufu, 1938–1944.

———. *Chōsen ni okeru kokumin seishin sōdōin* [National spirit mobilization in Korea]. Seoul: Chōsen Insatsu Kabushiki, 1940.

———. *Chōsen Sōtokufu seimu sōkan jimu hikitsugi mokurokusho* [Catalogue of Korean government-general civil governor's office transfer]. June 1942. Reprinted in *ICCCSC* 29, 316–545.

———. *Kanpō* [Official gazette]. 1938–1945.

———. *Shiganhei yori chōhei e* [From volunteer soldiers to the draft]. Seoul: Chōsen Sōtokufu Jōhōka, 1944.

Chōsen Sōtokufu, Dojimukan, and Okayuki Takeshi. *Rikugun tokubetsu shiganhei tokuhon* [Army special volunteer soldier reader]. Seoul: Teikoku Chihō Gyōsei Kakkai Chōsen Honbu, 1939.

Chōsen Sōtokufu, Jōhōka. *Zenshinsuru Chōsen* [Progressing Korea]. Seoul: Chōsen Sōtokufu, 1942.

Chōsen Sōtokufu, Jōhōkyoku. *Atarashiki Chōsen* [New Korea]. Seoul: Chōsen Gyōsei Gakkai, 1944.

———. "Chōsenjin ni taisuru chōheisei jikō junbi ni kansuru" [Regarding preparation for the conscription system for Koreans]. N.d. Reprinted in *ICCCSC* 55, 535.

Chōsen Sōtokufu, Kemukyoku. "Rikugun tokubetsu shiganhei shigansha boshū ni kanshi shoji bengi kyōyō kata iraino ken" [Request for matters of providing accommodation for special volunteer applicant recruitment]. October 30, 1941. Found in *SAJAN*, reel 215.

Chōsen Sōtokufu, Hōanka. *Chōsen ni okeru bōkyō undō* [Anti-communist movement in Korea]. Seoul: Maeil Sinbo, 1939. Reprinted in *ICCCSC* 52, 253–330.

Chōsen Sōtokufu, Rikugunhei Shigansha Kunrensho. *Shiganhei seido no genjō to shōrai e no tenbō* [Current situation of volunteer soldiers and views of its future state]. November 17, 1939. Reprinted in *Senji taiseika Chōsen Sōtokufu gaikaku dantai shiryōshū* [Collection materials of extragovernmental organizations of the Korean government-general under the war system, hereafter abbreviated *STCSGDS*], vol. 14., edited by Sin Chu-baek, 217–46. Seoul: Koryŏ Sŏrim, 1997.

Chōsen Sōtokufu, Rōmuka Kanshū. *Kokumin chōyō no kaisetsu: Shitsumon ni kotahete ichimon ittō shiki ni* [Inauguration of national labor conscription: Fashioned as detailed responses to questions one by one]. Seoul: Kokumin Sōryoku Chōsen Renmei, 1944.

Chōsen Sōtokufu Rōmukyōkai. *Chōsen rōdō gijutsu tōkei chōsa kekka hōkoku* [Statistical report on skilled Korean labor]. Seoul: Chōsen Sōtokufu, n.d. Reprinted in *Senjika Chōsenjin rōmu dōin kiso shiryōshū* 4, edited by Higuchi Yūichi, 9–423. Tokyo: Ryokuin Shobō, 2000.

Chōsen Sōtokufu, Saimu Kyokuchō, and Mizuta Naomasa. "Shōwa 19nendo Chōsen Sōtokufu yosan ni tsuite" [Regarding the 1944 government-general budget]. March 29, 1944. Reprinted in *Taiheiyō Senka shūmatsuki Chōsen no jisei*, vol. 2, edited by Kondō Ken'ichi, 1–206. Tokyo: Chōsen Shiryō Hensankai, 1961.

Chōsen Sōtokufu Teikoku Gikai setsumei shiryō [Explanatory materials for the Korean government-general Imperial Diet]. Reprint. Tokyo: Fuji Shuppan, 1994.

Chōsengun gaiyōshi [Outline history of the Korean Army]. Ca. 1954. Reprinted in *Chōsengun gaiyōshi*, edited by Miyata Setsuko. Tokyo: Fuji Shuppan, 1989.

Chōsengun Hōdōbu Kanshū. *Chōsen chōhei junbi tokuhon* [Preparatory reader on Korean conscription]. Seoul: Chōsen Tosho Shuppan, 1942. Reprinted in *Chōsen chōhei junbi tokuhon: Jūgonen Sensō jūyō bunken siriiju* [Reader on Korean conscription preparation: Important literature of the Fifteen-Year War], vol. 11, edited by Kim Yŏng-dal. Tokyo: Fiji Shuppan,1993.

Chōsengun Hōdōbu Kanshū, Sugiura Hiroshi. *Chōsen chōhei tokuhon* [Reader on Korean conscription]. Keijō: Tosho Shuppan, 1943.

Chōsengun Sanbōchō. *Chōsen shisō undō gaikyō* [General condition of Korean thought movement]. 1938–1940. Reprinted in *Jūgonen sensō gokuhi shiryōshū* [Collection of secret materials on the Fifteen-Year War], vol. 28, edited by Miyata Setsuko. Tokyo: Fuji Shuppan, 1991.

——. "Chōsenjin shiganhei seido ni kansuru ken" [Management of the Korean volunteer soldier system], no. 713, November 24, 1938. Available online at www.jacar.go.jp, ref. code c01004253900.

Chōsengun Sanbōchō and Koiso Kuniaki. "Chōsenjin shiganhei seido ni kansuru iken" [Opinion regarding the Korean volunteer soldier system], no. 354 (June 1937). Available online at www.jacar.go.jp, ref. code c01004599600.

Chōsengun Shireibu. *Chōhei jimu tekiyō* [Important points of conscription affairs]. Seoul: Chōsen Gyōsei Kakkai, 1944.

——. "Chōsenjin shiganhei mondai ni kansuru ken kaiketsu" [Settlement of the issue related to the Korean volunteer soldier problem]. June 1938. Available online at www.jacar.go.jp, ref. code, c01004253900.

——. "Chōsenjin shiganhei mondai ni kansuru ken kaitō" [Reply regarding the case of Korean volunteer soldier problem]. November 24, 1938. Available online at www.jacar.go.jp, ref. code, c01004253900.

——. "Chōsenjin shiganhei seido ni kansuru iken" [Opinion on the Korean volunteer soldier system]. June 1937. Found in *SAJAN*, reel 105, no. 678, f14254.

Chōsengun Shireikan, Rikugun Taishi. "Honendo saiyō suheki Chōsenjin shiganhei saiyō jin'in narabi nyūei mata ha meshiatsumeri butai ni kansuru ken" [Number of Korean volunteer soldiers recruited for this year and corps enlisted or drafted]. January 24, 1939. Available online at www.jacar.go.jp, ref. code c01004411700.

Cook, Haruko T., and Theodore F. Cook, eds. *Japan at War: An Oral History*. New York: The New Press, 1992.

Gakumushō. "Chōsenjin kōminka kihon hōsaku" [Basic measures of Korean imperialization]. N.d. Available online at www.jacar.go.jp, ref. code b02031285300.

Hayashi Eidai, ed. *Chōsenjin kōgun heishi: Nyūginiasen no tokushiganhei* [Korean imperial soldiers: Special volunteer soldiers of the New Guinea front]. Tokyo: Tsuge Shobō, 1995.

——. *Kesareta Chōsenjin kyōsei renkō no kiroku: Kanpu renrakusen to hidoko no kōfutachi* [Forgotten record of Korean forced displacement: Shimonoseki-Pusan ferry and miners of the fire broiler]. Tokyo: Akashi Shoten, 1989.

Higuchi Yuichi, ed. *Kyōwakai kankei shiryōshū: Senjika ni okeru zainichi Chōsenjin tōsei to kōminka seisaku no jittai shiryō* [Collection of materials related to the Kyōwakai: Materials on the actual conditions of Koreans in Japan during the war and assimilation policies]. 5 Vols. Tokyo: Rokuinsho, 1991.

——. *Senjika Chōsenjin rōmu dōin kiso shiryōshū* [Collection of basic materials on wartime Korean labor mobilization]. 5 vols. Tokyo: Ryokuin Shobō, 2000.

Kang Ch'ang-gi. *Naisen ittai-ron* [Treatise on Japanese-Korean unity]. Tokyo: Kokumin Hyōronsha, 1939.

Kang Man-gil, ed. *Ilcheha chŏnsi ch'ejegi chŏngch'aek saryo ch'ongsŏ* [Historical document collection of the policies of the wartime regime under Japanese imperialism]. 98 vols. Koyang: Han'guk Haksul Chŏngbo, 2000.

Kangje Tongwŏn Kusul Kirŏkchip. *Kapcha-ŭlch'uk saeng ŭn kunin e kayahanda* [If you were born in 1924 or 1925, you must join the military]. Seoul: Kangje Tongwŏn Kusul Kirŏkchip, 2006.

———. *Kulp'arŏ kundae kassŏ* [I went into the army to dig tunnels]. Seoul: Kangje Tongwŏn Kunsok Sugijip, 2008.

Kikuchi Kenjo. *Chōsenjin to heieki* [Koreans and military service]. Tokyo, 1943.

Kim Chun-yŏp. *Changjŏm: Na ŭi Kwangbokkun sijŏl* [A strong point: My Kwangbok Army experience]. Seoul: Nanam, 1987.

Kondō Ken'ichi, ed. *Chōsen kindai shiryō: Chōsen Sōtokufu kankei jūyō bunsho senshū* [Modern documents of Korea: Anthology of important documents related to the Korean government-general]. 5 vols. Tokyo: Chōsen Shiryō Hensankai, 1961–1964.

Kōseishō, Engokyoku. "Chōsen zaiseki kyūriku kaigun gun'in gunsoku shusshin chikibetsu tokeihyō" [A survey of registry origins of the old army and navy veterans and military civilians (with unit) by region]. 1962. Document 9-9 in Higuchi Yūichi, *Senjika Chōsen no minshū to chōhei*. Tokyo: Sōwasha, 2001.

Kōseishō, Engokyoku. "Chōsen zaiseki kyūrikugun gun'in gunsoku no tokoro sokubutai tokoro zaichi chiikibetsu tokeihyō" [Statistical chart of Koreans on the registry of the old army as soldiers and military civilians (with unit) by region]. 1962. Document 9-8 in Higuchi Yūichi, *Senjika Chōsen no minshū to chōhei*. Tokyo: Sōwasha, 2001.

Maeda Hajime. *Tokushu rōmusha no rōmu kanri* [Labor management of special laborers]. Tokyo: Sankai Dokan, 1944.

Mitarai Tatsuo. *Minami Sōtoku no Chōsen tōchi* [Governor-General Minami's Korea rule]. Keijō: Keijō Nippōsha, 1942.

Miya Kōichi. *Chōsen chōyō mondō: Kokumin chōyōrei kankei hōrei* [Questions and answers on Korean labor conscription: Statutes related to national labor conscription laws]. Seoul: Mainichi Shinbōsha Shuppanbu, 1944. Reprinted in *Senjika Chōsenjin rōmu dōin kiso shiryōshū*, edited by Higuchi Yūichi, 215–96. Tokyo: Ryokuin Shobō, 2000.

———. *Chōsen no rōmusha* [Korean laborers]. Seoul: Tōbu Shosekikan, 1945. Reprinted in *ICCCSC* 88, 489–542.

Miyata Setsuko, ed. *Jūgonen sensō gokuhi shiryōshū* [Collection of secret documents of the Fifteen-Year War]. Vols. 6, 15, and 28. Tokyo: Fuji Shuppan, 1987.

———. *Mikōkai shiryō Chōsen Sōtokufu kankeisha rokuon kiroku* [Unpublicized materials: (Sound) recording transcripts of people involved with the government-general of Korea]. Tokyo: Gakushūin, 2000.

Monbushō Kyōgakukyoku. "Jihenka ni okeru Chōsenjin shisō undō ni tsuite" [Regarding Korean idealogical activities during the (Sino-Japanese) incident]. 1941. Document 8 in *Zainichi Chōsenjin kankei shiryō shūsei* [Compilation of materials on Koreans in Japan], vol. 4, edited by Pak Kyŏng-sik, 1207–29. Tokyo: San'ichi Shobō, 1976.

Naikaku. "Kaigun tokubetsu shigan heisei jisshi no jiki oyobi tokubetsu shiganhei saiyō teiinsu" [Establishing the subject of the numbers of staff at the time of adopting the Naval Special Volunteer Soldier System]. July 22, 1943. Available online at www.jacar.go.jp, ref. code a03010086100.

Naikaku Sōridaishin. "Chōsenjin oyobi Taiwan hontōjin ni kaigun tokubetsu shiganheisei shin-setsu junbi no ken" [Establishing provisions of preparation for establishment of the Naval Special Volunteer Soldier System for the people of Korea and the Taiwan mainland]. May 8, 1943. Available online at www.jacar.go.jp, ref. code a03010132200.

Naimushō Kanrikyoku. "Chian jōkyō ni tsuite: Keisatsu buchō kaigi ni okeru hōankachō setsu-mei yōshi" [Explanatory summary of (a speech by the police) public peace section head at a police chief conference]. January 14, 1944. Found in *SAJAN*, reel 218, f88663.

———. "Chōsen oyobi Taiwan no genkyō" [Conditions of Korea and Taiwan]. July 1944. Reprinted in *Taiheiyō senka no Chōsen oyobi Taiwan* [Korea and Japan during the Pacific War], vol. 1, edited by Kondō Ken'ichi, 1–99. Chigasaki: Chōsen Shiryō Kenkyūkai, 1961.

Naimushō Kanrikyoku, Keihōbu. "Chōsenjin no idō bōshi ni kansuru ken" [Matter of Korean migration prevention]. Found in *SAJAN*, reel 215.

Nihon Shuppan Bunka Kyōkai. "Chōsenjin rōmu kanri no yōkō" [Outline of Korean labor control]. Tokyo: 1942. Reprinted in *Senji kyōsei renkō, rōmu kanri seisaku* [Wartime forced dislocation, labor control policies], vol. 1, edited by Pak Kyŏng-sik, 1–28. Tokyo: Ajia Mondai Kenkyūsho, 1982.

Ōmura Kenzō. *Tatakō hantō shiganhei* [Fighting peninsular volunteer soldiers]. Seoul: Tōbusho, 1943.

Pak Kyŏng-sik, ed. *Zainichi Chōsenjin kankei shiryō shūsei* [A collection of documents on Kore-ans in Japan]. Tokyo: San'ichi Shobō, 1976.

Rikugunshō, Chōboka. "Chōsenjin shiganhei mondai ni kansuru ken" [Issue of Korean volunteer soldier]. January 1938, frame 0800. Available online at www.jacar.go.jp, ref. code c01004411500.

Rikugunshō Fukkan. "Chōsen shusshinhei toriatsukai kyōiku no sankō shiryō sōfu ni kansuru ken" [Case regarding remittance participation materials of treatment education of soldiers from Korea]. Army Secret Order 2848, August 14, 1943.

Rikugunshō Heibika. "Daitōa Sensō ni kan wo wakajinteki no kentō" [An investigation of human resources in the Pacific War]. January 20, 1942.

Rikugunshō Jikan, Shibayama Kenshirō. "Chōsen shusshinhei no toriatsukka shidō sasshin kōjō ni kansuru ken rikugun ippan e tsuchō" [General army instructions on improving treatment of soldiers from Korea]. Army Secret Order 308, January 26, 1945. Available online at www.jacar.go.jp, ref. code, c01007867000.

Rikugunshō Sanbō Honbu Hensei Dōinka. *Shinajihen: Daitōa Sensōkan rikugun dōin gaikyō* [The China Incident: A general history of army mobilization during the Greater East Asia War]. Reprinted, Tokyo: Fuji Shuppan, 1988.

Sin Sang-chʼo. *Talchʼul: ŏnŭ chayujuŭija ŭi sugi* [Escape: Memoir of a liberalist]. Seoul: Nok-mungak, 1966.

Sohn, John Young. *Korean Gakuhei: My Life in the Japanese Army*. Stillwater, MN: River's Bend Press, 2007.

Takamiya Taira. *Hantō gakuto shusinfu* [A record of peninsular students sent to war]. Seoul: Keijō Nippō Shahakkō, 1944.

Takumushō, Yamao Dōni. "Rikugun shigansha no senkō wo ōsakashi ni oite jisshi suru no ken"

[Matter of enforcement of screening army volunteers in Osaka]. Kankei 835, November 15, 1941. Found in *SAJAN*, reel 215.

Takumushō Kanrikyokuchō. "Chōsen Sōtokufu rikugunhei shigansha kunreisho seito boshū ni kansuru ken" [Case regarding Korean government-general army soldier volunteer training camp pupil recruitment]. Kankei 1907, September 1, 1942. Found in *SAJAN,* reel 215.

Ueda Ryūdan. *Sumera Chōsen* [Imperial Korea]. Tokyo: Nihon Seinen Bunka Kyōkai, 1943.

Yun Ch'i-ho. *Yun Ch'i-ho ilgi* [Yun Ch'i-ho's diary]. Vols. 10–11. Seoul: National History Compilation Committee, 1989.

Zensen Gakudō Tsuzukatashū, ed. *Chōhei anisan* [Conscript brothers]. Seoul: Kōa Bunka Shuppan Kaisha, 1944. Reprinted in *STCSGDS* 16, 383–545.

SECONDARY SOURCES

1·20 Hakpyŏng Sagi Kanhaeng. *1·20 hakpyŏng sagi* [Chronicle of the January 20 student soldiers]. 3 vols. Seoul: 1·20 Hakpyŏng Sagi Kanhaeng, 1987.

Atkins, E. Taylor. *Primitive Selves: Koreana in the Japanese Colonial Gaze, 1910–1945*. Berkeley: University of California Press, 2010.

Baldwin, Frank. "The March First Movement: Korean Challenge and Japanese Response." PhD diss., Columbia University, 1969.

Balesi, Charles J. *From Adversaries to Comrades-in-Arms: West Africans and the French Military, 1885–1918*. Waltham, MA: Crossroads Press, 1979.

Brudnoy, David. "Japan's Experiment in Korea." *Monumenta Nipponica* 25, nos. 1/2 (1970): 155–95.

Bush, Barbara. *Imperialism, Race, and Resistance: Africa and Britain, 1919–1945*. New York: Routledge, 1999.

Byman, Daniel, and Matthew Waxman. *The Dynamics of Coercion: American Foreign Policy and the Limits of Military Might*. New York: Cambridge University Press, 2002.

Caprio, Mark. *Japanese Assimilation Policies in Colonial Korea, 1910–1945*. Seattle: University of Washington Press, 2009.

———. "Loyal Patriot? Traitorous Collaborator? The Yun Ch'iho Dairies and the Question of National Loyalty." *Journal of Colonialism and Colonial History* 7, no. 3 (2006). Available at http://muse.jhu.edu/journals/journal_of_colonialism_and_colonial_history.

Chang Kyŏng-ok. "Chingbyŏng t'alch'ulcha kkŭt ŏmnŭn miro" [Draft escapees with nowhere to go]. *Chŏnggyŏng munhwa* 234 (August 1984): 316–27.

Chen, I-te. "Japanese Colonialism in Korea and Formosa: A Comparison of Its Effects Upon the Development of Nationalism." PhD diss. University of Pennsylvania, 1979.

Chen Yingzhen. "Imperial Army Betrayed." In *Perilous Memories: The Asia-Pacific War(s)*, edited by Takashi Fujitani, Geoffrey M. White, and Lisa Yoneyama, 181–98. Durham, NC: Duke University Press, 2001.

Chi Yŏng-im. "Kusul ŭl t'onghae pon Ilcheha Chejudo nae kangje tongwŏn ŭi silt'ae wa t'ŭkching" [A look at the conditions and characteristics of the forced mobilization of Cheju Province under Japanese rule through oral statements]. *Sahoe wa yŏksa* 72 (2006): 73–94.

Choi, Kyeong-hee. "Another Layer of the Pro-Japanese Literature: Ch'oe Chŏnghŭi's 'The Wild Chrysanthemum.'" *Poetica* 52 (1999): 61–92.

Chŏn Ki-ho. *Chosŏn iranŭn uri nara ka issŏkkuna* [I did not know our country was called Chosen]. Seoul: Kangje Tongwŏn Kunsok Sugijip, 2008.

Chŏng Chae-jŏng. "Looking at the Economy and Society of Korea under Japanese Rule: Beyond the 'Theory of Development' and 'Theory of Exploitation.'" In *Korea under Japanese Rule Past and Current Research Results and Issues for Future Research,* edited by Matsuda Toshi-hiko, 39–60. Kyoto: International Research Center for Japanese Studies, 2009.

Chŏng Chin-sŏng and Yŏ Sun-ju. "Ilche sigi yŏja kŭl ro chŏngsindai ŭi silsang" [Conditions of the colonial era women's corps]. In *Hanilgan ŭi michŏngsan kwaje,* edited by Han'guk Chŏngsindae Yŏn'guhoe, 161–21. Seoul: Asea Munhwasa, 1997.

Chŏng Hye-gyŏng. *Chosŏnin kangje yŏnhaeng, kangje nodong* [Korean forced displacement, forced labor]. Seoul: Sŏnin, 2006.

———. "Ilche malgi Chosŏn kunnomuja ŭi silt'ae mit kwihwan" [A study on the Korean military employees in the late colonial period]. *Han'guk tongnip undongsa yŏn'gu* 20 (August 2003): 55–92.

Chŏng T'ae-hŏn and Ki Kwang-sŏ. "Ilche ŭi panillyunjŏk Chosŏnin kangje nomu tongwŏn kwa imgŭm t'alch'wi" [The Japanese imperialist's inhumane mobilization of Koreans and wage exploitation]. *Yŏksa wa hyŏnsil* 50 (2003): 403–28.

Chou, Wan-yao. "The Kōminka Movement: Taiwan under Wartime Japan, 1937–1945." PhD diss., Yale University, 1991.

Clayton, Anthony. *France, Soldiers, and Africa.* London: Brassey's Defence Publishers, 1988.

Cohen, Jerome B. *Japan's Economy in War and Reconstruction.* Minneapolis: University of Minnesota Press, 1949.

Confer, Vincent. *France and Algeria: The Problem of Civil and Political Reform, 1870–1920.* Syracuse, NY: Syracuse University Press, 1966.

Cumings, Bruce. *The Origins of the Korean War: Liberation and the Emergence of Separate Regimes, 1945–1947.* Vol. 1. Princeton, NJ: Princeton University Press, 1981.

Daws, Gavan. *Prisoners of the Japanese: POWs of World War II in the Pacific.* New York: Quill, 1994.

Dong, Wonmo. "Japanese Colonial Policy and Practice in Korea, 1905–1945: A Study in Assimilation." PhD diss., Georgetown University, 1965.

Duara, Prasenjit. *Culture, Power, and the State: Rural North China, 1900–1942.* Stanford: Stanford University Press, 1988.

Duus, Peter, Ramon Myers, and Mark Peattie, eds. *The Japanese Wartime Empire.* Princeton, NJ: Princeton University Press, 1996.

Echenberg, Myron. "Race, Ethnicity, and Social Class in the French Colonial Army: The Black African *Tirailleurs,* 1857–1958." In *Ethnic Armies: Polyethnic Armed Forces from the Time of the Habsburgs to the Age of the Superpowers,* edited by N. F. Dreisziger, 50–68. Waterloo, ON: Wilfrid Laurier University Press, 1990.

Eckert, Carter J. *Offspring of the Empire: The Koch'ang Kims and the Colonial Origins of Korean Capitalism.* Seattle: University of Washington Press, 1991.

——. "Total War, Industrialization, and Social Change in Late Colonial Korea." In *The Japanese Wartime Empire*, edited by Peter Duus, Ramon Myers, and Mark Peattie, 3–39. Princeton, NJ: Princeton University Press, 1996.

Eckert, Carter J. et al. *Korea Old and New: A History*. Cambridge, MA: Harvard University Press, 1990.

Effendi, M. Y. *Punjab Cavalry: Evolution, Role, Organisation, and Tactical Doctrine: 11 Cavalry (Frontier Force), 1849–1971*. Karachi: Oxford University Press, 2007.

Ellinwood, DeWitt C., and S. D. Pradhan, eds. *India and World War I*. Columbia, MO: South Asia Books, 1978.

Endō Akira. "Senjika no Chōsenjin rōdōsha renkō seisaku no tenkai to rōshi kankei" [Wartime Korean labor displacement policy development and labor and management]. *Rekishigaku kenkyū*, no. 567 (May 1987): 1–15.

Farwell, Byron. *The Gurkhas*. New York: W. W. Norton, 1984.

Foucault, Michel. *The History of Sexuality*. Trans. Robert Hurley. New York: Pantheon Books, 1978.

Fujitani, Takashi. "The Masculinist Bonds of Nation and Empire: The Discourse on Korean 'Japanese' Soldiers in the Asia Pacific War." *Senri Ethnological Studies* 16 (2000): 133–61.

——. "Right to Kill, Right to Make Live: Koreans as Japanese and Japanese as Americans During WWII." *Representations* 99, no. 1 (2007): 13–39.

——. "Senka no Jinshu Shugi" [Wartime racism]. In *Kanjō, Kioku, Sensō, 1935–1955* [Emotion, remembrance, war, 1935–1955], edited by Narita Ryūichi, 235–80. Tokyo: Iwanami Shoten, 2002.

Fujitani, Takashi, Geoffrey M. White, and Lisa Yoneyama, eds. *Perilous Memories: The Asia-Pacific War(s)*. Durham, NC: Duke University Press, 2001.

Garon, Sheldon. *Molding Japanese Minds: The State in Everyday Life*. Princeton, NJ: Princeton University Press, 1997.

Gershovich, Moshe. *French Military Rule in Morocco: Colonialism and Its Consequences*. Portland, OR: Frank Cass, 2000.

Grajdanzev, Andrew J. *Modern Korea*. New York: Institute of Pacific Relations, 1944.

Grundlingh, Louis. "'Non-Europeans Should Be Kept Away from the Temptations of Towns': Controlling Black South African Soldiers during the Second World War." *The International Journal of African Historical Studies* 25, no. 3 (1992): 539–60.

Ha ŭn-jin. "Ilche p'asijŭm (1937–1945): Chosŏn minjung ŭi hyŏnsil insik kwa chŏhang" [Japanese colonial fascism (1937–1945): Korean people's reality understanding and resistance]. PhD diss., Koryŏ University, 1998.

Hanil Munje Yŏn'guwŏn. *Ppaeakkin choguk kkŭllyŏgan saramdŭl: Ch'ilbaengman Chŏsonin kangje tongwŏn ŭi yŏksa* [Stolen country, taken-away people: A history of seven million Koreans' forced mobilization]. Seoul: Asia Munhwasa, 1995.

Haron, Nadzan. "Colonial Defence and British Approach to the Problems in Malaya, 1874–1918." *Modern Asian Studies* 24, no. 2 (1990): 275–95.

Hayashi Eidai, ed. *Chōsenjin kōgun heishi: Nyūginiasen no tokushiganhei* [Korean imperial soldiers: Special volunteer soldiers of the New Guinea front]. Tokyo: Tsuga Shobō, 1995.

———. *Kyōsei renkō, kyōsei rōdō: Chikuho Chōsenjin kōfu no kiroku* [Forced dislocation, forced labor: A record of Chikuho's Korean miners]. Tokyo: Gendaishi Shuppan, 1981.

Henry, Todd A. "Cheguk ŭl kinyŏm hago, chŏnjaeng ŭl tongnyŏhagi Singminje malgi (1940nyŏn) Chosŏn esŏ ŭi pangnamhoe [Celebrating empire, fighting war: The 1940 exposition in late colonial Korea]. *Asea yŏn'gu* 51, no. 4 (Winter 2008): 101.

Hicks, George. *The Comfort Women: Japan's Brutal Regime of Enforced Prostitution in the Second World War.* New York: W. W. Norton, 1995.

———. *The Comfort Women: Sex Slaves of the Japanese Imperial Forces.* London: Souvenir Press, 1995.

Higuchi Yūichi. *Kōgun heishi ni sareta Chōsenjin: 15nen Sensōka no sōdōin taisei no kenkyū* [Koreans who were forced to be imperial army soldiers: Study on the general mobilization system during the Fifteen-Year War]. 1992 ed. Tokyo: Shakai Hyōronsha, 1991.

———. *Kyōwakai: Senjika Chōsenjin tōsei soshiki no kenkyū* [Kyōwakai: Study of an organization that controlled Koreans during war]. Tokyo: Shakai Hyōronsha, 1986.

———. *Senjika Chōsen no minshū to chōhei* [Korean people and conscription during the war]. Tokyo: Sōwasha, 2001.

———. "Taiheiyō Sensōka no josei dōin: Aikokuhan wo Chūshin ni" [Women mobilization during the Pacific War: An emphasis on the Women's Patriotic Association]. *Chōsensa kenkyūkai ronbunshū* 32 (October 1994): 119–38.

Hŏ Su-yŏl. "Chosŏnin nodongnyŏk ŭi kangje tongwŏn ŭi silt'ae: Chosŏn nae esŏ ŭi kangje tongwŏn chŏngch'aek ŭi chŏn'gae rŭl chungsim ŭro" [Conditions of the forced mobilization of the Korean labor force: Centering on the development of the forced mobilization policies within Korea]. In *Ilche ŭi Han'guk singmin t'ongch'i* [Korea under Japanese imperial control], edited by Ch'a Ki-byŏk, 289–349. Seoul: Chŏmŭmsa, 1985.

———. "'Kaebal kwa sut'al' ron pip'an: Singminji sanŏphwa wa haebang hu sanŏphwa ŭi yŏn'gwansŏng pigyo" [A criticism of development and exploitation: A comparison of colonial development and development after liberation]. *Yŏksa pipyŏng* 48 (1999): 127–67.

Holbrook, Wendall P. "British Propaganda and the Mobilization of the Gold Coast War Effort, 1939–1945." *Journal of African History* 26 (1985): 347–61.

Im Hye-bong. *Ch'inil sŭngnyŏ paekp'arin: Kkŭnnaji anŭn yŏksa ŭi murŭm* [108 Pro-Japanese monks: A historical question that never ends]. P'aju, South Korea: Chŏngnyŏnsa, 2005.

Judd, Denis. *Empire: The British Imperial Experience, from 1765 to the Present.* London: Harper-Collins, 1996.

Ka Kaoru. "Sōryoku senka no Chōsen josei" [Korean women under total war]. *Rekishi hyōron,* no. 612 (April 2001): 2–17.

Kajiyama Toshiyuki. *Clan Records: Five Stories of Korea.* Translated by Yoshiko Dykstra. Honolulu: University of Hawaii Press, 1995.

Kang Deok-sang. See Kang Tŏk-sang.

Kang, Hildi. *Under the Black Umbrella: Voices from Colonial Korea, 1910–1945.* Ithaca, NY: Cornell University Press, 2001.

Kang Man-gil. "Ch'imnyak chŏnjaenggi Ilbon e kangje tongwŏn toen Chosŏn nodongja ŭi chŏhang" [Resistance of Korean laborers who were mobilized against their will in Japan during the aggressive war period]. *Han'guksa hakbo* 2 (March 1997): 239–63.

Kang Tŏk-sang. "Background to History-Related Conflicts between Korea and Japan." In *The Historical Perceptions of Korea and Japan*, edited by Hyun Dae-song, 325–48. Paju, South Korea: Nanam Publishing House, 2008.

———. *Chōsenjin gakuto shujjin: Mou hitotsuno wadatsumino koe* [Korean students go to war: Another voice of the sea]. Tokyo: Iwanami Shoten, 1997.

Kang, Young Hoon. "Personal Reminiscences of My Japanese School Days." In *Korea's Response to Japan: The Colonial Period, 1910–1945*, edited by C. I. Eugene Kim and Dorthea E. Mortimore, 286–90. Kalamazoo: Western Michigan University, 1977.

Katō Yōko. *Chōheisei to kindai Nihon, 1868–1945* [Conscription system and modern Japan, 1868–1945]. Tokyo: Yoshikawa Kōbunkan, 1996.

Kawashima, Ken C. *The Proletarian Gamble: Korean Workers in Interwar Japan.* Durham, NC: Duke University Press, 2009.

Killingray, David. "Labour Exploitation for Military Campaigns in British Colonial Africa, 1870–1945." *Journal of Contemporary History* 24 (1989): 483–501.

———. "Military and Labour Recruitment in the Gold Coast during the Second World War." *Journal of African History* 23 (1982): 83–95.

Killingray, David, and David Omissi, eds. *Guardians of Empire: The Armed Forces of the Colonial Powers, c. 1700–1964.* New York: Manchester University Press, 1999.

Kim, C. I. Eugene, and Dorthea E. Mortimore. *Korea's Response to Japan: The Colonial Period, 1910–1945.* Kalamazoo: Western Michigan University, 1977.

Kim, Choong Soon. *A Korean Nationalist Entrepreneur: A Life History of Kim Sŏng-su, 1891–1955.* Albany: State University of New York Press, 1998.

Kim, Han-Kyo. "The Japanese Colonial Administration in Korea: An Overview." In *Korea under Japanese Colonial Rule: Studies of the Policy and Techniques of Japanese Colonialism*, edited by Andrew Nahm, 41–53. Kalamazoo: Western Michigan University Press, 1973.

Kim, Janice C. H. *To Live to Work: Factory Women in Colonial Korea, 1910–1945.* Stanford: Stanford University Press, 2009.

Kim, Michael. "The Aesthetics of Total Mobilization in the Visual Culture of Late Colonial Korea." *Totalitarian Movements and Political Religions* 8, nos. 3–4 (September–December 2007): 483–502.

Kim Hak-tong. "Chang Hyŏk-chu ŭi minjokchŏk kwa ch'inilchŏk chakp'um ŭi pigyo koch'al: Haebang ijŏn Ilbonŏ chakp'um ŭl chungsim ŭro" [A comparative study of Chang Hyŏk-chu's nationalist works and his pro-Japanese works: With a focus on his Japanese language works before liberation]. *Ilbŏn yŏn'gu* 34 (December 2007): 191–210.

Kim Hyo Soon and Kil Yun Hyung, "Remembering and Redressing the Forced Mobilization of Korean Laborers by Imperial Japan," *Asia-Pacific Journal: JapanFocus*, February 15, 2010. Journal available online at www.japanfocus.org.

Kim Min-yŏng. *Ilche ŭi Chosŏnin nodongnyŏk sut'al yŏn'gu* [Research of Japan's Korean manpower exploitation]. Seoul: Hanul, 1995.

Kim To-hyŏng. "Haebang chŏnhu Chaba chiyŏk Han'gugin ŭi tonghyang kwa kwihwan hwaltong" [Korean repatriation activities from Java and Indonesia prior to and after liberation]. *Hanguk kŭnhyŏndaesa yŏn'gu* 24 (Spring 2003): 152–74.

———. "Ilche malgi Taegu 24 pudae hakpyŏng t'alch'ul ŭi ko" [A study on the Korean soldiers' escape from the twenty-fourth battalion of the Japanese military in Taegu]. *Kunsi* 65 (December 2007): 204–31.

———. *T'aep'yŏngyang chŏnjaenggi kyŏkchŏnji wa Chosŏnin hŭisaengja e kwanhan yŏn'gu: Nyuginia chiyŏk ŭl chungsim ŭro* [Research on the Pacific War battlefront and Korean victims: The New Guinea area]. Seoul: Ilche Kangjŏmha Kangje Tongwŏn Pi'hae Chinsang Kyumyŏng wiwŏnhoe, 2006.

Kim Yong-gwŏn, ed. *Kkŭllyŏgan saramdŭl, ppaeakkin saramdŭl: Kangje chingyongja wa chonggun wianbu ŭi chŭngŏn.* [Hauled-off persons, snatched-away persons: Forced conscriptees and the testimony of comfort women who followed the troops] Seoul: Haewadal, 2000.

Knez, Eugene I. "Sam Jong Dong: A South Korean Village." PhD diss., Syracuse University, 1959.

Kobayashi Ei. "Chōsen Sōtokufu no rōdō ryoku seisaku ni tsuite" [On the Korean government-general's labor force policies]. *Keizai to Keizaigaku* 34 (1974): 55–80.

Koshō Tadashi. "Nihon Seitetsui Kaisha no Chōsenjin kyōsei renkō to sengo shori" [Korean forced labor by Nippon Seitetsu Corporation and their demand for compensation]. *Kaizaigaku ronshū* 25, no. 1 (June 1993): 1–37.

Kratoska, Paul H., ed. *Asian Labor in the Wartime Japanese Empire: Unknown Histories.* Armonk, NY: M. E. Sharpe, 2005.

Lawler, Nancy E. *Soldiers of Misfortune: Ivoirien Tirailleurs of World War II.* Athens: Ohio University Press, 1992.

Lee, Chong-sik. *Japan and Korea: The Political Dimension.* Stanford: Stanford University Press, 1985.

Lee Sun-jin. "The Feature Films in the Colonial Period: Discontinuity and Continuity." In *The Past Unearthed: Collection of Feature Films in the Japanese Colonial Period.* Trans. Kim Su-hyŏn. Seoul: Korean Film Archives, n.d.

Lynn, Hyung Gu. "Limits of the Colonial State: Interest Intersections and the State in Colonial Korea, 1919–1942." PhD diss., Harvard University, 2001.

Matsuda Toshihiko. *Korea Under Japanese Rule Past and Current Research Results and Issues for Future Research.* Kyoto: International Research Center for Japanese Studies, 2009.

Matthews, James K. "Reluctant Allies: Nigerian Responses to Military Recruitment, 1914–1918." In *Africa and the First World War*, edited by Melvin E. Page, 95–114. London: Macmillan, 1987.

Mazrui, Ali A., ed. *General History of Africa.* Vol. 8, *Africa since 1935.* Heinemann, CA: University of California Press, 1993.

Minami Jirō Denki Kankōkai. *Minami Jirō.* Tokyo: Minami Jirō Denki Kankōkai, 1957.

Mitarai Tatsuo. *Minami Sōtoku no Chōsen tōchi* [Governor-General Minami's Korean rule]. Seoul: Keijō Nippōsha, 1942.

Miyata Hiroto. *Tatakō Chōsen.* Tokyo: Shinkansha, 2007.

Miyata Setsuko. *Chosŏn minjung kwa "hwangminhwa" chŏngch'aek* [The Korean people and the "imperialization" policy]. Transated from Japanese to Korean by Yi Hyŏng-nang. Seoul: Ilchogak, 1997.

———. *Chōsen minshū to "kōminka" seisaku* [The Korean people and the "Japanization" policy]. Tokyo: Miraisha, 1985.

Morrow, John H., Jr. *The Great War: An Imperial History.* New York: Routledge, 2004.

Nahm, Andrew, ed. *Korea under Japanese Colonial Rule: Studies of the Policy and Techniques of Japanese Colonialism.* Kalamazoo: Western Michigan University Press, 1973.

Namiki Masahito. "Singminji sigi Chosŏnin ŭi chŏngch'i chamyŏ" [Korean political participants during the colonial era]. In *Haebang chŏnhusa ŭi chaeinsik* [A rediscovery of history before and since liberation], edited by Chi-hyang Pak, Kim Chŏl, Kim Il-yŏng, and Yi Yŏng-hun, 655–97. Seoul: Ch'aek Sesang, 2006.

Narita Ryūichi, ed. *Kanjō, kioku, sensō, 1935–1955* [Emotion, remembrance, war]. Tokyo: Iwanami Shoten, 2002.

No Yŏng-chong. "Ilche malgi Chosŏnin ŭi Pukhaedo chiyŏk kangje yŏnhaeng kwa kŏbu t'uchaeng" [The Hokkaido forced repatriation and resistance of Koreans at the end of Japan's imperialism]. *Hanguk kŭnhyŏndaesa yŏn'gu* 17 (Summer 2001): 153–88.

Page, Melvin E., ed. *Africa and the First World War.* New York: St. Martin's Press, 1987.

Pak Chi-hyang et al., eds. *Haebang chŏnhusa ŭi chaeinsik* [A rediscovery of history before and since liberation]. Seoul: Ch'aek Sesang, 2006.

Pak Kyŏng-sik. *Chōsenjin kyōsei renkō no kiroku* [A record of the forced displacement of Koreans]. Tokyo: Miraisha, 1965.

———. *Nihon teikoku shugi no Chōsen shihai (ka)* [Japanese imperialistic domination of Korea]. Vol. 2. Tokyo: Aoki Shoten, 1975.

———. "Taiheiyō Sensō toki ni okeru Chōsenjin kyōsei renkō" [Forced relocation of Koreans during the Pacific War]. *Rekishigaku kenkyū* 297 (February 1965): 30–46.

———. *Tennōsei kokka to zainichi Chōsenjin* [The emperor system state and Koreans in Japan]. Tokyo: Taihei Insatsusha, 1986.

Park, Soon-won. *Colonial Industrialization and Labor in Korea: The Onoda Cement Factory.* Cambridge, MA: Harvard University, 1999.

———. "The Politics of Remembrance: The Case of Korean Forced Laborers in the Second World War." In *Rethinking Historical Injustice and Reconciliation in Northeast Asia: The Korean Experience,* edited by Gi-Wook Shin, Soon-won Park, and Daqing Yang, 55–74. New York: Routledge, 2007.

Rew, Joung Yole (Yu Chŏng-nyŏl). *Japanese Colonial Government of Korea: Empire Building in East Asia.* P'aju, South Korea: KSI, Han'guk Haksul Chŏngbo, 2008.

Ryang, Sonia. "Inscribed (Men's) Bodies, Silent (Women's) Words: Rethinking Colonial Displacement of Koreans in Japan." *Bulletin of Concerned Asian Scholars* 30, no. 4 (1998): 3–15.

Saaler, Sven, and Victor Koschmann, eds. *Pan-Asianism in Modern Japanese History: Colonialism, Regionalism, and Borders.* New York: Routledge, 2007.

Scott, James C. *Weapons of the Weak: Everyday Forms of Peasant Resistance.* New Haven, CT: Yale University Press, 1985

Selth, Andrew. "Race and Resistance in Burma, 1942–1945." *Modern Asian Studies* 20, no. 3 (1986): 483–507.

Shillony, Ben-Ami. "Universities and Students in Wartime Japan." *The Journal of Asian Studies* 45, no. 4 (August 1986): 769–87.

Shin, Gi-Wook. *Peasant Protest and Social Change in Colonial Korea.* Seattle: University of Washington Press, 1996.

Shin, Gi-Wook, and Michael Robinson, eds. *Colonial Modernity in Korea*. Cambridge, MA: Harvard University Press, 1999.

Shin, Michael D. "Introduction." In *Landlords, Peasants, and Intellectuals in Modern Korea*, edited by Pang Kie-chung and Michael D. Shin, 1–19. Ithaca: Cornell University Press, 2005.

Shiota, Shōbei. "A 'Ravaged' People: The Koreans in World War II." *Japan Interpreter* 8, no. 1 (Winter 1971): 43–53.

Shirai Atsushi. *Daigaku to Ajia Taiheiyō Sensō: Sensōshi kenkyū to taiken no rekishika* [Universities and the Asia Pacific War: Historicizing research and experiences historical]. Tokyo: Nihon Keizai Hyōronsha, 1996.

Shirakawa Yutaka. "Chan Hyokuchyu 'Iwamoto shiganhei' ni tsuite" [On Chang Hyŏk-chu's "*Iwamoto shiganhei*"]. In *Iwamoto shiganhei*, by Chang Hyŏk-chu, with postscript by Shirakawa Yukata. Seoul: Kōa Bunka Shuppan Kabushiki Kaisha, 1944. Reprint, Tokyo: Yumani Shobō, 2001.

Sin Chu-baek. "Ilche malgi Chosŏnin kunsa kyoyuk, 1942–1945" [Korean military education in the late colonial period, 1942–1945]. *Hanil minjok munje yŏn'gu* 9 (December 2005): 153–86.

Smith, William Donald, III. "Ethnicity, Class, and Gender in the Mines: Korean Workers in Japan's Chikuhō Coal Field, 1917–1945." PhD diss., University of Washington, 1999.

Soh, C. Sarah. "Aspiring to Craft Modern Gendered Selves: 'Comfort Women' and the Chŏngsindae in Late Colonial Korea." *Critical Asian Studies* 36, no. 2 (2004): 175–98.

———. *The Comfort Women: Sexual Violence and Postcolonial Memory in Korea and Japan*. Chicago: University of Chicago Press, 2008.

Sohn, John Young. *Korean Gakuhei: My Life in the Japanese Army*. Stillwater, MN: River's Bend Press, 2007.

Stoler, Ann Laura. *Capitalism and Confrontation in Sumatra's Plantation Belt, 1870–1979*. Ann Arbor: University of Michigan, 1995.

Strachan, Hew. *The First World War in Africa*. New York: Oxford University Press, 2004.

Takaki, Ronald. *Democracy and Race: Asian Americans and World War II*. New York: Chelsea House Publishers, 1995.

Tansman, Alan, ed. *The Culture of Japanese Fascism*. Durham, NC: Duke University Press, 2009.

Thomas, Martin. *The French Empire at War, 1940–1945*. New York: Manchester University Press, 1998.

Toyonaga Keisaburō. "Colonialism and Atom Bombs: About Survivors of Hiroshima Living in Korea." In *Perilous Memories: The Asia-Pacific War(s)*, edited by T. Fujitani, Geoffrey M. White, and Lisa Yoneyama, 378–95. Durham, NC: Duke University Press, 2001.

Ts'ai, Hui-yu Caroline. *Taiwan in Japan's Empire Building: An Institutional Approach to Colonial Engineering*. New York: Routledge, 2009.

Tsuboe Senji. *Zainihon Chōsenjin no gaikyō* [Overview of Koreans in Japan]. Tokyo: Byōi Hōkichi, 1953.

Uchida, Jun. "'Brokers of Empire': Japanese Settler Colonialism in Korea, 1910–1937." PhD diss., Harvard University, 2005.

Ulrich, Herbert. "Forced Laborers in the Third Reich: An Overview." *International Labor and Working Class History* 58 (October 2000): 192–218. Available online at http://journals.cambridge.org/action/displayJournal?jid=ILW.

United States, Office of Strategic Services, trans. *Programs of Japan in Korea.* Honolulu: Office of Strategic Services, 1945.

United States, Office of Strategic Services, Research, and Analysis Branch. *Manpower in Japan and Occupied Areas.* Vol. 1. Honolulu: Office of Strategic Services, 1944.

United States Strategic Bombing Survey. *Coals and Metals in Japan's War Economy.* Washington, DC: United States War Department, 1947.

——. *The Effects of Strategic Bombing on Japanese Morale.* Washington, DC: United States War Department, 1947.

Unno Fukuju. "Chōsen shokuminchi ni okeru nōgyō seisaku no tenkai: Toku ni rōdōryoku seisaku to no kairen ni tsuite" [The development of the agricultural policy in colonial Korea: Centering on its relation to the labor policy]. *Meiji Daigakuin bunkagaku kenkyūjo kiyō* 32 (December 1992): 254–309.

Utsumi Aiko. *Chōsenjin "kōgun" heishitachi no sensō* [The Korean "imperial army" soldiers' war]. Tokyo: Iwanami Shoten, 1991.

——. "'Daitōa kyōeiken' to Chōsenjin gunjin/gunzoku" [The "East Asia Co-Prosperity Sphere" and Korean soldiers and military civilians]. *Samchŏlli* 31 (Winter 1982): 82–91.

——. *Kimu wa naze sabakareta no ka: Chōsenjin BC-kyū senpan no kiseki* [Why was Kim tried? The trajectory of Korean BC-class war criminals]. Tokyo: Asahi Shinbun Shuppan, 2008.

——. "Lee Hak Rae, the Korean Connection, and 'Japanese' War Crimes on the Burma-Thai Railway." Trans. Herbert Bix. *Asia-Pacific Journal: JapanFocus,* August 26, 2007. Journal available online at www.japanfocus.org.

Utsumi Aiko and Murai Yoshinori. *Chosŏnin panhang* [Korean resistance]. Translated from Japanese to Korean by Pak Nam-ch'ul. Seoul: Kukmun Publishing Co., 1981.

Weiner, Michael. *Race and Migration in Imperial Japan.* New York: Routledge, 1994.

Yamada Shōji. "Chōsen joshi kinrō teishintai no dōin to tenkōgyō e no Chōsenjin danshi no senji dōin tono hikō kentō" [A comparison of the wartime mobilization of the Korean women's *teishintai* and Korean men in mining]. *Hanil minjŏl munjae yŏngu* 9 (December 2005): 117–52.

Yamada Shōji, Tadashi Koshō, and Higuchi Yūichi. *Chōsenjin senji rōdō dōin* [Korean wartime labor mobilization]. Tokyo: Iwanami Shoten, 2005.

Yi Ki-baik. *A New History of Korea.* Trans. Edward W. Wagner and Edward J. Schultz. Seoul: Ilchokak, 1984.

Yi Ki-dong. "Ilbon chegukkun ŭi Han'gugin changgyodŭl" [Korean officers of the Japanese army]. *Sin Tong-a,* no. 299 (August 1984): 452–99.

——. *Pigŭk ŭi kunindŭl: Ilbon yuksa ch'ulsin ŭi yŏksa* [Soldiers' tragedy: A history of Japanese military school graduates]. Seoul: Ilchogan, 1982.

Yi Myŏng-jong. "Ilche malgi Chosŏnin chingbyŏng ŭl wihan kiryu chedo ŭi sihaeng mit hojŏk chosa [Resident registration system enforcement and family registry system investigation for the draft in late colonial Korea]. *Sahoe wa yŏksa t'onggwŏn* 74 (June 2007): 75–106.

Yi Sang-ŭi. "1930 nyŏndae Ilche ŭi nodong chŏngch'aek kwa nodongnyŏk sut'al" [Imperial Japan's labor policy and the exploitation of workers in the 1930s]. *Han'guksa yŏn'gu* 94 (September 1996): 151–91.

Yi Se-il. *Hawai p'oro suyongso Hanin p'oro e kwanhan chosa* [A survey on Korean POWs in Hawaiian POW camps]. Seoul: Ilche Kangjŏmha Kangje Tongwŏn P'ihae Chinsang Kyumyŏng Wiwŏnhoe, 2008.

Yong, Tan Tai. *The Garrison State: The Military, Government, and Society in Colonial Punjab, 1849–1947*. London: SAGE Publications, 2005.

Yoo, Theodore Jun. *The Politics of Gender in Colonial Korea: Education, Labor, and Health, 1910–1945*. Berkeley: University of California Press, 2008.

Yun, Hae-dong. *Singminji kŭndae ŭi p'aerŏdoksŭ* [The paradox of colonial modernity]. Seoul: Hyumŏnisŭt'ŭ, 2007.

Yun, Hae-dong, et al., eds. *Kŭndae rŭl tasi ingnŭnda: Han'guk kŭndae insik ŭi saeroun p'aerŏdaim ŭl wihayŏ* [Another reckoning of modern time: For the realization of a new paradigm in modern Korea]. Seoul: Yŏksa Pip'yŏngsa, 2006.

NEWSPAPERS AND JOURNALS

Asahi shinbun

Bunkyō no Chōsen

Chogwang

Chōsen

Chōsen gyōsei

Chōsen nenkan

Chōsen rōmu

Chōsen shakai jigyō

Chōsen shisō undō gaikyō

Chōsen Sōtokufu shisei nenbō

Hokkaidō shinbun

Honolulu Advertiser

Honolulu Star-Bulletin

Hyōgoken shakai jigyō

Japan Times & Advertiser

Joong-ang ilbo [Chungang Ilbo] (available online at www.joongang.co.kr)

Keijō ihō

Keijō nippō

Kokumin bungaku

Kokumin sōryoku

Korea Herald

Korea Times

Koseki

Kyōwa jigyō
Kyōwa jigyō nenkan
Maeil sinbo
Midori hata
Naganoken kōsei jibō
New York Times
Nippon Times
Nippu jiji
Oriental Economist
Osaka Mainichi and Tokyo Nichinichi
Samch'ŏlli
Shisō geppō
Shokugin chōsa geppō
Sōdōin
Tokkō gaiji geppō
Tokkō geppō
Tōyō no hikari

INDEX

CPSIA information can be obtained at www.ICGtesting.com
Printed in the USA
BVOW08s1926281013

334865BV00002B/26/P